Musical Visions

Selected Conference Proceedings from

6th National Australian/New Zealand IASPM

and Inaugural Arnhem Land Performance Conference

Adelaide, Australia, June 1998

Edited by Gerry Bloustien

Contributors – Phil Bagust, Gerry Bloustien, Andrew Bradley, Jenjo Brown, Mark Evans, Jon Fitzgerald, FRUIT, Nancia Guivarra, Philip Hayward, Shane Homan, Kipps Horn, Bruce Johnson, Jardine Kiwat, Adé Kukoyi, Richard Margetson, Tony Mitchell, Jennifer K. Newsome, David Page, Catherine Palmer, Motti Regev, Robin Ryan, Paulene Thomas, Mandy Treagus, Ashley Turner, Graeme Turner, Gordon Williams

Wakefield Press

Wakefield Press
17 Rundle Street
Kent Town
South Australia 5071

First published 1999

Cover designed by Liz Nicholson, design BITE, Adelaide
Book design and typesetting by Hyde Park Press, Adelaide
Printed and bound by Hyde Park Press, Adelaide

National Library of Australia
Cataloguing-in-publication entry

Musical visions: selected conference proceedings from the 6th National Australia/
New Zealand IASPM and the Inaugural Arnhem Land Performance Conference.

Includes index.
ISBN 1 86254 500 6.

1. Music and society – Congresses. 2. Aborigines, Australian – Music – Congresses. 3. Popular music – Social aspects – Congresses. 4. Popular music – History and critcism – Congresses. I. Bloustien, Gerry. II. Title.

306.484

Wakefield Press thanks Wirra Wirra Vineyards and Arts South Australia
for their continued support.

Musical Visions

To my mother
who loved to sing and dance

CONTENTS

EDITOR'S PREFACE

Be not afeard; the isle is full of noises,
Sounds, and sweet airs, that give delight and hurt not.
(The Tempest: Act III, Scene II)

Musical Visions '98, was an exciting and unique international event held in Adelaide, South Australia, June 25 – 28 1998. In combining the 6th National Australian/New Zealand IASPM (The International Association for the Study of Popular Music) and the Inaugural Arnhem Land Performance conferences, it brought together different disciplines, fields of interest and areas of academia. A diverse group of practitioners from the media and music industries and many Indigenous and non-Indigenous groups such as researchers, sociologists, anthropologists, ethnomusicologists, cultural critics, journalists, educators and musicians attended. Delegates came from institutions around the country and included researchers from Israel, Germany and America. As might be expected, the company and the presentations were eclectic, but the overarching theme of the *complexity* of music as sound, image and movement enabled the various perceptual threads to successfully integrate and intertwine. Two fascinating collections of papers have emerged from this successful event: the first is this one, *Musical Visions,* which explores the wider issues of popular music and cultures; the second, to appear later this year, focuses more specifically on the Arnhem Land performances themselves.

This volume attempts to resonate with the aims and atmosphere of that original conference. It is above all a sensitive coming-together of Indigenous and non-Indigenous voices and perspectives, a particularly important, timely and positive statement for the media organisations and academic institutions to be making in light of the current concerns about equality and equity for all cultures in Australian and overseas.

The conference, *Musical Visions,* was fittingly opened by Lewis O'Brien, an Aboriginal elder who extended a traditional welcome to Kaurna Land (the original name for Adelaide, South Australia) through ritual song and dance by members of his community. Gatjil Djerrkura, Chairperson of the Aboriginal and Torres Strait Islander Committee (ATSIC) then responded, introducing ritual and secular music by Yolngu performers from Arnhem Land. The music for the rest of the opening ceremony, and indeed the whole conference, brought together the ancient and the emerging cultural musical expression. Many of the contributors in this volume preface their papers by acknowledging the generosity of the Kaurna people for permitting the conference to take place on their land.

The three main key-note addresses, included in this volume, set the tone for the rest of the papers, performances and workshops to follow. Graeme Turner, Motti Regev, and Adé Kukoyi each highlighted the main strands of discussion to be picked up and explored in various ways by the other presenters and panellists — issues of globalisation, appropriation, nationalism and contested identifications are all to be found debated in these pages. Yet like the conference itself, the research and discussions to be found here are in a form that is accessible to both the lay-reader as well as to those with a scholarly or professional interest in the field. Such diverse topics as gumleaf playing, new and emerging forms of Indigenous music, hip hop, new technologies, music in science fiction films, punk, pop, Japanese ritual drumming and jazz music follow, delightfully articulating the common interests of the practitioners and the researchers. And as so many of our presenters suggest, the conference and the papers that are reproduced here, also bridge the cultural divides that so often appear in our societies.

The participants of the original event were also privileged to hear several well-known Indigenous musicians and performers, such as David Page (Bangara Dance Theatre and Nikinali Music), the members of Trochus (an Indigenous fusion group) and Soft Sands (a Yolngu rock band). Several of those performances and presentations, where the performers spoke eloquently and movingly about their art and its spiritual significances, are reproduced here. Along with other musicians from Western traditions, such as Fruit (a funk band) and The Fuglemen (hip hop), these musicians talked about their styles, their influences and their inspirations.

The chapters are ordered simply according to the alphabetical order of the authors' names, enabling the readers to spin their own webs of relevancies and connections, their own 'musical visions'. The papers have been deliberately left 'raw' and unrefined to reflect the colloquial tone and atmosphere of collegial debate that flowed through the original presentations. If contradictions sometimes emerge and differences arise between the papers, that complexity is perfectly in keeping with what may be expected from such a stimulating and open gathering.

A volume like this only comes together with a great deal of assistance and encouragement. Thanks are due in the first instance to the University of South Australia for generously providing some funding and technical assistance towards the coordination and production of this book. The contributors themselves, of course, deserve very special thanks, not only for their fascinating topics and their wonderful music which inspired the collection but also for their patience, collegiality and their cooperation.

In terms of the production process itself, a very special thanks are due to Michael Bollen and Stephanie Johnston from Wakefield Press for supporting the publication of this book. I am particularly grateful for their advice, support and technical expertise. We are grateful also to Liz Nicholson from Design Bite for creatively designing our wonderful cover to reflect the flow and mood of the collection. Thanks too to Elaine Maloney and Phil Gibson from Hyde Park Press for designing and typesetting the manuscript

I am particularly indebted to my colleagues at the School of Communication Studies: Ruth Trigg for her invaluable advice, and Karah Hogarth, Emma Masters, Rita Reitano, and Jacki Bloustien who have been a magnificent editorial team, generously providing expertise, support and indefatigable good humour.

Finally, I wish to express my gratitude to Mark Bloustien. Without Mark's remarkable expertise, continual generosity, practical help and good humour, I would never have survived such daunting tasks as convening the original conference and editing this book.

Gerry Bloustien
Adelaide, 1999

POOR FM: A DECADE IN ADELAIDE PROGRESSIVE COMMUNITY RADIO

PHIL BAGUST

History/Background

3D radio was born 20 years ago as 5MMM-FM, otherwise known as the Progressive Music Broadcasting Association. The immediate community impetus for its birth was the decision in 1978 of the then sole FM broadcaster, ABC-FM, to restrict its format to the classical end of the music spectrum. A 'seeding' grant of $62,000 courtesy of the then Dunstan government secured the fledgling organisation's future and MMM's license was granted in October of that year. It is not often remembered that MMM was the first alternative rock format station to hit the Adelaide airwaves.

After many difficulties the station began broadcasting in December 1979 from a converted undertaker's premises in Norwood, approximately 2km from Adelaide Central Business District (CBD). This building was to prove to be an important element in creating the right 'aura' for an 'alternative public broadcaster'.

Magill Road 1979–1990

In its early years the station regularly had over one thousand subscribers and hundreds of members and volunteers, and managed to sustain a vibrant level of on and off-air activity, with fundraisers, regular station gigs at local venues, and live-to-air broadcasts, all featuring local artists. The station released a compilation album of unsigned Adelaide bands and managed to publish a monthly free street-zine called 'Airwave' that was, in many ways, a precursor to the street-zines so common today.

Franklin Street 1990–1995

It didn't last. As the 1980's wore on, things started to sour. Other FM stations hit the airwaves, the first chills of economic rationalism and the withdrawal of government from the arts sector began to manifest themselves and the number of subscribers began to fall.

In 1990, government asset sales sealed the fate of MMM's much loved premises. The funeral home was being sold. After much fruitless searching the former 5KA commercial radio studios in the heart of the Adelaide CBD was selected. To many of us this seemed ideal — a ready made studio right in the centre of town!

However, the move proved to be exceptionally draining on the volunteer spirit of the station. The new premises lacked the character that allowed the volunteers to feel part of a radio community. Management clashed with volunteers and volunteers clashed with management. Subscribers left in droves, dropping below five hundred by the early 1990s. Triple J's arrival at this time did not help either.

By 1993, the station was in debt and on the brink of closure. It was at this stage that luck intervened. We were offered a considerable sum of money by the national Austereo network for our callsign, an offer we had little hesitation in accepting in October that year. This callsign buyout saved the station's bacon, but it also meant that a new name had to be chosen and that 13 years of public identification with the Triple M logo would be lost. Thus 3D was born and virtually had to start selling its bona fide's as a station from scratch.

Since that time the station has moved again, leaving behind high CBD rents for the considerable charm of a historic two story villa at Stepney, ironically just around the corner from the station's original location. This place feels much more like a public radio station should, although it suffers from being somewhat remote.

Although it is coming off a very low and demoralised base, 3D has once more become a pleasant place for volunteers to 'hang out' and soak up the ambience of public radio. Nevertheless, direct financial listener support has remained flat, and the station has had to look carefully at its expenditure. Only one staff member is currently employed — and the current manager has demonstrated that a real enthusiasm and empathy for both the alternative economy and voluntarism is essential for the survival of this kind of operation in a media competitive environment.

Who listens to the station?

Determining the listener demographic has always been a problem — even for commercial radio stations. Public radio stations are not differentiated on commercial listener surveys and so it is difficult to determine levels of listenership.

Nelson Street, Stepney 1998

Suffice to say that the 1989 'Capital Media' report by the Public Radio Advisory Committee noted that '... 5MMM-FM has consistently, in independent surveys, the largest audience of all of the public stations, yet has not converted that into income'. In other words, having a lot of listeners does not necessarily translate into financial support — an internal phone survey of three hundred and five listeners in April 1989 revealed that only 27 percent of these 'loyal listeners' were current subscribers or members. Suffice to say that internal surveys have loosely centred the station's audience in the 18-35 age group, slightly biased towards males. Crucially, listeners are likely to be students, single and not high income earners.

The on air sound of 3D radio

Whether the emphasis should be on the 'progressive' or the 'music' has been a problem within the station right from its beginning. Back in the 1970s the media diversity that is now obvious was not there and the committees that brought about the station's birth were inevitably coalitions of alternative music lovers, left wing and gay activists, journalists and feminists. Right from the station's beginning this diversity has been reflected in the on-air programming, and has been the cause of endless clashes and disagreements within management. Are we a music or spoken word station? 3D, unlike many other community radio stations, attempts to maintain a balance between spoken word and music in its schedule.

3D has remained unusual in other respects too. The station retains its commitment to alternative progressive music not simply by airing a raft of specialist genre programs (i.e. blues, dance, jazz, metal) but by maintaining a policy of 'general music' during prime listening hours. Other time slots are reserved for spoken word programs (environment shows, alternative current affairs, new age, gay support and information and so on) and specialist music shows (jazz, blues, experimental and dance).

Our 'general music' shows are meant to be just that — a deliberately eclectic mixture of alternative music sounds in each show. An ideal show might include a dash of metal, a pinch of indie pop, a slather of punk, and dollops of dance and grunge — or tracks from any number of other rock genres that have sprung up over the years. Not only that, but the show still has to be presented in adherence with 3D's quota system, which does not tell DJ's what to play, but does insist that roughly 40% of any general music show be Australian music, 20% locally released music and 10% unsigned demo tapes. On top of this is the expectation that at least 25% of any show's music will have some female content.

This system is at once both one of 3D's strengths and weaknesses. A general music show that really runs the gamut of music styles requires not only a wide appreciation of music but also an ability to resist the temptation to play a preponderance of one's own musical tastes. So it is inevitable that general music tends often to become a series of shows that can be best identified with the tastes of individual presenters. Nevertheless, the idea of general music is a brave one, even if it has proved hard to market.

The other factor that makes public radio's on-air sound very different from commercial radio is what I call the 'wank factor'. 3D DJ's, who are all volunteers, are everything commercial DJ's are not. They are not slick, they do not embellish their voices in false and fatuous ways and, being relatively untrained and totally unpaid, they do stumble, make mistakes and 'umm and err' sometimes. Yet it is precisely this laid back feel that can be so endearing and 'real' to many of our listeners. Occasionally self-indulgent, 3D announcers still manage to pull together moments of magic that would be difficult in more controlled environments and are able to supply the kind of information that can only come from an active love of the music they play.

Keeping the place running — management realities at 3D radio

There are two management principals that have always dominated the worldview at 3D:

1. Where is the next dollar coming from?
2. Is my management committee not plotting against me?

Having spent two years on the management committee I can say that station power politics is about the only area that bears any similarity with what was portrayed on the ABC TV series 'Raw-FM'. Dark conspiracies, covert lobbying and threats of legal retribution have all been rampant at various times and I doubt it is any different anywhere else in public radio. People who think that community radio is all about sweetness and cooperation need to do some time in management themselves. It has been my observation that politics is politics no matter how small the pyramid of power is and that passions can swell to amazing proportions even in places like 3D.

Social networks and community

Overall, it is the social networks that come out of public radio that I really want to discuss. I am sure I do not need to remind you that one of the pernicious tendencies of postmodern life is to isolate people as individual consumers. With the continuing breakup of the nuclear family, more alienating work environments, and the kind of nomadism that goes with a casualised workforce — meaningful expressions of face to face cooperation and community seem to be increasingly hard to find.

It is this community aspect of 3D that, in spite of all the grumbles and cynicism, has made a great difference to my life in the last ten years. In addition, I think I can say with some certainty, that it has made a difference for hundreds of other volunteers. It is why I joined in the first place, and it is why I stay. It has been my alternate non-nuclear family if you like.

The station has brought together friends in music, and fired them with a sense of purpose that has always secured the station's existence in spite of the many threats it faces. I have met people who have become great friends and who I can not imagine having lived without knowing. This sense of collective belonging — between people who often ostensibly belong to different 'style tribes' (punks, goths, jazz freaks, metal heads, ravers, the list goes on) is finally, just as, if not more important than the sound the station puts out. Time after time the station has acted as a 'surrogate' home, and even social worker, for people who find it a centre point for their lives.

Working at 3D is working at the coalface of dynamic music culture. Time and time again I have seen music styles (and their associated subcultures) pop into being at 3D, infect the station workers like a virus, and quickly spread to mass culture, and be rejected by the station as a result. The rise and fall of 'grunge' is a perfect example. General music DJ's were playing Mudhoney, and bands of that ilk, years before Nirvana became a household word and a stock item at K-mart. You can call this elitism if you like, I call it expert fandom and it is what sets 3D station workers and listeners apart from the mass audience. 3D consistently plays music styles six to eighteen months before the mass market appropriates them.

It is this fandom, tied with a spirit of voluntarism, that sets alternative radio apart and is what ultimately connects its disparate music cultures — a willingness to explore and be open to what is perceived to be the cutting edge — and an acceptance that it is the dynamism and continual change of music culture, the knowledge that what you love today will not be what you love next year, that is the heart of the station aesthetic. To put it another way, individuals at the station might not like other volunteers' musical preferences, but they will fight for their right to have them — as long as they are 'alternative'. That is not to say that there are not major disagreements between the music subcultures at the station — because there are. I could go on about the flux of forces that direct station culture towards one music style, dress style, haircut style (I kid you not) and away from others. What's hot at the moment? It is so-called new country, as personified by Palace Music. As unlikely a trend as I have seen in a long time — but that is the perversity of this continual mining for new 'alternative' cultural capital.

One of the unique aspects of 3D culture is the studio logbook. For over fifteen years log books have sat in the on-air studio at 3D and guests and presenters alike have used them as an uncensored forum for their current internal political concerns — as a drawing board, an information service, a dating service (I kid you not) and as a place to polemicise current musical debates. These log books illustrate living station culture — both irreverent, hilarious and at times deadly serious, the logs now run to thousands of pages and probably deserve to be published in their own right.

In addition to the logbooks, hundreds of demo tapes at 3D represent an Adelaide local music history of the last twenty years that thousands of individuals have participated in. It is a unique cultural record of changes in genre and style that is unmatched in Australian public radio. Unfortunately, given the perishable nature of the tape medium, it is also a history that is rapidly deteriorating.

Finally, the on air studio 'wonderwall' is a more recent innovation. As bands and other performers have come into the station they have signed their names on the wall and left messages. The list is impressive — a piece of constantly evolving graffiti and a constant reminder to station workers of the continuing relevance of public radio.

"Wonderwall"

The future of public radio in Adelaide — some factors

Finances

Many social factors have changed in Australia in the last twenty years, but as far as 3D is concerned the most important one is the progressive withdrawal of government funding. The station would not have started without an injection of public money and it is fair to say that it has struggled ever since these moneys have been withdrawn. 3D now goes through the yearly rituals of applying for individual grants from a plethora of different bodies — something that absorbs an inordinate amount of time for no guaranteed return. Revenues from gigs, station parties, merchandising and appeals have all declined — at least in part because that pool of volunteers that helped make these things happen has also declined. The ability of the station to earn sponsorship revenue has always been limited given our listener demographic, and I do not believe that it is likely to change.

Triple J's arrival in Adelaide was definitely one of the things that put the station on the back foot. At that stage, Triple J's playlist and on-air style was similar to 3D's and it had so much national promotional muscle that local fundraising immediately became harder to do. It has been ironic, if I may say so, to see the Triple J playlist progressively 'bland out' over the intervening years. Such is the fate of a government funded body in increasingly conservative times perhaps?

Of course needing to move premises twice in the last eight years has not helped 3D either. For a volunteer organisation, this is a huge drain on goodwill and a diversion from the day to day duties of providing good on-air sound.

Social

One of the nice things about 3D was always its ability to mobilise support from people in the community who did not 'fit in'. Back in the 1970s and 1980s these people, who were often unemployed for long periods, were able to be virtually full-time volunteers. These people helped keep the place humming with social activity.

As economic rationalism and a general hardening of community and governmental attitudes has progressed through the 1990s, these people — the lifeblood of the culture and community feel of the station — have drifted away. Potential volunteers find themselves working longer hours in less secure jobs. Those on social security find themselves threatened or harassed by employment agencies. People in general seem to have less time to give to a voluntary passion. It is a strange phenomenon that does not augur well for so-called civil society. Of course our present government would say its not 'real work' anyway.

Cultural comparisons with interstate public radio

One of the constant things I hear about the alternative music scene is how healthy it is interstate — and as a consequence how healthy the alternative radio scene there is as well.

The most successful public alternative music stations in Australia are probably Triple M and PBS, both in Melbourne. There are good reasons for this. Melbourne is the home of the live music scene in Australia. Maybe it is the weather, I do not know, but as far as making it in a band is concerned, Melbourne is the first, and often the last port of call. When bands move to Melbourne, so do friends and partners. So do arts graduates. So do people who just want to hang out on Brunswick Street. It is the kind of vicious circle that is gradually turning Australia into Sydney/Canberra/Melbourne. As a result of this talent drain the station (and Adelaide in general) loses the very people that could help to revitalise it.

So as far as the vibrancy of its arts and music cultures are concerned, Adelaide suffers from a 'far outer suburb syndrome'. Why struggle in Adelaide when Melbourne is so close and Sydney is not much further? As a result, a large expatriate Adelaide community develops in Melbourne and Sydney and helps reinforce the 'alternative' scene there. Every time I travel east I meet ex-Adelaidians who could have made a difference if they had stayed, but instead deserted the sinking ship and moved to Prahan or Surrey Hills.

What about Brisbane you may ask? In Brisbane, 4ZZZ is probably, in my opinion, the personification of anti-establishment — grotty but lovable, up-yours public radio. But 4ZZZ has survived by being campus lifestyle based in a city where students have always had something to really fight against — be it Bjelke and his draconian drug laws or just the general social attitudes of the deep north. In Adelaide, the so-called progressive 'Athens of the south', alternative public radio was born in an environment of official support, and that safe attitude persists amongst those who remain today.

Demographic

It is not just the size of the total radio market; Adelaide is losing the people who are most likely to listen to 3D. Its demographic is shrinking naturally because of our aging population, and as I have mentioned, those that are left tend to leave. It was not always that way. At present Adelaide is simply not an expanding market for the type of product that 3D broadcasts. This is a city with a static population and one where the type of people that are likely to become loyal alternative radio listeners are just as likely to be drawn away to the eastern states by improved job/study opportunities. Losing people like this happens all the time at the station. Blame the media, blame globalisation — it is just the way it is.

New media

When 3D began there were no video games, the computer was something nerds fiddled with in their bedrooms, and the Internet was still nestled in the military's bosom. It is easy to forget just how much things have changed in the last twenty years. Back in the late 1970s, people interested in non-commercial music had to rely on a few magazines and record stores to get their information. A radio station that played the kind of music they wanted to hear, said the kind of things they wanted to hear, and generally acted as a support network for the alternative community was a real innovation.

It is not that way now of course. We suffer, if anything, from too much media. Markets have diversified and specialised tremendously. Now, you can get the latest information about your favourite band direct off the Internet, and hear the latest music for that matter. Cable television has arrived. The video/computer game scene is a separate subculture in its own right. And desktop publishing has meant that personal fanzines are cheap and easy to make and distribute. Public radio now has far more competition than it did two decades ago. It is an ever changing market that seems to be aligning itself, more and more, with a kind of screen culture. That does not mean that public radio has lost its special charms, it just means that there is a lot more noise and clutter to compete with out there.

Dance culture

A final factor I want to mention is the changing taste of the alternative audience. What passes for alternative these days is more likely to be one of the many permutations of dance music and culture as

Helen 'Hellbound' on air 1997

it is some kind of rock based style. This is, as has already been mentioned, the basis of many bitter debates within the station.

There is little doubt that, for a large number of young people, dance music and dance culture represent the rebellious or alternative. 3D comes from a rock background which is dismissed as passe by the rave scene. It does program a fair bit of dance music, but it does so as 'specialist music' (i.e. like jazz, blues, metal et cetera) rather than 'general music'. Dance is not really part of the station culture. This unofficial policy may come back to haunt the station if it does not incorporate the dance scene into its makeup.

Conclusion

This may have seemed like a litany of woes. Not so. It is just a recognition that things are changing rapidly in public radio, and 3D's future into the next century is not assured . If I was to place bets — I would say that it will still be here in 10 years time, but that in the kind of fragmented market we are likely to see by then, 3D will never again be the focus of a generation of people like it was in 1978. From a volunteer point of view though, the work of 3D and similar organisations in giving a sense of worth to people is likely to become even more important in the next century. A recent article in *The Australian* put expenditure in the non-profit sector in this country at $27 billion p/a and employment at 560 000 (Gunn 1998). Something to think about, something worth protecting.

References

Gunn, M. 1998, 'Who can spend $27bn without making profit?' *The Australian*. June 20-21.

ON NOT DANCING LIKE A 'TRY HARD'

GERRY BLOUSTIEN

❖

It follows that an identity is always already an ideal, what we would like to be, not what we are... And what makes music special in this familiar cultural process is that musical identity is both fantastic — idealising not just oneself but also the social world one inhabits — and real; it is enacted in activity... music gives us a real experience of what the ideal could be (Frith 1996:274).

Music, mimesis and methodology

Pat, identified herself as a 'Raver'. As both a producer and consumer of Techno music, she spoke with scorn of the 'Townies' who seemed to try and appropriate her cultural identity simply by dressing in similar clothes and attending the same venues. She expressed this clearly to me one evening when I was invited to attend one of the Raves with her. I was holding a video camera as Pat hadn't wanted to be seen personally filming on that night but she wanted the event to be filmed. While we were standing on the edge of the main dancing 'circle', Pat drew my attention to a girl dancing flamboyantly in the middle of the area. Her white luminous blouse was catching the lights from the lasers and her movements were large and exaggerated. 'She's not a Raver', hissed Pat in my ear, 'She's a Try-Hard'. I asked how she knew. 'Look at the way she's moving her arms. And look at the clothes. She's not here to dance. She's here to pick up guys'.

To an outsider, Pat's insistence and anxiety are almost comical. Yet perhaps her words also point to something far more poignant, something she is 'guarding' jealously — her precarious sense of self; something often termed 'the *real* me'. This paper is concerned with the nexus between such notions of personal 'authenticity' and popular music — exploring the moments where the values and philosophies underpinning these concepts intertwine. Such moments, I argue, frequently underpin the process of young people's simultaneous representation and constitution of self. More specifically I am looking at the ways in which music was produced and consumed in the everyday lives of a particular number of teenagers living in Adelaide in the early 1990s in order to represent and epitomise integral aspects of this sense of 'self' — who they felt they were, who they wanted to be.

The material used here is drawn from my much larger ethnographic study where I looked at the significance of popular music and other related cultural texts in the everyday lives of ten young women undertaken over a period of three years from 1993-1996 (see Bloustien 1996, 1998, 1999). Pat, Mary, Janine, Sara, Grace, Hilary, Diane, Claire, Kate and Fran, as I shall refer to them throughout this paper, were all aged around 15 at the start of the fieldwork. They hailed from different social backgrounds, inflected through a range of ethnic identifications. As an integral aspect of my methodology — and ultimately as the lynch pin of the resulting reflexive analysis — the girls had all been invited to document on video any aspect of their lives, and their wider social networks, that they wished for a period of fifteen months. The resulting footage could also be shot and edited in any way that they wished. Through my relationship with the girls over this period, both on and off the camera, I learnt a great deal about how they perceived their microworlds within their wider social networks. Sixty-five young people and over fifty significant adults in their lives ultimately formed the basis of the study. The original research looked at many aspects of these lived realities and how particularly the teenagers negotiated the contradictions in their lives.

Lack of space and this particular forum requires that I narrow that focus; it is also important to state immediately that not all of the girls would have understood or sympathised with Pat's sense of 'the real me' so dramatically articulated above. For example, the concept of personhood for Janine and her friends, who identified as *Nunga*, South Australian Aboriginal, and for Mary, from Papua New Guinea, seemed to resonate with notions of relatedness and kinship rather than a Western sense of independent individualism. Nevertheless, I would still argue that for all the teenagers in my study, their sense of self, however it was inflected, was integrally enabled either through the production or consumption of the music or indeed through being able to engage in both practices.

To underpin my case, I will use Pat's concerns as a tantalising thread to unravel two aspects of personal identity and notions of 'authenticity'. I will look at the ways in which ideas of what constitutes *musical* authenticity has changed with developments in technology and how that change is reflected in the way the young women in my research, as practitioners and consumers of popular music, used music to constitute their sense of personal identities. I begin with another look at the pivotal place of music in everyday life.

Why music matters

Right from the earliest moments of my fieldwork, the participants in my research project revealed the centrality of popular music in their lives — through their first discussions with me, in their casual conversations with their friends, in the way they dressed, decorated their rooms, in the ways in which they 'carved out' and appropriated private spaces, in their music-making and in their music consumption and indeed, in *all* their social activities. Undoubtedly, music was central because it is an effective vehicle for establishing and sustaining an idealised identity (Frith 1996). More importantly, this identity itself relies upon shades of difference within similarity to express a sense of individuality and personhood. These were girls of approximately the same age, living in the same city, sometimes attending the same school and going to similar places for leisure activities but they were not from exactly the same social and ethnic backgrounds. Significantly, their musical 'tastes' and musical activities highlighted and maintained these differences, to emphasise both distinction (Bourdieu 1984) and, in post-structuralist terminology, *différance* (Derrida 1978).

Elsewhere (1996, 1998), I have highlighted the powerful and serious role of play in the lives of the young women in my wider research. I argued that play is hard work because it is the basis for the constitution and representation of the 'real me' or the 'authentic' self, that ethereal, slippery concept which eludes definition and closure.[1] On the surface, especially in the late 1990s in post-industrial societies, that 'self' seems even harder to pin down as it has become impossibly fragmented. Former social categories and symbolic boundaries that attempted to define who we are to ourselves and to others, have become suspect; ethnicity, gender and class all seem less stable in a world where communications, customs and allegiances are constantly shifting. Paul Patton refers to this as 'authentic inauthenticity' for 'it is not that postmodern lives lack meaning, but rather that the meanings are multiple, temporary and unstable... They involve investment in the image or the idea of the moment, insecure in the knowledge that it is only of the moment' (Patton 1988: 91).

In the midst of this 'sea-change', one of the ways people attempt to demonstrate who they are is through their fealty to particular social groupings, through their clothes, their demeanour, their argot, their activities, their music and their style. Polhemus suggests that 'we are, as our most distant ancestors were, dependent on style — in our dress and our dance — as the definitive means by which we can crystallise our social experiences into cultural realities' (Polhemus 1993:14). Yet perhaps inevitably, the symbols themselves, appropriated to express those social realities, also have become fragmented. Indeed, it has been argued that today's youth, frequently 'jumbling geography as well as history' in fashion, dance and music, often attempt to express that idealised self, in a 'supermarket of style' (Polhemus 1997:150).

That resulting cacophony or *bricolage* of style and symbol does not make the search any less serious, however. In fact, despite the association with trivia, with 'a sort of street-style theme park' (Polhemus 1997:149), young people's expressions of cultural identities through fashion, style, dress and dance could be considered particularly important and serious *because* they represent attempts to embody a stable, 'authentic' sense of self *despite* the shifting, segmented cultural contexts. To cite Paul Willis: 'symbolic creativity is not only part of everyday human activity, but also a... part of *necessary work*' (1990:9). Willis identifies three interrelated elements of 'necessary symbolic work' — language, bodily praxis and drama — which underlie symbolic creativity. All these aspects of self-making were integral to the young participants in my research project and their engagement with popular music, for 'it is symbolic work and creativity which realise the structured collectivity of individuals as well as their differences' (Willis 1990:12). So, music is essential to constituting an authentic sense of self both in relation *to*, and in distinction *from* others, a powerful, 'magical' vehicle of mimesis. It is akin to what Raymond Williams termed 'sympathetic magic' in advertising and other media texts (1975, 1981).

Gilbert Rouget's writings on music and trance broadly and empirically defined music as 'any sonic event... that cannot be reduced to language... and that (which) displays a certain degree of rhythmic or melodic organisation' (Rouget 1985:63).[2] Rouget confined his discussion to the way music is used in non-Western traditions in religious rituals that involve trance-like or ecstasy-induced states. Yet, many of his insights and observations can just as readily be applied to many young people in 1990 South Australia in their engagement with popular Western musical forms and genres. They too use music as an essential part of their bodily praxis to establish symbolic boundaries between self and other, the 'me' who is both like me and yet 'not-me', indicating that music clearly plays as central a part of contemporary (post)industrialised Australia, as it did in the societies and cultures which Rouget investigated.

For the teenage participants in my fieldwork, their musical allegiances and expressions of fandom were also another manifestation of the hard work of play. Music informed their sense of space, their relationship to their idealised selves and, by its very plasticity, allowed for a dialogic engagement with others. It was indeed the major vehicle for what has been identified as 'serious play' and fantasy, mimetic exploration and mimetic excess in their everyday lives (see Handelman 1990; Schechner 1993; Taussig 1993).

Music and bodily praxis

It is important to realise that much of the pleasure and power of music is that it produces emotions and affective states of mind (Levi-Strauss 1972; Willis 1990). Furthermore, recent research suggests that the affective qualities of music are universal. That is, despite common sense and academic assumptions that musical aesthetics are culturally specific, one of the most interesting aspects of current musicological research has been to point to the way certain pieces of music can arouse similar kinds of emotional states in the listeners without the listeners knowing a great deal about the context of the music or its original purpose (Storr 1992:24). Indeed, there are aspects of music which seem to be common to all cultures; a lullaby or a funeral dirge can evoke appropriate emotions in quite divergent listeners, even when they are not familiar with the type of music and its usual social context (Storr 1992; Blacking 1976, 1987). Of course, not all states of arousal by music are equally pleasant; they can be disturbing emotions such as intense grief, fear, rage or sexual excitement, as Catherine Palmer suggests in her paper in this volume. Or they can be gentler emotions that induce peace, sleep or relaxation. The point is that *all* music evokes some emotional reaction in the listener and this emotional arousal manifests itself in various physiological changes (Harrer & Harrer 1977). Again, we are reminded that physical and social identities are only possible through bodily praxis.

Certainly for younger people in contemporary Australian society, existing simultaneously in a local and a global cultural post-industrial context, music permeates and shapes everyday experiences. It is, in fact, *the* defining social context and often the 'social *glue*' through which teenagers, in particular, study, shop, relax, communicate and socialise. Particular music is used to define specific experiential cultures and social groupings, even when, to an outsider, the same music seems common to several groupings. In fact, it is the arbitrary nature of the symbolism of a particular piece of music, the connection between the signifier and its particular referent, that points to another vitally important aspect of music, that is, its ability to blur cultural boundaries and move beyond historical time and space. Storr points out the ironic ease with which the same tune, 'God Save the Queen' – the British national anthem, is used in the U.S.A. for 'My Country, 'tis of Thee'. Similarly the Christian hymn 'Abide With Me' is often played at football matches for its emotional and spiritual power without the singers feeling that they have to subscribe to Christian beliefs or even perhaps knowing that the music originally indicated such values (Storr 1992:22; see also Mark Evans, this volume). Similarly it is common practice now for advertisers to appropriate particular songs associated with original ideologies of rock music — freedom, rebellion, youthful exuberance, anti-materialism — and to re-ally these feelings with very commercialised products from multi-nationals, commodities such as denim jeans, *Coca Cola* and cigarettes. This is only possible because of the arbitrary nature of the sign and helps explain why, despite the insistence on identifiable differences and distinctions between the diverse teenage social groupings by insiders, the same music was often appropriated by different clusters as their own.

The fluidity of the nature of music in fact enables its seemingly effortless appropriation by different groups for diverse purposes. The way the teenagers in my project talked about and demonstrated their allegiances to 'their' kind of music points to the way specific music genres and styles become commonly associated with groupings, whether these are what are usually considered as teenage 'subcultures', sporting affiliations, or wider national cultures.[3]

The rhymes and the repeated rhythms of music which are an invaluable aid to memory, could explain another facet of musical pleasure: that of its nostalgic quality. Birthdays, anniversaries and ritual events are almost always associated with particular pieces or forms of music. Music habitually accompanies religious ceremonies and other rituals; it has a collective importance in many cultures, underlying and interlinked with so many disparate activities that sometimes, as in ancient Greece, 'there is no separate word for music as such' (Storr 1992:17; see also Shepherd & Wicke 1997).

So music is vitally interwoven with cultural identities both on the collective and the personal level. For the teenagers participating in my research, their very definition of self often pivoted upon their music allegiances. These allegiances were expressed in the way they spoke about their favourite musicians, singers and bands, how and where they danced or listened to these musical styles and what activities they engaged in through their favourite music. Out of this kaleidoscope of symbolic work, out of all of these aspects of their engagement with music, emerged their idealised selves, seemingly temporally 'crystallised' at that moment, simultaneously both 'fantastic' and 'real' — 'a real experience of what the ideal could be' (Frith 1996:274). In other words, music is central to both the materiality of social context and the symbolism of the self for a number of related reasons.

Music and cultural identity

Firstly, music is universally tied tightly into concepts of cultural identity and community. Musical appreciation, the critical and aesthetic response, is but a part of the whole experience of music for 'music gives us a way of being in the world... music doesn't represent values but lives them' (Frith 1996:272). These values, however, are broader than those of the immediate social groupings, being tied, in fact, into much larger aspects of culture. That is, although rock and pop are commonly perceived as being particularly *teenage* music, for the young people themselves such music enables a particular pathway to linking in with broader *adult* cultural activities. It allows them 'to situate themselves historically, culturally and politically in a much more complex system of symbolic meaning than is available locally' (Frith 1992:77; see also Finnegan 1989). So, rather than seeing such associations as *sub*cultural and by definition, *oppositional* to adult values, I argue that youth affiliations are very much *micro*cultural; simply aged, gendered and ethnically-nuanced perspectives and distillations of their larger parent cultures.[4]

Secondly and perhaps at first sight, somewhat paradoxically, music is an intensely personal bodily experience, 'a subjective sense of being sociable'. Through the way our senses engage in song, dance, performance 'we absorb songs into our own lives and rhythm into our own bodies' (Frith 1996:273). So music is powerful because it brings together both the experience of the intensely subjective and personal with the external, cultural and collective.

> *Music is concerned with feelings which are primarily individual and rooted in the body, its structural and sensuous elements resonate more with individuals' cognitive and emotional sets than with their cultural sentiments, although its external manner and expression are rooted in historical circumstances* (Blacking 1987:129).

John Blacking argues that music arouses intense bodily feelings that emphasise our inherent *humanness*; in other words 'feeling with the body' enables the individual to symbolically *merge* into 'the other'— the 'me' whom I identify as simultaneously *the same as* and yet *different* from me.

The physicality that can be expressed through music is not simply through dance, although that is clearly one of its most common manifestations.[5] In the processes of musical production and consumption, through listening, singing, instrument playing, taping or dance, the body is employed through specific practices as a symbolic resource. Indeed, the body becomes not only a way of experiencing but also a way of *knowing*, a 'site of somatic knowledge' (Willis 1990:11). A similar concept is developed in Bourdieu's notion of *cultural* and *symbolic* capital. He argues that what is manifested as 'taste' is also, in fact, *physical* capital; not just an intellectual way of asserting who one is, but also a way of asserting *authenticity,* constituting and 'proving' who one *is* or who one would like to be, through bodily praxis. So for Mary, one of my teenage participants, her demeanour, assertiveness, dress and hair style indicated to others that she was strong, tough, street-wise and proudly from Papua New Guinea. Her preferred choice of music, reggae, like that of the Aboriginal girls, indicated her affinity with a proud, assertive transcultural 'black culture'.

Referring to the Indigenous South African band, Ladysmith Black Mambazo (particularly popularised overseas after their musical collaboration with Paul Simon on *The Graceland* album), Timothy Taylor (1997) also perceives the same creation of experiential and affective cultural communities. He argues that 'wider spread commodification of musical forms allows distant solidarities to be fashioned, even "across the ocean"' (76). Similarly, examples in Philip Hayward's 1998 collection of essays in *Sound Alliances* point to the cultural complexities of musical appropriation. For example, John Castles writes of the Australian Indigenous band, No Fixed Address, 'embracing reggae as an expression of solidarity with black people everywhere' (1998:16).

But if music is to do with the boundaries of the local, material body, it is also concerned with the 'out of body', the blurring of historical and geographical boundaries, as indicated above. Music transcends the local to be in several places at the same time, simultaneously *transforming* physical and social space; it becomes a way of appropriating and distinguishing space. Undoubtedly, on one level, that is why music is so central to most religious rituals in all cultures. It explains the ways the music of one culture can be appropriated by another expressing a powerful political affinity. On another level, it explains the ubiquitous popularity of radios, the Walkman and personal tape and CD players in contemporary life (Hosokawa 1984; Thornton 1995). As each new technology develops, new ways of producing, consuming and marketing music have had marked effects on the *meanings* that are understood to emanate from all of its forms. One of the first issues that then emerges and is debated, is almost always from the question of the musical 'authenticity' of that particular style and its attendant cultural forms and meanings.

The technologised self (?)

The advent of electronic media and new technologies has other implications for concepts of musical authenticity and therefore also the perceived 'authenticity' of the performer and consumer of that music. It means that the performance and consumption of music can be undertaken far from the original place of origin. As Jody Berland reminds us, 'music is now heard mainly in technologically communicated form, not live, and its circulation through these spaces (in connection with that of its listeners), along with its assimilation to and appropriation of previous contexts for musical performance, is part of the elaboration of its forms and meanings' (Berland 1992:39; see also Rosing 1984:119-149). Music, in other words, has become completely mobile, moving with us from room to room, country to country, from work to leisure. It can also move us emotionally, as from depression to elation. Moreover, it can be endlessly reproduced without any loss in quality. Indeed, as Frith points out, 'the "past" of music is endlessly re-experienced in its presence; the most distant or strange music is heard in our most familiar surroundings... music is now the everyday (and silence becomes the mark of the special moment)' (Frith 1996:236-237).

In these ways, contemporary practices of engaging with music particularly through new technologies, through ever evolving 'mimetic machinery' (Taussig 1993:20), can blur our sense of time and space. Music connects the private experience into the public. It blurs the self and other; the song I listen to expresses *my* feelings even though I did not write it. When I perform someone else's music, I express their feelings although I am a different person. So music is indeed a powerful, 'magical' vehicle of mimesis.

In Sarah Thornton's (1995) study of British club cultures she argues that 'the cultural form closest to the lives of the majority of British youth is in fact music. Youth subcultures tend to be music subcultures' (19). In my own research, as indicated above, I discovered a similarly-perceived centrality of music — although I would challenge this definition and interpretation of a 'microculture' as a 'subculture'. Rather I found that music took the form of symbolic capital in a variety of arenas to represent many different aspects of everyday practice, knowledge and experience. It was a way for the young people to situate themselves within wider cultural contexts.

These cultural contexts have become even more complex however with the advent of each new way of performing, producing and listening to music, noted above. New technologies, for example, have brought about particular changes in the way we *engage* with music. The use of modern engineering devices highlights the way we no longer simply 'listen' to music (Frith 1996).[6] The music we hear is affected by the choices *we* make on the turn-table, the dial, the mixer and the player. In the dance clubs and Rave scenes, the DJ and MC who skilfully mix and sample the pre-recorded sounds to create new music have become the revered artists of the 1990s (Haslam 1997). Their performances remind us that we too can become such musicians, for here the body and the technology blend to form a different kind of instrument. They also alert us to the way DJs have become the linking medium between the music and the audience.

As with the advent of the VCR and its effect on television watching, CD players and burners, the Walkman, and computer terminals, can all recreate audiences of a different kind. They encourage and enable the consumers to produce, rearrange and recreate the kind of music they listen to.[7] They can have new political meanings such as in the parody of the leader of the One Nation party's (Pauline Hanson) racist speeches, resampled in Pauline Pantsdown's CD and music video, 'I Don't Like It'.[8] Hence, the lines between consumption and production, between the original and the copy, become blurred. In other words, like those ephemeral self identities that we struggle to 'fix', music itself has become a *process* of becoming, something we now experience as fragmented and unstable (Hosokawa 1990; Berland 1992).[9]

Such examples point to the connection between on-going, popular concepts of 'self' and musical authenticity, the nexus between the 'real' and representation in the enormity (some would say the impossibility) of the search for 'the real me'. They resonate with the insights of Walter Benjamin and Michael Taussig. Benjamin had believed that in 'the age of mechanical reproduction', uniqueness, or what he termed the 'aura', would cease to be considered the most important quality of a work of art. New technologies, he hoped, would bring about a new democratisation of cultural goods. Yet, as he suspected, the desire for uniqueness would be difficult to dismiss and indeed, the magical 'aura' has not disappeared with the diffusing of what was previously thought of as high culture. It hasn't even been demystified but has disseminated and dispersed into other cultural forms (Thornton 1995). The goal posts have moved. Now the 'authentic' has switched from the original to the copy. For example, the new technological methods of producing music from the 1970s meant that original music was created in the studio not on the stage; the authentic was the recorded. Furthermore, Benjamin saw the advent of technology bringing about the rebirth of the mimetic faculty: 'the nature that culture uses to create a second nature, the faculty to copy, imitate, make models, explore difference, yield into and become Other' (Taussig 1993:*xiii*).

These two related notions, the power of the mimetic faculty and the dissemination of 'the aura', lead us back to the concepts of musical authenticity and cultural identity and where these intertwine. The concept of 'authenticity' is perhaps the most fundamental aspect of musical meaning with its embeddedness in the 'rhetorics of self-making' (Battaglia 1995). It permeates discussions of Western popular music, fandom, fanzines, and dance clubs because, ultimately, it is concerned with the expression of the individual vision, the individual self, the 'real me' which is seen simultaneously to be part of a particular cultural perspective.[10] Indeed, popular music for most of the young women in my research project seemed to be valued above everything else for its underpinning and linking of the concept of musical authenticity and their own refracted sense of selfhood.[11]

Desperately seeking authenticity

A particularly vivid example of this link occurred during my field work. The occasion was when I met one of the teenage participants in my research, a young woman called J.D. It served for me as an immediate and dramatic reminder of the vital nexus between music and bodily praxis.

The incident took place during that part of my fieldwork spent at several Blue Light discos. One evening, Wendy, one of the young police constables on duty that night, pointed out a young girl whom she said had been 'acting strangely'. Addressed by adults and teenagers alike as J.D., this young teenager, probably aged thirteen, was also identified by the police as a 'trouble maker'. I looked carefully and with a new respect at this petite, young woman who, at first sight, seemed far too small and insipid to have such an awesome reputation. Wendy soon discovered that J.D. was '*illicitly* attending the dance' that night, in that she had absconded from a correctional services' half-way house just to attend the disco.[12] By the time the police realised who she was, they felt it was too late to send her back again straight away and allowed her to stay until the end of the evening. When not on the dance floor or chatting in the toilets, J.D. and her friends stood just outside the main door talking to the young *male* 'offenders' who had not been permitted to attend that week. Apparently, they hadn't been as wily as J.D. to get in unidentified.

What J.D. lacked in physical size, she apparently made up for in personality and sheer dynamism. On closer inspection, she seemed to be a tiny bottle of energy just waiting to explode, rarely standing completely still, even in the confined space of the women's toilets. Even when Wendy challenged her about her attendance at the disco, J.D. stood swaying slightly, eyes half-closed, as though her energy was just simmering under the surface of a temporarily quiescent body. Ostensibly, however, J.D.'s behaviour was not to attract the attention of the police or other authority figures, but mainly to draw the notice of boys at the dance through a very dramatic display of self. At one point she appeared by my side while I was talking to her friend, Emma. Without ceremony and ignoring me, she grabbed

Emma's arm. 'Quick, come in', she urged, 'Jessica's getting all the heap cool guys. There'll be no heap cool guys for us to get off with'. She then dragged Emma back into the dance area. It was there that she suddenly performed a most amazing display of dancing.

The song being played was 'The Time Warp', the popular track from *The Rocky Horror Picture Show*. As usual, it was a dance that the teenagers danced in unison, most participants knowing the steps. However, in the middle of this symmetry, J.D. danced flamboyantly and idiosyncratically. A space cleared around her as others stopped to stare and admire. Emma herself made no attempt to join in or dance at this point. She just stood and watched J.D.'s display in manifestly stunned admiration. J.D.'s dance was an exaggerated parody of usual steps and movements but here there was also something splendid! This tiny figure had suddenly erupted into an excessive expression of uninhibited movement. What came to my mind was that, above all, J.D. was presenting her admirers with an extraordinary expression of freedom through dance movements, despite (or perhaps because of) the fact that she would shortly be returned to the juvenile detention centre. After all, this was hardly an attempt to escape the notice of the authorities on duty. The underlying paradox was that her expression of authenticity and individual personhood was expressed through a particularly self-conscious and stylised *representation* of freedom. The movement had to indicate to all around her that *this* was freedom! *This* was uninhibited movement. Its very self-consciousness rendered it a particularly fine example of mimetic excess.

Music and other bodies

J.D.'s display was excessive. Yet it brought to my mind many other examples throughout my fieldwork of the way music was used by the teenagers to explore, to underpin and to experiment with the very *physicality* of their self-making. I have described elsewhere, how Grace had danced silently and alone in front of the video camera, watching and recording herself dancing to her favourite band; how Diane and her friends exaggeratedly mimicked the movements of the models and dancers on the Peter André video as they danced and postured in front of Diane's television set; how Janelle and her friends practised dance steps before the mirrors in their school hall (see Bloustien 1996, 1998).

Dancing to Peter André

It is easy to overlook the significance and the wider implications of such play. Behind the obvious fun and pleasure lie very purposeful reflections, explorations and (self) creativity; 'The imaginative is self-validating!' (Willis 1990:10).

Through their bodies, individuals experience and claim as their own a sensation of being (appropriately) *other;* 'appropriately' because such a claim and adherence must reflect and help *constitute* the self within a framework that one *already* accepts for oneself. Diane, for example, in her claims of fandom to Peter André or to New Kids on the Block ('I'm a *really* big fan of theirs') was creating and affirming in herself the sensation of bathing in the glow of a romantic (heterosexual) ideal. In her situation, with her particular style of music, the romantic lyrics and the overt 'maleness' of the stars are particularly important. In her video footage, for example, she suddenly interrupted her own flow of direct address to the camera to listen more closely to the music she had been playing in the background.

> *I'll leave you with this song 'Dream a Little' by Peter André (eyes closed for a moment in an extravagant gesture of immense pleasure). It is such a beautiful, beautiful song (Diane, direct to camera).*

In the same way that she had previously indicated that her choice of popular brand-named clothes pointed to her knowledge of fashion and taste ('I can hold my head up') so her selection of music here indicates her knowledge of and embeddedness in discourses of romance and heterosexual love. In contrast, Fran's declared choice of popular music allowed her a different kind of knowledge. *Her* exaggerated dance movements and her accompanying raunchy language, as for example when she directed her friends' attentions to another girl's dance style at a party ('Hey, everyone, look at M.! She's fucking a pole') indicated her worldliness and her casual sexual knowledge.

In contrast, Wanda, Janine's cousins and one of her closest friends, told me quite seriously and unselfconsciously that 'music is in my soul'. She and her friends were part of an teenage Aboriginal rock band called Black Image. Her friend, Janelle, did not verbally articulate her love of particular music on camera but she demonstrated her embodiment of knowledgeable 'authentic' musician as she played the drum in her band practice. As she played she suddenly closed her eyes, slowly moved her head from side to side as though immensely moved by the music. It was a wonderful moment of 'striking a pose', a simultaneous representation and constitution of the 'real-me-as-musician' that she was portraying at that moment.

Janelle strikes a pose

So in these ways, the teenagers in my research project used their musical fealties to express and constitute a self that was associated with a particular musical style, genre or star. It was vitally important to them that this sense of belonging was seen as 'real', part of their whole being, even if sometimes, as with Janelle, I also caught their self-conscious reflexive gaze in *my* camera lens.[13] The musical style selected was not simply an expression of what they *liked* but who they *were*; not simply who they *were* but also who they *would like to be*. It was a dialectic exploration of 'being' and 'becoming' at the same moment — identity as process.

Polhemus, in fact, argues from a different perspective. He suggests that today young people are far less committed to a particular style or musical taste. He states, 'back in 1964 you *were* a Mod or a Rocker. Today you are *into* Techno, Reggae or Acid Jazz. It's the difference between swimming and sticking your foot in the pool to check out the temperature — an exploratory dalliance versus immersion and commitment' (1997:149). My experience and observations were very different. For the young people who participated in my research, how they dressed, moved and danced were used as particularly clear pointers of their struggle to constitute 'authentic' selves, even if today those selves are perhaps even more difficult to 'fix' than those of people in the 1960s. It separated the 'real' from the 'fake'. The 'authentic' is what distinguishes the 'Real' from the 'Try Hards' although what exactly constitutes the 'real thing' differs from group to group, and girl to girl, even within one cultural activity. Association with a particular musical style, grouping or fashion is an attempt to 'prove' one's established authenticity. But that authenticity also is founded on wider cultural links than just the music. It could be argued that a greater understanding of those links is provided by Bourdieu's concept of *habitus*.

> *What is called 'creation' is the encounter between a socially constituted* habitus *and a particular position that is already instituted or* possible *in the division of the labour of cultural production* (Bourdieu 1993:141).

As Bourdieu points out, to sociologically analyse cultural 'tastes', including those of popular music, 'means understanding, on the one hand, the conditions in which the products on offer are produced, and on the other hand, the conditions in which the 'consumers produce themselves'' (1993:112). In other words, musical 'tastes' and the underpinning relationship created between musical and personal 'authenticity', depends upon the emotional investments that the individual has already established. Moreover, Bourdieu defines 'investment' as:

> *the propensity to act that is born of the relation between a field and a system of dispositions adjusted to the game it proposes, a sense of the game and of its stakes that implies at once an* inclination *and an* ability *to play the game*[14] (Bourdieu & Wacquant 1992:118).

In other words, to make sense of those musical distinctions of the young women in my fieldwork, one has to search beyond the teenager's immediate perspective and look into their established familial and social networks. The allegiances are not separate nor, more importantly, are they trying to be. So for example, Pat's sense of self through her participation in Raves and techno music in her 'dance club scenes'; Diane's fandom of New Kids on the Block and Peter André; Fran's attraction to 'new age' music; Sara's passion for 'world music'; Grace's love of Violent Femmes; Janine's playing and Mary's enjoyment of reggae, were significant *precisely* because they expressed an aspect of each girl's sense of an idealised, individualised self while *simultaneously* intertwining with each girl's wider social allegiances.

Music production and the search for the real me

The search for distinction between the 'real' and the 'inauthentic' and the struggle to manifest the difference, are also tacitly behind the respective bodily praxes, the (playful) 'practices' of styles of dance and movement of the teenagers in front of mirrors or cameras. It also helps explain the different forms of music *production* that the girls were engaged in. Apart from involvement with music as consumers, several of the teenagers were also actively engaged with making or producing music. Kate played a trombone and electronic keyboard, Sara played the violin, Diane played a guitar, Janine played guitar and some keyboard within her rock band, Pat worked in a voluntary capacity at a techno radio station and learnt how to MC at Raves. Their choices of instrument and musical production were not as arbitrary as appears at first sight if examined in the light of their familial contexts and 'investments'. Firstly of course, the kind of instrument they selected was determined partly by finances and educational opportunity and access, for all of the teenagers who played an instrument were taught to play them through an educational institution. Pat's development of her techno production skills was only gained after she saved up to take a suitable training course. So what instrument they chose was partly determined by what choices were made available to them within those institutions and within the financial constraints of their personal situations.

Yet secondly, even within these constraints were other factors. Janine's choice of instrument and style of music is perfectly in keeping with a paradigm acceptable to her Aboriginal family and wider social network. During my fieldwork I attended several of Black Image's concerts and performances. At many of those performances, Janine's band would play amongst other Indigenous musicians, even sometimes including those who have become very widely appreciated, such as Archie Roach or the members of Trochus. During WOMADelaide, a biennial world music event held in the city parklands, I often saw Janine and her friends wandering the grounds, enjoying the music and attending some of the Aboriginal performances. In other words, they could attend not only as consumers of the music, but also knowing they could be part of the 'scene' as Indigenous musicians in their own right.[15]

In a similar way, Kate's trombone was used to express her sense of self that fitted within *her* familial schema for an idealised self. Kate was brought up to see herself as an independent, non-conformist, feminist young woman. Kate demonstrated this representation and constitution of herself through her clothes, her activities, her great ebullient physicality. She took great pleasure in showing me her musical ability on the trombone, delighting, of course, in its size, its awkwardness, its loud noise and its unconventional image for a fifteen-year old girl. The loud farting noise that she could produce from it also added greatly to her sense of fun and incongruity. Like Kate herself, her brass instrument and its sound in the house was physically excessive, appropriating space and deliberately unsettling domesticity through its noise and sheer presence.

Conclusion

The central concerns in this paper have been the ways in which music underpinned the process of each teenager's simultaneous representation and constitution of self, the nexus between concepts of 'musical' and personal (cultural) authenticity. I have explored just some of the ways in which serious play and its more extreme, theatrical manifestation of mimetic excess enabled explorations of each girl's sense of self to be constituted and performed, both materially and symbolically. Through their bodily behaviours, gestures, dress and musical 'tastes', the girls tested out their 'being' in the world within preconceived boundaries, as gendered, classed, ethnic and aged agents. All of these aspects of self-making: the physical, the emotional, the sexual, the material and the symbolic, are, of course, intricately linked. The sense of one's 'place' in the world is about how one 'relocates' oneself and about how one's social identities are established within discursive contexts and within moral and political hierarchies. In Giddens' phraseology, it is also how we 're-embed' ourselves, as spaces become 'phantasmagorically' separated from place (Giddens 1990:88). As a consequence of modernity, places become 'thoroughly penetrated by and shaped in terms of social influences quite distant from them' (18). These influences, expressed through diverse activities and practices, highlight the way they both reflect and *create* social groupings.

In other words, on the one hand it is clear that popular cultural activities emerge as an expression of particular values from social groupings — clearly, they have a material social origin. On the other hand, and perhaps more importantly, the social groupings themselves are *created* and shaped through the shared aesthetic expression of specific cultural activities. These activities and social performances have to be understood as practices 'in which meanings are generated, manipulated and even ironised, within certain limitations' (Stokes 1994:4). Particularly in the case of young people, they are always underpinned by, and expressed through, popular music.

But, as suggested earlier, the musical tastes and distinctions of my teenage participants were both derived from their familial and social backgrounds and simultaneously helped to form them. So, for example, rather than music and musical taste *reflecting* aspects of a preconceived sexuality or conventional gendered or 'classed' behaviour, we need to see that the forms and aesthetics of popular music are signifying *practices* through which discourses of sexuality, gender, ethnicity and 'class' are negotiated (Frith 1996).

Most research carried out on youth cultures does not incorporate the whole of the teenagers' worlds, both within their home and their extramural activities. It is only on closer everyday contact across these different contexts, through a thoroughly ethnographic approach and thus by engaging with the participants in their different contexts and social 'fields' (Bourdieu 1992, 1993), that one can see that the concept of the 'authentic' that seems to be idiosyncratically linked to a particular music taste and youth microculture, was in fact firmly embedded in each girl's parent culture.

Notes

1 Also see Handelman 1990.

2 There seem to be very few appropriate all-encompassing definitions of music available in the literature as concise as this one. I am concerned with the cultural significance of the various forms of popular music in the processes of self-making in the lives of the young women in my research project. For this purpose, although perhaps limited as an overall account of musical forms, Rouget's definition is an excellent spring-board.

3 Again, see Catherine Palmer's, Motti Regev's and Tony Mitchell's contributions to this volume.

4 While like Motti Regev, I draw on Bourdieu's insights in this claim, I have deliberately not included the category of class in this perspective as I feel that this concept is far more complex and heterogeneous than is usually understood. As I have already discussed, the girls in my research project often came from what would usually be identified as the same 'class' but their *self*-identification, consciousness and modes of expression of this social positioning were quite different.

5 See Bruce Johnson this volume. Several essays in Helen Thomas's collection *Dance, Gender, Culture* also make this point, that 'there is evidence to suggest that dancing not only plays an important role in the life of a number of pre-industrial societies, but it also performs a significant function in the process of gender construction and identification' (Thomas 1993: 71).

6 Of course, it is a matter of contention if we were ever 'merely' listeners, at least to popular music. Appreciation of classical music is traditionally expressed through the stillness and control of the body whereas the listener of popular music (jazz, folk, pop, rock and so on) expresses her enjoyment through bodily movement. As my own teenage daughter exclaimed in exasperation at a rock concert when she was told by the bouncers to 'sit down', 'How can you listen to this (rock) music and *not* dance?'

7 Henry Jenkins' work frequently studies this aspect of fandom. He explores the way audiences and consumers are active cultural 'poachers'. See for example 1992.

8 Pauline Pantsdown, a drag artist, changed his stage name and dressed like Pauline Hanson to attend all her political rallies. He then produced the music clip from the political leader's own words to parody, highlight and ridicule One Nation's political stance. The CD and video clip were played continuously on ABC radio and TV (Triple J and *Rage*) until Hanson brought an injunction against their airing. In the meantime many young people had watched and listened to the parody — even if they had failed to attend to the original racist arguments. How effective the strategy was as a political tool is perhaps debatable but humour and carnival, of course, can always seem empowering!

9 That is, although in common usage and in the writing of music critics, distinctions and definitions are made between different types of musical genres, on the ground, young people are very aware that such distinctions as, for example, between techno, hip hop and 'dance music' are not so finely drawn.

10 So Billy Bragg's music is seen to represent a particular neo-Marxist, working class stance while Ani DiFranco's music portrays a young feminist vision. It is these wider cultural and collective affinities that their fans can hold on to and appropriate as their own.

11 Although as indicated earlier that 'self' could be profoundly enmeshed with a wider cultural identity rather than resonating with Western individualism.

12 These were assessment centres where those people officially designated/identified as 'young offenders' were placed for a short period of time while the assessment team, youth workers, psychologists and legal representatives, decided between them where the young person should be sent — to a remand home or back into the community.

13 I have only room here to signal the issues of reflexivity embedded in this methodology. Further discussion can be found particularly in Bloustien 1996 and 1998.

14 It is also important to realise that both ability and inclination to 'play the game' are not the same for every person but are 'socially and historically constituted' (Bourdieu & Wacquant 1992:118).

15 The tickets for WOMAD were always expensive but in the first few years of its establishment as a biennial event in Adelaide, children under fifteen were admitted free with their fee-paying parents or adult family members. Even after that time, the families and friends of the performing musicians were usually given some complimentary entrance tickets.

References

Battaglia, D. (ed) 1995, *Rhetorics of Self-Making,* Berkeley: University of California Press.

Benjamin, W. 1969, *Illuminations,* New York: Schocken Books.

Berland, J. 1992, 'Angels Dancing: Cultural technologies and the Production of Space', in Grossberg, L., Nelson C. & Treichler, P. (eds) *Cultural Studies,* New York: Routledge.

Blacking, J. 1977, *The Anthropology of the Body,* New York: Academic Press.

Blacking, J. 1976, *How Musical Is Man?* London: Faber and Faber.

Blacking, J. 1987, *A Common-Sense View of All Music,* Cambridge: Cambridge University Press.

Bloustien, G. 1996, 'Striking a Pose: Girls, Cameras and Deflecting the Gaze' in *Youth Studies Australia,* 15:3.

Bloustien, G. 1998, 'It's Different To a Mirror 'Cos It Talks to You' in Howard, S. (ed) *Wired Up : Young People and The Electronic Media,* London: Falmer Press, Media Education and Culture - Series Editor: David Buckingham.

Bloustien, G. 1999, 'The Consequence of Being a Gift', in TAJA, 10:1.

Bourdieu, P. 1984, *Distinction: A Social Critique of the Judgment of Taste,* Cambridge, Mass.: Harvard University Press.

Bourdieu, P. & Wacquant, L.J.D. 1992, *An Invitation to Reflexive Sociology,* Chicago: University of Chicago Press.

Bourdieu, P. 1993, *Sociology in Question,* London: Sage Publications.

Castles, J. 1998, 'Tjungaringanyi: Aboriginal Rock (1971-91)' in Hayward, P. (ed) *Sound Alliances: Indigenous Peoples, Cultural Politics and Popular Music in the Pacific,* London: Cassell.

Derrida, J. 1973, *'Différance'* in *Speech and Phenomena,* Illinois: Northwest University Press.

Derrida, J. 1978, 'Structure, Sign and Play in the Discourse of Human Sciences' in *Writing and Difference,* London: Routledge.

Finnegan, R. 1989, *Hidden Musicians,* Cambridge: Cambridge University Press.

Frith, S. 1992, 'The Cultural Study of Popular Music' in Grossberg L., et al (eds) *Cultural Studies,* London: Routledge.

Frith, S. 1996, *Performing Rites,* Cambridge, Mass.: Harvard University Press.

Giddens, A. 1990, *The Consequences of Modernity,* Cambridge: Polity Press.

Handelman, D. 1990, *Models and Mirrors: Towards an Anthropology of Public Events,* Cambridge: Cambridge University Press.

Harrer, G. & Harrer, H. 1977, 'Music Emotion and Automatic Function' in Critchley, M. & Henson, R.A. (eds) *Music and the Brain,* London: Heineman.

Haslam, D. 1997, 'DJ Culture' in Redhead, S. (ed) *The Club Cultures Reader,* Oxford: Blackwell.

Hayward, P. (ed) 1998, *Sound Alliances: Indigenous Peoples, Cultural Politics and Popular Music in the Pacific,* London: Cassell.

Hosokawa, S. 1984, 'The Walkman Effect' in *Popular Music IV.*

Hosokawa, S. 1990, *The Aesthetics of Recorded Sound,* Tokyo: Keisó Shobó.

Jenkins, H. 1992, *Textual Poachers,* London: Routledge.

Levi-Strauss, C. 1972, [c1966] *The Savage Mind,* London: Weidenfeld & Nicholson.

Patton P. 1998, 'Giving Up the Ghost: Postmodernism and Anti-nihilism' in Grossberg, L. (ed) It's a Sin: Essays on Postmodernism, Politics and Culture, Sydney: Power Publications.

Polhemus, T. 1978, (ed) *Social Aspects of the Human Body,* Harmonsworth: Penguin Books.

Polhemus, T. 1993, 'Dance Gender and Culture' in Thomas, H. (ed) *Dance Gender and Culture,* London: Macmillan.

Polhemus, T. 1997, 'In the Supermarket of Style' in Redhead, S. (ed) *The Club Cultures Reader,* Cambridge: Blackwells.

Rosing, H. 1984, 'Listening Behaviour and Musical Preferences in the Age of Transmitted Music' in *Popular Music, 5: Continuity and Change.*

Rouget, G. 1985, *Music and Trance: A Theory of Relations Between Music and Possession,* Chicago & London: The University of Chicago Press.

Schechner, R. 1993, *The Future of Ritual,* Routledge: London.

Shepherd, J. & Wicke, P. 1997, *Music and Cultural Theory,* Cambridge: Polity Press.

Stokes, M. (ed) 1994, *Ethnicity, Identity and Music: The Musical Construction of Place,* Oxford: Berg.

Storr, A. 1992, *Music and The Mind,* London: Harper Collins Publishers.

Taylor, T. 1997, *Global Pop: World Music, World Markets,* London, New York: Routledge.

Taussig, M. 1993, *Mimesis and Alterity,* New York: Routledge.

Thornton, S. 1995, *Club Cultures: Music, Media and Subcultural Capital,* Cambridge: Polity Press.

Williams, R. 1975, *Television, Society and Cultural Form,* New York: Schocken Books.

Williams, R. 1981, *Culture,* London: Fontana.

Willis, P. 1990, *Common Culture,* Buckingham: Open University Press.

DRIVEN BY THE SONIC LANGUAGE PASSION

ANDREW BRADLEY

This paper is a transcription from a discussion panel held at the University of Technology, Sydney (1998) for 'Urban Xpressions', an annual festival celebrating local hip hop culture. Transcribed and edited by Emma Masters.

I've only been back in Australia for two weeks now, going on three weeks. I was in New York for just over a month and I guess that is what I am really here to talk about. As an Australian who has been involved in hip hop — I came up doing bad graffiti when I was a younger dude and moved into the music area (I picked up MC'ing in the early 1990's and… here I am) — for me, I thought it was essential that I got out of Australia and experience other countries. I had been to Europe previously where I had gone to Germany and I was incredibly vibed by the way that hip hop lives and breathes in Germany. You would go to a jam and you would see guys breaking, next to guys painting the wall, next to freestyle cyclists, everything. For me, coming from Australia where that is such a remote thing, that was inspirational and I knew when I did that trip that I would have to get back overseas, and primarily, get to New York.

New York is the spot where hip hop began. It is the point where it was named. It was the region where scratching was invented, and all the early bombers, graffiti writers, came from. The whole culture is essentially straight forth from New York. I felt it essential that I got there and that I understood why it was that I was so deeply involved in this culture, why I loved it so much and what I could learn from people whose experience has been very, very different from mine here in Australia. And the hip hop experience that I found in New York is one that is very different to here, in all sorts of ways. I mean, you step off the plane in New York and you are literally attacked by hip hop. You walk into every shop and you hear it on the speakers in the store, you walk down the street and every pole is covered in stickers for the latest material that's being dropped. Every few days, every few nights there is an event happening in the record stores, there are appearances by artists whose records most people in this room go out and buy.

So, for the first week or so, I kind of found myself wandering around in this sort of daze. Like, 'my god, where do I start'… I mean, where do you start? First of all, as someone who buys records, I suddenly had this incredible option open, of like 'shit man, I've got all this vinyl I can get into'. So that was one of the first things that struck me.

When the experience of being there and the sensations and the vibes sort of died back, a little, I guess I started to look at myself as an artist; as someone who attempts to craft themselves as a lyricist. I classify myself as an lyricist or MC and I do believe that I have some ability. What I wanted was to discover and understand what ability I have in regards to the rest of the world, in regards to being in New York where it was invented. So I was very, very surprised at the way that I was received.

Firstly, when I approached record companies and artists to try to do interviews for my writing, and also for a radio show (93.7 Degreez in the Shade, 3D Radio), I was very, very surprised at the way I was

Andrew (Quro) performing with the Fuglemen at the 'Resuscitation' album launch

taken in. People were like: 'Word, you from Australia? Come in, come in here and talk to us, tell us what's happening there'. People know that they sell records in Australia but they have no idea of what happens here. There is this absolute mystique about Australia and that cuts right across the board — through our film and through other music, art, everything. Australia is looked at like this bizarre place that nobody knows anything about. So, suddenly these people are sitting down with somebody that, for the first time, they can talk to on a personal level in the same room about what is happening in Australia. It also made me think about what we have here, from another perspective.

I'll be straight up about this. Before I left Australia in November I was at the point where I was really questioning my contribution to hip hop in this country. The time and the energy that I invest in writing, in putting on a radio show, in writing lyrics, in freestyling… I was questioning the time and energy because what we get back in this country is very limited. We don't sell records. Straight up. I don't think there is a hip hop artist in this country that can say they've probably sold more that a thousand copies of any release. So anyone, put up their hand… Def Wish Cast maybe, sorry. But it is still limited. What I am saying is that — we do not sell records, we do not sell a lot of records. We do not have any internal structures in this country. We do not have a record company that is devoted to promoting and pushing Australian talent, we do not have a national radio show, we do not have a national magazine. We do not, for the most part, have a great deal of contact between the cities. There are obviously people here who talk, converse, but for the most part, how many people in this room that are performers perform in Melbourne, Adelaide, Perth. For the most part we're so separated. But!

We're here — we are having a 10 day festival celebrating hip hop and hip hop culture in this country. We put out records. They may not sell, but we put out records. We have, in my opinion, some of the most gifted turntablists in the world. We have some of the most gifted producers. We have some of the most amazing rhymers that are absolutely on their own level, working on material that is unique, that is on a vibe that nobody else, in the world, that I have heard is doing. It is essentially Australian. I do believe that somehow, in some bizarre manner, we have managed to create a culture which is like nowhere else.

Australian hip hop can, and will, continue to survive and grow if people are prepared to continue to invest their time and energy in not only themselves, but in respecting and purchasing other peoples material… there's a whole series of things. If people in Australia that are involved in hip hop culture, whether they are aerosol artists, DJ's, producers, rhymers, or whether they are a kid on the street who loves it, if we can all somehow channel what we have — all our abilities and strengths that we have come to have through the hard work and time and energy that we have invested — if we can somehow harness that, then we can truly all start to push each other. I feel that it's time that people put aside their personal ambitions as artists work together. Then will come a point where we have a structure where there is a company who can distribute our material, when there is a magazine where you can read about our latest releases, where there is a TV show, where there is a radio show. After all, just about every other country in this world has their own TV show or radio show, why don't we have one in Australia?

Basically what I am saying is that we all, as artists, have something to offer. We all have unique talents and abilities and it is essential we understand that we are the ones who have to build the structures. That is something that I feel myself, Madcap and Jain in Adelaide have been actively trying to do for years... put on shows, put out our own material, support one another. I believe that once we have established some sort of structures, then we can take our stuff to the world and we can say 'listen — we've done this with help from each other, this is what we have done in Australia'. We really do have the talent to really make some power moves, I think that once we get the actual structures to distribute material overseas and to get the publicity right, I believe Australian hip hop can go a long way.

QUEERYING THE VOICE: ELECTROVOCALITY AND THE DOMESTICATED MUSIC STUDIO

JENJO BROWN

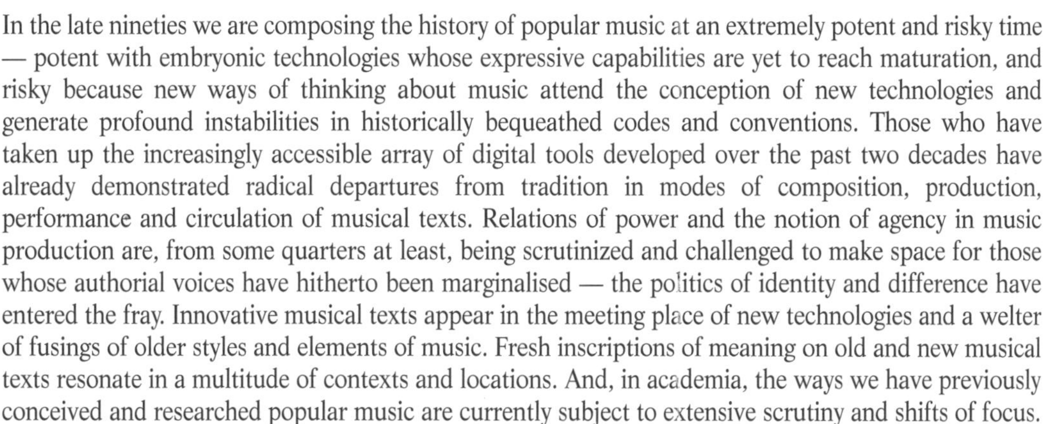

In the late nineties we are composing the history of popular music at an extremely potent and risky time — potent with embryonic technologies whose expressive capabilities are yet to reach maturation, and risky because new ways of thinking about music attend the conception of new technologies and generate profound instabilities in historically bequeathed codes and conventions. Those who have taken up the increasingly accessible array of digital tools developed over the past two decades have already demonstrated radical departures from tradition in modes of composition, production, performance and circulation of musical texts. Relations of power and the notion of agency in music production are, from some quarters at least, being scrutinized and challenged to make space for those whose authorial voices have hitherto been marginalised — the politics of identity and difference have entered the fray. Innovative musical texts appear in the meeting place of new technologies and a welter of fusings of older styles and elements of music. Fresh inscriptions of meaning on old and new musical texts resonate in a multitude of contexts and locations. And, in academia, the ways we have previously conceived and researched popular music are currently subject to extensive scrutiny and shifts of focus.

Herman, Swiss and Sloop (1998) refer to this process as a reconceptualisation within popular musicology from a framework based on three distinct areas of emphasis — namely, production, text and consumption — to a spatialized analysis of popular music which maps the social dynamics of production and consumption as a terrain of power and difference. They refer to the work of Jacques Attali, Henri Lefebvre and others to develop the notion of 'mapping the beat' between spaces of noise and places of music. For Attali, music is the endowment of noise with form and is conceived as a space of harmony for those within its boundaries, providing a structure of interpretation and identity through which a dominant ordering of power and difference are articulated.

> *For those in positions of musicianship and listenership that are located within the dominant code of music, noise is 'unlistenable' static and interference, a cacophonous anarchy of sound. Thus noise, as an element of the aural soundscape of society, can challenge positions of power and difference that are assumed to be 'natural'. On the other hand, if a dominant aural framing of power and difference is to be maintained, noise must either be silenced, contained, or domesticated and incorporated in the dominant culture. Accordingly, the history of music in general and of popular music in particular can be understood in terms of this dynamic tension between the popular noise of subordinate or marginal groups and the popular music of dominant culture (Herman, Swiss & Sloop 1998: 19).*

The leaky margin between noise and music is a potent and risky site from which the sounds of the not-yet-popular and the never-to-be popular are pitched and echo noisily off the brittle walls that fortify musical virtue (however that may be conceived in particular instances of time and place). For the past forty years, the electroacoustic avant-garde have been experimenting noisily with electronically processed vocal sounds to create pieces which have been referred to variously as sonic poetry, electrovocal music, sound-text or sonic art, depending on the institutional context in which a particular text is produced and circulated. The works I refer to here are those in which the processed voice is the only instrument used or is dominant in the timbral palette. The original means of electronically manipulating the voice was the tape recorder in the 1950s and 1960s. This was followed by the mainframe computer with elaborate programming in the 1960s and 1970s, and by the development of MIDI in the early 1980s. In the late 1990s, hard-disk recording and sound processing with softwares ready-made for the personal computer are becoming commonplace. All of these technologies have been utilised in popular musics, along with electric instruments and synthesisers and indeed, vocal sounds are commonly subjected to electronic manipulation in terms of amplification, compression and the addition of effects such as echo and reverb, and equalisation. However, radical manipulations of vocality and its centralisation within the musical form remain relatively unexplored in popular music, despite Laurie Anderson's chart success with 'O Superman' (1981).

It would seem that, in the context of popular music discourse, electrovocal musics have largely been consigned to those spaces beyond the boundaries of accepted musical convention as 'noise', despite their legitimisation as 'music' in the electroacoustic avant-garde. I want to suggest that this is no coincidence, that certain 'truths' are currency across a multitude of sites in which popular music circulates and effectively re/produces very particular kinds of relationships among bodies, artifacts and texts in such a way as to marginalise vocality itself within the audible terrain. A central theme of this discourse, in white western contexts at least, is a dualistic rendering of vocality and virtuosity as binary opposites with virtuosity in the privileged and valourised position. Vocality aligns with the body, the emotions, the intuitive, the disorderly, the unpredictable, the non-white and the feminine. Virtuosity is strongly associated with technology, the rational mind, order, skill, whiteness, and the masculine. Such classic dualisms (Gatens 1991:122-123) serve to re/produce existing power relations by presenting culturally constructed hierarchical categories of difference in productive roles as if they were 'natural' and 'normal' divisions of skill and space.

In this dominant discourse, music technologies and the spaces in which they are materially and culturally located are normalised in multiple sites around the industry as masculinist domains and the feminine, represented most coherently by the female body, is marginalised, even totally absent.[1] Since those in the privileged position of a binary may appropriate roles and resources from its Other without censure, white male bodies are not only legitimated as virtuosos (in composition, instrumental performance, and sound engineering) but also as vocalists. Women and others on the intersecting undersides of such hierarchical categories as race, class and age typically negotiate musical agency from the margins as vocalists and meet with censure if this condition of participation is transgressed.

This pronounced vectoring of gender around modes of agency in popular music is highly problematic to a post-feminist framework that destabilises notions of fixity and essence adhering to the body. And indeed it is foregrounded as an equity issue for female music practitioners, many of whom have devised elaborate strategies to subvert and dismantle restrictive and fixed notions of 'the feminine' in production and performance. Some women simply refuse to be contained and forge their way resolutely across masculinised terrains to write and produce their own work, perform as instrumentalists and work as engineers. Others, as singers, subvert dominant regimes of normalised feminine appearance and conduct by simply refusing to mould their bodies into Barbie-like contours or by performing (multiple) stereotypical feminine representations to excess. There has been, and is, ongoing resistance against restrictive codes and controls designed to render only certain sounds, certain bodies and certain kinds of female agency as 'normal' and 'natural' in the commodification of bodies, instruments and texts for circulation in the market place.

A strategy which I find appealing is a combined approach of appropriating the masculinist domain of the 'high-tech' and of playing the voice — the feminine instrument — to parodical excess. Electrovocal composition using personal computers situated in the domestic sphere offers very particular advantages to those who have been marginalised in relation to technology and virtuosity in a public arena, which positions performances of the white male virtuosic body as normative.

In digital processing, the notion of a 'natural' voice attached to a socially located body may be abandoned. Traditional sound engineering works to enhance vocal qualities associated with embodiment rather than to subvert them and, on both the stage and in music video, the recorded voice is frequently rejoined to images of the body in such a way as to create an illusion of naturalised vocal performance. Electrovocal music may also be juxtaposed with bodies but hardly in an attempt to suggest naturalised links, indeed such work is usually not singable in real time. Electrovocal sounds may refer to the body that originally produced them, to other imaginary bodies, or to no recognisable bodies at all. As Hazel Smith commented in a paper given at the *Resonances* conference in Sydney last September:

> *... technological manipulation of the voice can splinter male/female oppositions into multiple sites along the whole continuum of sex and gender. These complex configurations displace gender extremely radically, and liquidate the materiality of the voice as a sexual marker (Smith 1997: 7).*

Timbre, pitch, and temporality of the sounds may be readily altered with a mouse click through the application of a variety of filters. Multitrack layering of the same or different voices may produce complex and novel textures and rhythms; highly flexible cut and paste editing makes for fluid and experimental compositional processes; transgressive and transgendered voices suggesting multiple subject positions emerge and resonate with contemporary mythologies of the cyborg.

Haraway's[2] (1990) cyborgian vision encourages us to take advantage of the instabilities in boundaries that new technologies expose and provides a conceptual framework for exposing essentialist notions which adhere to biological bodies and gendered expectations. Radical reconsideration of traditional and fixed notions around sexed and gendered bodies is highly relevant to exploring the musical possibilities that may emerge in new conjunctions of voice and technology. The struggle between authorised and unauthorised sounds occurs across a potent and risky border which attempts to distinguish the acoustic from the electronic, the organic from the technological, the female from the male, noise from music. What is called for here are more diverse and hybrid imaginaries of the feminine in which differentiated women might imagine and perform themselves against the grain of the stereotypical female vocalities re/produced by an industry with highly regulated and restrained visions of *legitimate* femininity.

Yet the erasure of the materiality of the voice as sexual marker is only one strand of the political potential of the digital processing of vocal sounds. At the human-computer interface — in the volatile matrix of hardware, software and wetware — the roles of composer, singer, musician, engineer, and producer may fuse and make redundant nonsense of masculinist techno-hegemony. One person could conceivably perform all these roles in authoring a sonic piece, undermining traditional notions of agency and authority with their adherence to male bodies. Ironically sound recording has led, on the one hand, to the death of the singer — recordings outlive the original performance and listeners can interpret and use these texts in their own way; they can be also be copied, cited, sampled, and manipulated to become part of other compositions (see Hanna Bosma 1996). Yet, on the other hand, the recording of a live performance also offers the possibility of reiterating that moment in time when the performer usurps the authorial voice of the (normatively male) composer and completes the work with his/her own interpretation.[3]

That digital technologies are becoming increasingly accessible to the populace in terms of cost and ease of use is also highly significant to a claiming of techno-territory by its Others. It is now within the reach of many more pockets to set up a professional studio at home. This domestication of the technology and technological spaces represents a major disruption to the established order between private and public spheres in which recorded musical texts have traditionally been produced and circulated. Attali was concerned that recording technologies have led to an individualisation and privatisation in the reception of musical texts and decried this as a deanimation of music, making it devoid of spirit and sociability (Herman, Swiss & Sloop 1998). A similar concern could be expressed over the production of music in the domestic sphere. Yet for women (and others) who have been disenfranchised in the public sphere and accorded legitimacy only in the private, very different perspectives emerge. Not only is it now possible to set up a room of one's own for electronic play in the familiarity of the domestic sphere, but composition, performance and circulation of musical works (via the Internet) can all be carried on at a distance from the oppressive constraints of conservative music industry discourse. The domestication of noise in this sense can be an immensely liberating prospect for women, though to embrace and deploy its potentials to our own ends we will need to rework received masculinist mythologies and relationships with computers and their accompanying array of digital paraphernalia.[4]

As a sonic praxis, I work with a computer using ready-made softwares to record directly to disk, process and compose sounds into pieces which currently are all derived from the sounds of my own voice. I play with the 'popular' imaginary by composing pieces that are rhythmic and danceable. I sing and speak this particular female voice to parodic excess, partly as a ploy to draw attention to the 'fixing'of the feminine in popular music but also to push out the boundaries of my own known world of subjectivity and vocality. This process is a potent means of exploring the tensions between essentialist and non-essentialist conceptions of gender[5] — on the one hand the choice of a specifically female vocal body from which to sample sounds and, on the other, the queering of those sounds through digital filtering to create a sense of multiple voices and subjectivities. I hope that the sonic texts I produce queery all voices, not only by fusing the 'organic' with the 'technical' in creating a complex postmodern cyborgian instrument, but by calling into question the very means by which the genderedness of vocal bodies is constituted.

Notes

1 An exploration of discourses around gender, power and technology in contemporary music is the subject of my Master thesis — see Brown, J. 1995, *De-Gendering the Electronic Soundscape: Women, Power and Technology in Contemporary Music,* Masters thesis, Lismore: Southern Cross University. Also see Bradby, B. 1993, 'Sampling Sexuality: Gender, Technology and the Body in Dance Music' in *Popular Music* 12, 2:156-157.

2 Haraway writes: '... my cyborg myth is about transgressed boundaries, potent fusions, and dangerous possibilities which progressive people might explore as one part of needed political work... a cyborg world might be about lived social and bodily realities in which people are not afraid of permanently partial identities and contradictory standpoints'.

3 Abbate (1993), discusses the notion of the 'female authorial voice' in relation to performance in opera and, following Barthes, demonstrates ways in which the controlling authorial voice outside and prior to the text it seems to produce may be re-created and dispersed among an array of multiple voices which perform the text (229-236).

4 Zoe Sofia (1993, 1995) demonstrates the usefulness of psychoanalytic tools in exploring the 'sexio-semiotics' of technology — a playful deconstruction of the ways in which tools may come to represent gendered meanings through bodily associations.

5 Smith (1997:7) makes this point in relation to her own sonic writing in a literary context.

References

Abbate, C. 1993, 'Opera, or the Envoicing of Women' in Solie, R. *Musicology and Difference: Gender and Sexuality in Music Scholarship,* Berkeley & Los Angeles: University of California Press.

Anderson, L. 1981, *Big Science,* compact disc, Warner Bros.

Attali, J. 1985, *Noise: The Political Economy of Music,* Minneapolis: University of Minnesota Press.

Bosma, H. 1996, 'Authorship and Female Voices in Electrovocal Music' in *Proceedings of the International Computer Music Conference* Hong Kong 1996, http://www.let.uva.nl/~hannah/icmc96.htm.

Bradby, B. 1993, 'Sampling Sexuality: Gender, Technology and the Body in Dance Music' in *Popular Music* 12, 2:156-157.

Brown, J. 1995, *De-Gendering the Electronic Soundscape: Women, Power and Technology in Contemporary Music,* Masters thesis, Lismore: Southern Cross University.

Gatens, M. 1991, *Feminism and Philosophy: Perspectives on Difference and Equality,* Bloomington & Indianapolis: Indiana University Press.

Haraway, D. 1990, 'A Manifesto for Cyborgs: Science, Technology, and Socialist Feminism in the 1980s' in Nicholson, L.J. (ed.), *Feminism/Postmodernism,* New York: Routledge:190-233.

Herman, A., Swiss, T. & Sloop, J. (eds) 1998, *Mapping the Beat: Popular Music and Contemporary Theory,* Malden, Massachusetts: Blackwell Publishers.

Lefebvre, H. 1991, *The Production of Space,* Malden, Massachusetts: Blackwell Publishers.

Smith, H. 1997, *Sonic Writing and Sonic Cross-Dressing: Gender, Language, Voice and Technology,* unpublished paper, University of NSW: School of English.

Sofia, Z. 1993, *Whose Second Self? Gender and (Ir)rationality in Computer Culture,* Geelong: Deakin University.

Sofia, Z. 1995, 'Of Spanners and Cyborgs: De-Homogenising Feminist Thinking on Technology' in Caine, B. & Pringle, R. (eds), *Transitions: New Australian Feminisms,* Brisbane: Allen & Unwin.

BE WHO YOU WANT TO BE: IDENTIFYING (WITH) VERNACULAR MUSIC

MARK EVANS

Introduction

Some recent quarters of popular music academia may have us believe that a paper dealing with Christian music, particularly that music which would commonly be found in an average church, is offensive and should not be tolerated. It is opinions such as these that have propelled my interest in analysing Christian music in such a setting as this.

What I wish to do in this paper is explore current views on Christian music within academia, and more recent ideas about the popular music studies in general. I will begin by looking at a debate which took place on the Pacific Music Research email list during September 1997. I will move on to discuss recent ideas developed by Bruce Johnson in his seminar paper *Watching the Watchers.* In it Johnson identifies several key relevancies in the study of popular music (and more importantly for this paper, the inclusion of Christian music in that study). Johnson's paper centres around the notion of vernacular music, and our academic indifference to discourse derived from it. In light of the debate around the scholarly merit of Christian music, it would appear that an (un)fortunate example has been created to support this observation.

This paper will finally centre around identification and the attempt to understand how it is we identify with certain music. The case study utilised will be contemporary Christian worship music, though I believe the theory presented operates more widely than this genre alone. Whilst still in the hypothesis stage, I wish to develop notions of psychoanalytical identification in popular music, particularly in relation to vernacular music. These ideas have their origin in film theory though I believe an interesting adaptation within popular music studies is possible. The aim of such theorisations is to locate Christian music, and indeed all vernacular music, within an intellectual framework which enhances the dissection of these valuable musical forms.

The debate

In September 1997, I placed a posting to the Pacific Music Research list calling for contacts and/or information regarding my doctoral thesis topic 'Church music in Australia'. As with most calls on such lists this produced a wealth of useful information in private email and phone communications. What was unexpected was the reaction by a minority to the posting itself which, in computer parlance, can be described as a good flaming.

One particularly irate academic posted a response indicating that they thought it inappropriate to discuss Christian music in an objective, and secular, forum. After others attempted to quell his angst the academic responded thus:

> *I am sorry... but I refuse to allow Christians to run the world. They have had a go at it for about 2000 years and continue to make a monumental mess of it. I am disinclined to create a space in the world of popular music for support of Christianity. I know we live in conservative times but whatever happened to critique?*[1]

The problematic nature of this statement is quite apparent. For, despite advocating an objective space for serious critique and analysis, the respondent here enforces his/her own subjectivity into that space. As Trimillos noted in response:

> *A scholar, because of his or her own cultural biases, may choose to ignore these facts [being those surrounding the influence of Christian music on contemporary regional musics] and this truly 'fundamental' aspect of most Pacific cultures in the twentieth century. Doesn't this represent another form of 'Western' domination, in which the biased scholar constructs the Pacific Other according to his or her notions of political (or in this case, religious) correctness?*

The scholar claims to be wary of supporting Christianity through a study of Christian music. Many ethnomusicologists may stumble at this point if, in view of their musical analyses, they are deemed to intrinsically support entire cultures or cultural groups. Once again the issue of analytical objectivity is at stake. That subjective positioning should be assumed within critical study seems unwarranted. Yet the postings continued, and the tenor of the argument became more pronounced.

> *Surely there is a world of difference between analysis and critique of popular music recordings and what seems to be the uncritical engagement with the tools of western culture — Christian music making and values.*

This raises a valid and pertinent point; the 'serious' study of any music needs to involve critique and analysis. This is, I believe, exactly the process I am involved in. What is the value of compartmentalising popular music into those areas deemed worthy of study and those not, and looking at any music or phenomenon without the tools of critique and analysis? What this statement does authenticate however, is Johnson's observation that we 'turn away in academic embarrassment from the everyday truth of music practices which deface our discourses of authenticity' (1998:3).

Vernacular music

The study of local Christian music fits with Bruce Johnson's categorisation of vernacular music as:

> *A kind of music activity which is fragmented into insignificance when approached generically... vernacular music is largely generated at the local level and expresses the sense of immediate, lived experience, of individual and collective regional identity...It refers to conditions of production and consumption, [and] their relationship to the community that produces them* (1998: 8).

'Amazing Grace' is no doubt easily identifiable as a traditional religious hymn. With this example of Christian music, a generic depiction would sit adequately, and in many senses may be accepted as suitable fodder for critique and analysis. The version of the song I am referring to in this paper can be found on *Acapella Hymn Classics.* One reason this song may commonly find its way into secular popular music critique is due to the apparent distance particular productions of the song place between producers and consumers. This version of the song under scrutiny has clearly been produced *for* an audience, rather than attempting to instigate any audience participation. It is precisely arranged, ready for any 'formal' performance venue — in sharp contrast to the original 'informal' venue in which it was conceived. Yet interestingly it is the informal performance space that marks much vernacular music.

Perhaps the formality of the song is due in part to the southern Baptist acapella presentation. Surely such an inflection in arrangement is worthy of investigation. But what if I had seconded a few souls from the local Anglican church to sing the hymn live and recorded them? Would this be deemed more authentic — a live field recording — or rather would such a display come closer to fulfilling Marcus Breen's nightmare of singing *'Jesus Loves Me'* at IASPM conferences?[2]

My point may be highlighted by a hypothetical situation. Assume I was to travel to Fiji to study local church music there. Fiji has one of the largest Methodist congregations (as a percentage of population) in the world. To understand current popular music trends in Fiji is to attempt to understand the influence of current trends in their religious worship music. For, as Stillman insightfully notes:

> *Insofar as church music was the conduit for rudiments of western music into many indigenous societies, and those rudiments and repertoire provided materials for the evangelized to pick and choose from among, scholars who ignore musical impacts of missionization do so at the peril of basing conclusions about the subsequent development of popular musics in such societies on incomplete histories.*

Continuing with the hypothetical, assume that whilst in Fiji I collected a variety of field recordings, taken from actual religious meetings. Surely, and even as I think about it now, those recordings would be marvellous to investigate in a paper such as this. One gets the definite sense that, should those recordings exist, I would have no hesitation in deconstructing them over and above recordings from a local church in Sydney. What is being consciously and unconsciously activated here is the preferencing of the other over the everyday. As Johnson notes:

> *The everyday music of Elsewhere is haloed with an aura of authenticity, and the dedicated study of ethnomusicologists and anthropologists. Everyday music in my own community remains unseen or so scorned that up to now our own music scholars, policy makers, historians scarcely think of it. And because it remains invisible as such, we are scarcely aware of it when we are experiencing it* (1998: 5).

'The Stone's Been Rolled Away' is a song from Hillsongs music in Sydney — one of the largest local Christian music producers in Australia. It is taken from the album of the same name which was released in 1993 and became a huge hit within the Christian music community. In fact, that album, and the four of similar ilk that succeeded it, achieved gold sale status in Australia. Music from the album was largely adopted in churches throughout Australia and remains commonplace today. This CD represents a field recording of local Australian Christian music. The version being considered here was recorded live during a church service in 1993. It thus minimises the distance between producer and consumer — with the audience (the lived experience) present in the mix as participant/performer. It is the everyday music of our community.

What can be noticed from a brief analysis of the song? As Stillman notes in regard to current Hawaiian hymnody, 'the instrumental accompaniment style associated with popular music (has) been applied to hymns and hymn repertoire (and) thereby brought into the mainstream of... popular music.' This song represents a perfect example of vernacular music, of that which could be 'fragmented into insignificance when approached generically'. By way of a simplistic categorisation the following unfolds:

Hip hop — in keeping with various hip hop traditions and stereotypes, the vocal leader (a worship leader in the lingo) includes several statements (or calls) to the audience. These include 'everybody in the house', 'come on' and 'in the house'. At one point the leader instructs the audience to 'lift those hands!' — the religious equivalent of 'wave your arms' and other overly common hip hop phrases. After adopting his call he interacts again with the audience informing them that, 'you look great!' This takes place within, and simultaneously external to, the music text. It also occurs outside of the experience of the distanced listener, further highlighting the 'lived experience' of vernacular music.

Jazz funk — this is clearly referenced in the click organ solo, a feature common to such styles of music yet quite foreign to traditional interpretations of religious music. Calvinists everywhere are no doubt dismayed.[3] The solo is followed by applause (called for by the leader who also announces the soloist before the solo) for the virtuosity of the player. This removes the traditional focus of church music (i.e. God) and replaces Him with a human counterpart — once again to the dismay of many theological schools of thought.

Another significant feature in regard to this genre is the inclusion in the musical construction of the song of chromatic passing chords. Exemplified by James Brown and other funk performers, such a device further clouds the generic intent of the song.

Blues — In keeping with the standard blues scale the song incorporates flattened 3rds, 5ths and 7ths throughout. It also relies heavily on the harmonic construction of 7th and 9th chords.

Pop — Unmistakable is the ascendant chordal progression of tonic to sub-dominant. Though an inversion of the classic plagal (religious) cadence, such a progression has now become synonymous with contemporary pop music. Pop supergroup U2 utilises such a progression relentlessly.

Religious worship — This is the obvious purpose of Christian music. The lyrics content is directed towards this purpose. There are many sub-genres or categories of Christian music, this song is a member of the personal praise sub-genre where the individual worshipper is called to subsume the identity of the songwriter and give thanks for the work of God in their own life.

Note again the presence of a leader to guide the congregation through the song (traditionally a transparent role with the attention of the congregation drawn towards God rather than the singer themselves). As mentioned above, the presence and participation of the congregation within the acoustic space posits the religiosity of the piece.

Thus, what can be gleaned from this brief generic analysis, is substantiation of the fragmentary nature of vernacular music. The inconclusiveness of such an analysis is revealed in the difficulty of generically pinpointing the song. This raises additional questions about the dissection of vernacular music generally. It is at this point that I wish to change the focus of this paper. For if vernacular music is going to become part of 'mainstream' academia, then attention needs to be paid to the possible approaches to studying it. It would be a brave soul to attempt a field recording of the infamous 'shower singer'.

I believe that one possible avenue of investigation lies in the theory and practice of identification within popular music. For identification represents one commonality between various forms of vernacular music. Whether it is in church (identifying with God, with other members, with the songwriter), or at the World Cup Soccer (identifying with your team, or with your fellow supporters, or soccer lovers in general), or even in the shower (identifying with the [imaginary] audience) — the process of identification is integral to vernacular music, and quite possibly popular music in general.

Identification

This theorisation of identification skips over many basic principles of psychoanalytical theory. Indeed, I intend to proceed straight to notions of psychoanalytic identification itself. Within psychoanalysis, one of the simplest and most accessible definitions of identification is that it 'involves a process of assimilation by the subject of an other, either in its totality (as in identifying with an individual), or partially (as in the assumption of a physical trait or characteristic)...[in identification] the subject is transformed, wholly or partially, after the model the other provides. It is by means of a series of identifications that the personality is constituted and specified' (Stam et al, 1992:149).

Both Lacan and Freud recognise two types of identification, primary and secondary. Primary identification involves an idealisation of the self, usually prior to any complete formation of distinctions between the self and the other. Secondary identifications are those whereby the subject both constitutes itself in the symbolic (ie in language and culture) as well as establishing its individuality in relation to cultural 'others'. It is secondary identification that we normally associate with empathy towards certain characters in a movie or play, and it is these secondary identifications that I believe underlie many popular music constructions today. The notion of the star text, the latest teen pop sensation, and your favourite World Cup Soccer anthem all appear to this level of psychoanalytical involvement. Yet this level is problematic in that it involves the 'unconscious processes of the psyche rather than... cognitive processes of the mind' (ibid:150).

In seeking to further extend these ideas in the realm of film theory, Lacan developed his conceptualisation of the gaze. It is at this point that I believe popular music can intersect and interact with psychoanalytical identification. The most forceful argument concerning the gaze from within a Lacanian perspective is presented by Joan Copjec.

Observing Lacan's two interpenetrating triangles, Copjec reminds us that the subject is trapped in the imaginary, trapped in that they can imagine nothing outside it; 'the imaginary cannot itself provide the means that would allow the subject to transcend it' (Copjec, 69). However, representation of something other attracts the gaze and causes the subject to imagine something other. Thus Lacan argues that the subject sees the (imaginary) walls and is constructed by something beyond them (ibid). Yet this point beyond is an 'unoccupiable point, the point at which the subject disappears' (ibid). Thus the image itself becomes terrifying for the subject who can no longer see themselves in the representation.

At what point do we integrate popular music to this established model? Precisely at the point of the subject and the (its) representation. To do so obviously involves transformation of the 'gaze' to an aural gaze, an acoustic similitude if you like. This, I would argue, is the imaginary created by the unconscious interaction with the music. Whether it be the desire for stardom, for the star, or for the imaginary realm in which they phantasmagorically exist, it nonetheless becomes the enclosed acoustic similitude gaze. As noted, Lacan suggests that the subject is constructed via something beyond its own imaginary walls. What is this? He feels that 'beyond the signifying network, beyond the visual field, there is, in fact, nothing at all. The veil of representation actually conceals nothing... The subject is the effect of the impossibility of seeing what is lacking in the representation, what the subject therefore, wants to see' (ibid). It is here that I return to my case study of local Christian music. For what the subject involved in this music has the impossibility of seeing, yet desires to see, is the Deity himself. What for Lacan existed nihilistically behind the screen is for those identified in Christian music a real and living being.

The extension of this model of identification to this distinct vernacular music becomes more pronounced as Copjec reminds us that:

> *the subject identifies with the gaze as the signifier of the lack that causes the image to languish. The subject comes into existence, then, through a desire which is still considered to be the effect of the law, but not its realization. Desire cannot be a realization because it fulfills no possibility and has no content; it is, rather, occasioned by impossibility, the impossibility of the subject's ever coinciding with the real being from which representation cuts it off'* (70).

In terms of contemporary Christian music such identification is often reinforced theologically. The subject/participant is constantly called upon to live a life worthy of the calling; to look beyond the walls of representation and seek to live as he who occupies the space beyond the walls lives. In Christian theology, for one example, the subject is aware that 'there is no one righteous, not even one... there is no one who does good' (Romans 3:10ff, New International Version). Yet the subject is called to 'Be holy as I [God] am holy' — ie the subject is called to live outside of the walls of representation and often in church music it is this ideal which is being appealed to. The doctrinal element of sanctification is propelling the subject to transcend their current representations of themselves.

The example cited earlier, 'The Stone's Been Rolled Away' begins 'I've been delivered, I've been set free. Restored and sanctified in Christ I've been released and I am free'. Here the subject transcends through singing about their experience, transporting themselves to the place beyond their own representation. As Lacan revealed, 'Narcissism... seeks the self beyond the self-image, with which the subject constantly finds fault and in which it constantly fails to recognise itself' (Copjec, 70). Within such a view of identification as presented above, the subject is now unfettered, free to recognise itself as that which it can never be. Encouraged, at least in Christian music, to identify itself with that which exists unattainably outside of representation.

Though this exemplifies but one type of process within one type of vernacular music, I would propose that similar theorisations could be drawn to other areas of previously unresearched musics. How dissimilar is the place of representation beyond the screen for the 'shower singer'? That place where the individual is free to succeed creativity, or free to experience an 'ideal' life unimpeded from the realities of drugs, divorce and desperation.

Yet for all this theoretical postulating one must remember the transitory nature of such identifications and representations. The return to the flawed self is absolutely essential for the continuing pleasure of the identification, for the suspension of disbelief to continue to exhilarate. As Copjec finally reminds us:

> *The subject's visions and revisions, all its fantasies, merely circumnavigate the absence that anchors the subject and impedes its progress. It is this desire that must be reconstructed if the subject is to be changed* (71).

The subject's desire to be changed, within the Christian culture, will be an on-going one. The doctrine of sanctification — that process whereby the Christian is slowly transformed to be more like the God they serve — will ensure the continual release and renewal of the subject. Simultaneously however, the subject will gain a growing awareness of their unworthiness, and their need to be transformed, to know that which is beyond the screen. Throughout the subject's life it will often be music, the vernacular music sung and re-sung at church, that leads them through this motile identification process.

Conclusion

The growing awareness of vernacular music and the formation of a serious body of inquiry concerning it would surely make discussions like that presented at the beginning of this paper a thing of the past. With the continued postmodern fragmentation of culture, understanding the everyday music that surrounds us may become more vital to understanding the musical culture as a whole. Though church music may seem, at least to some, a safe critical option, there remains an absence of investigation into music of sporting fixtures, of the music which invades public spaces, and of course that which exists solely in the personal sphere.

Psychoanalytical identification is but one theoretical model that can be applied to vernacular music. Its engagement with church music becomes interesting in helping to understand the processes at work in participants. Such applications need to be contained in critical discourses in order for deconstructions of that which ordinarily receives no discourse to be understood more broadly. As highlighted above, former methods of generic inquiry and the like may no longer achieve the goals they set out to when applied to the music which has so long avoided analysis. In some cases however, the first step required appears to be a cleansing from the subjective positioning that has hampered previous attempts at 'serious' inquiry.

Notes

1 This and subsequent PMR postings all occurred during September, 1997. As I am concerned with the process rather than the people, the anonymity of contributors has been upheld. Unless otherwise indicated, all quotes following come from this source.

2 An idea Breen apocalyptically postulated as the outcome of continued concern with Christian music in formerly respectable critical spaces. Comments summarised from the PMR email list.

3 Theologian John Calvin even feeling that the use of organ to accompany religious singing was inappropriate.

References

Copjec, J. 1989, 'The Orthopsychic Subject: Film Theory and the Reception of Lacan', in *October* 49 (Summer): 53-71.
Johnson, B. 1998, *Watching the Watchers,* unpublished IASPM seminar paper, Sydney.
Stam, Burgoyne & Flitterman-Lewis. 1992, *New Vocabularies in Film Semiotics*, London: Routledge.

Discography

Various Artists, *Australia's 25 Favourite Praise and Worship Choruses*, Focus, 1996.

MUSICAL FORM
AND THE EARLY 1960S POP SONG

JON FITZGERALD

In recent years popular music scholars have increasingly begun to speak out in support of the detailed consideration of musical texts. For example, in the introduction to *Rock, the Primary Text: Developing a Musicology of Rock,* Moore (1993:1) argues:

> *Within 'rock' criticism and commentary in general, insufficient attention is paid to what I call the 'primary text', i.e. that constituted by the sounds themselves, as opposed to commentaries on them, which constitute the 'secondary text'.*

Paralleling these calls for musical text analysis have been a number of publications which provide examples of how this type of analysis might be undertaken. Studies such as Brackett's (1992) consideration of timbre, Middleton's (1993) theory of gesture and Tamlyn's (1995) research into the rhythmic roots of rock and roll all provide useful insights into aspects of musical texts.

Despite this timely activity there remains a relative paucity of information about the musical parameters of popular song and, as a result, observations about musical texts have often been based on what Moore (1993:73) describes as 'speculation rather than analytical insight'. In addition, researchers who have concerned themselves with musical text analysis have been hindered by a lack of comparative information that might be used to lend weight to some of their conclusions.

This paper emanates from my doctoral project which involved detailed examination of more than three hundred and seventy songs written by more than forty of the most successful writers of US top forty hits from the period 1963 - 1966. My doctoral work reflected my belief that music analysis can play an important role in providing empirical data which might inform and challenge critical theorists as they attempt to formulate a comprehensive account of the development of popular music. As Keightley (1991:5) suggests, 'theoretical overviews and textual instantations are necessary and ongoing parts of the study of popular culture. They are complementary, not opposite; one approach should not dominate to the detriment of the other'.

The focus of this paper is popular song form. In particular, I propose to briefly examine the development of three different song forms: firstly, what I have called the 'blues-derived' form; secondly, the AABA form and thirdly, what I describe as the 'gospel-pop' form. In so doing, I hope to raise some issues relating to the interpretation of the history of early 1960s popular music.

Firstly to the blues-derived form. Many of the best known early rock and roll hits, such as 'Rock Around the Clock', 'Johnny B. Goode', 'Tutti Frutti', 'Good Golly Miss Molly', 'Hound Dog', 'Heartbreak Hotel', 'Whole Lotta Shakin' Goin On', 'Peggy Sue' (I could go on) employed song structures which incorporated a literal version of a twelve (or 6/24) bar blues form, or an adaptation of this form. In fact, it is probably fair to say that this form still most typifies early rock and roll to many listeners. (I was recently reminded of this at the Lismore Highland Ball when I endured a night of a

1950s rock cover band while my son partnered a young debutant — yes, it does still happen in the country). It remains one of the great ironies of popular music history that, while the rhythm and blues-derived form was the mainstay of early rock, it was virtually impossible for more traditional black rhythm and blues artists to gain access to white mainstream pop audiences. Shaw (1978:525) explains the difficulties black rhythm and blues artists had in crossing over to the pop mainstream, when confronted by young white musicians who copied the style:

> *The (rhythm and blues) records that crossed over invariably had a young, if not amateurish sound... and most rhythm and blues artists were men of experience who did not sound young and could not look at the world through the misty eyes of an adolescent.*

In addition, as Hoffman (1982:56) observes: 'White audiences did not prove receptive to the earthy lyrics and raw exuberance characterizing the most indigenous black styles such as jazz and rhythm and blues'. When added to raw vocal and instrumental sounds, these features made traditional rhythm and blues unattractive to many white listeners.[1]

When one examines the US pop charts between 1963 and 1966, it becomes apparent that the blues-derived form cannot be said to pervade the popular mainstream at this time. Of the three hundred and seventy-three songs in the song field, only twenty-eight (one in thirteen) employ a literal or adapted 6/12/24 bar blues form. Table 1 provides a list of these songs grouped within some notional genres. Table 1 illustrates several aspects relating to the use of the blues form at this time.

Although black artists employed the blues-derived form most often, the form was associated with a very small number of performers and songwriters. Of Motown's considerable roster of artists, Marvin Gaye was the only performer regularly associated with the form. The songs written for Gaye were invariably uptempo twenty-four bar blues featuring shuffle feels, prominent call-response elements, and a relative light, sweet vocal quality in the lead voice. Motown's most successful songwriters, Holland-Dozier-Holland and Smokey Robinson (who between them wrote more than fifty top forty hits between 1963 and 1966) were each responsible for only two songs, both written for Gaye. The other black artist to construct blues-based songforms was James Brown. In contrast with the songs written for Gaye, Brown's songs feature a raw, emotional vocal delivery, and sparse rhythm-oriented textures which are unique within the popular mainstream at this time.

The songwriters who most often utilised blues-based songforms were Brian Wilson and John Lennon-Paul McCartney. Wilson's surf and hot rod songs, written for his band the Beach Boys, or other artists such as Jan and Dean, often involve original and creative adaptations of the standard blues form, and in this sense Wilson should be accorded more credit as the songwriter who was best able to create a logical development of 1950s rock, and surf groups should be considered to be updated 1960s rock and roll bands.

Wilson's use of the blues-based form is deserving of some detailed attention. He rarely used the form for a complete song, preferring instead to use it for one section only. Most of Wilson's songs are verse-chorus forms, while in some songs (such as 'Little Deuce Coupe', 'Little Honda') the blues form is employed in the verse but not the chorus. In others (like 'Dance Dance Dance', 'Drag City', and 'Surf City') the reverse applies. The other technique employed by Wilson was to vary the standard chord progression over the last four bars of the form, thereby creating a striking hook effect, usually in combination with prominent multi-part vocals and a strong lyric hook. This technique is evident in 'Shut Down', 'Drag City', 'Surf City' and 'Three Window Coupe'.

Lennon-McCartney also used (copied?) this latter technique, most notably in 'Daytripper' and they too created some idiosyncratic adaptations of the form. 'I Feel Fine' incorporates an unusual ten bar form. Like Wilson, Lennon-McCartney rarely employed the form for a complete song. Their normal procedure was to use the blues scheme for the A section of the typical AABA form, and to create a strongly contrasting B section by using a progression totally unconnected with the blues idiom, as in songs such as 'I Feel Fine', 'Can't Buy Me Love', and 'She's a Woman'. No other writers make significant use of the form, and it should also be noted that use of the form appears to be in decline

Table 1: Blues-derived song forms 1963 - 1966

	Song title and year	Performer	Songwriter(s)
Black pop/soul	Can I Get A Witness	Marvin Gaye	HDH*
	You're a Wonderful One	Marvin Gaye	HDH
	One More Heartache	Marvin Gaye	Robinson, Moore, Tarplin, Rogers, White
	Ain't that Peculiar	Marvin Gaye	Robinson, Tarplin, Rogers
	Hitch Hike	Marvin Gaye	Gaye, Paul, Stevenson
	Shake	Sam Cooke	Sam Cooke
	Devil With a Blue Dress	Mitch Ryder	Stevenson, Long
	Out of Sight	James Brown	James Brown
	Papa's Got a Brand New Bag	James Brown	James Brown
	I Got You	James Brown	James Brown
Surf/hot rod	Dance, Dance, Dance	Beach Boys	Wilson, Christian
	Shut Down	Beach Boys	Wilson, Christian
	Little Deuce Coupe	Beach Boys	Wilson, Christian
	Three Window Coupe	Rip Chords	Berry, Christian
	Surf City	Jan and Dean	Berry, Wilson
	Drag City	Jan and Dean	Berry, Wilson, Christian
	Little Honda	Hondells	Wilson, Love
British Invasion	I Feel Fine	Beatles	Lennon-McCartney
	Daytripper	Beatles	Lennon-McCartney
	Can't Buy Me Love	Beatles	Lennon-McCartney
	She's a Woman	Beatles	Lennon-McCartney
	19th Nervous Breakdown	Rolling Stones	Jagger-Richards
Brill Building/ Philadelphia	Hanky Panky	Tommy James and the Shondells	Greenwich, Barry
	Let's Turkey Trot	Little Eva	Goffin, King
	Hey Bobba Needle	Chubby Checker	Mann, Appell
	Twist It Up	Chubby Checker	Mann, Appell
Other	Twinkle Toes	Roy Orbison	Orbison
	Rainy Day Women	Bob Dylan	Bob Dylan

* Holland-Dozier-Holland

when one compares their output over 1963 - 1964 (seventeen songs) and 1965 - 1966 (eleven songs). The next form I wish to briefly discuss is the AABA form. This form has been widely employed by popular songwriters since the beginning of the century. Middleton (1990:46) observes that 'thousands of Tin Pan Alley[2] tunes share this scheme' and he describes the AABA form as 'totally predictable' to mid-century listeners. The AABA form proved popular with Broadway songwriters, and many of the songs which have come to be regarded as pop standards (like 'Ain't Misbehavin' and 'On the Sunny Side of the Street') utilise this structure. Middleton (1990:46) describes the typical AABA song as consisting of four eight-bar sections. The B section is commonly referred to as the 'middle eight' of the song, and typically incorporates new lyrical and musical material.

In the early 1960s many of the so-called 'Brill Building'[3] songwriters continued to utilise the AABA form in writing songs for the teen idols and girl groups who were popular at the time. Writers such as Gerry Goffin-Carole King and Ellie Greenwich-Jeff Barry found this form, with its early statement of the lyric hook (usually in the last line of the A section), was ideally suited to the simple, direct teen romance dramas which formed the staple lyric fare of their songs. Typical AABA hits include 'Then He Kissed Me', 'Da Doo Ron Ron' (by Greenwich-Barry), 'I'm Into Something Good', and 'One Fine Day' (Goffin-King).

Subsequently, when Lennon-McCartney began their well-documented assault on the US pop charts in 1964, they demonstrated a marked preference for the AABA form (see Table 2, which is based on the analysis of all of the US top forty songs written by several of the most successful songwriters or songwriting teams between 1963 and 1966). Lennon-McCartney's use of the form does bear some close examination. Firstly, in addition to those songs which feature the lyric hook as the last line of the A section, a number of the early Lennon-McCartney hits take the notion of the early statement of the song hook one step further, by placing the main lyric hook in the very opening line of the song, thereby providing a focal point, and what might be seen as a type of instant gratification for the listener. Typical examples include 'Love Me Do', 'Hard Day's Night', and 'Do You Want to Know a Secret'.

Table 2: Use of the AABA and verse-chorus forms by the most successful writers of US top forty hits, 1963-1966.

Writers	No. of hits	AABA	Verse/chorus	Other
Lennon-McCartney	(34)	76%	24%	0%
Goffin-King	(15)	54%	38%	8%
Barry-Greenwich	(17)	47%	53%	0%
Brian Wilson	(24)	29%	59%	12%
Smokey Robinson	(23)	26%	65%	9%
Bacharch-David	(19)	21%	63%	16%
Mann-Weil	(18)	17%	67%	16%
Holland-Dozier-Holland	(35)	0%	86%	14%

Note: Percentage figures are rounded off to the nearest whole number

In addition, the Lennon-McCartney songs are notable for their distinctive middle eight sections. Almost without exception, Lennon-McCartney's middle eights introduce notable new hooks, with the result that they become as memorable as the A sections of the songs. In creating these distinctive middle eights, Lennon-McCartney employed a wide range of melodic, rhythmic, lyric and harmonic techniques. I will briefly summarise some of these techniques, but for further detail, see my article: Fitzgerald, J. 1996 'Lennon-McCartney and the middle eight' in *Popular Music and Society*, 20, 4:41-52.

Lennon-McCartney's melodic style almost invariably involved setting the B section melody at a contrasting pitch level to the A section melody (a low-set A section melody is followed by a higher B section melody, and vice-versa). In a number of songs, for example 'P.S. I love You', 'A Hard Day's Night' and 'Ticket To Ride', Lennon-McCartney incorporate changes of mode between the A and B sections of AABA songs. Rhythm also plays a very important role in the creation of distinctive B section melodies. Lennon-McCartney regularly employ prominent changes in melodic rhythm to achieve variety and contrast between the A and B sections of AABA songs. Typically, a contrasting bridge melody involves a significant increase or decrease in rhythmic activity.

Lyrical contrasts often go hand in hand with these rhythmic changes. In a number of instances, lyrics appear to be employed for their value as sound rather than meaning, and contrast is achieved by increasing or decreasing the number of syllables and rate of delivery of these syllables ('Please Please Me', 'We Can Work It Out'). 'We Can Work It Out' also provides an example of a song which involves a contrasting lyric tone between the A and B section. The conversational nature of the A section lyrics contrasts with the more reflective, philosophical tone of the B section lyrics.

Harmonic elements also play an important role in the creation of interesting and unpredictable B sections. A wide range of chords are employed to begin these sections, and the particular chord featured at this point in the song sometimes creates a distinctive effect. Contrasts between the A and B sections in the area of vocal harmony are also effectively employed by Lennon-McCartney. All of these elements contribute to the effectiveness of the Lennon-McCartney middle eights, which in turn make important contributions towards the overall success of Lennon-McCartney's AABA songs.

It is therefore interesting to note that the collaboration between the two writers often consisted of a contribution by one writer to a song which was largely written by the other writer. In particular, interviews with both Lennon and McCartney reveal that the editing role of each writer often consisted of a contribution to the middle eight of the song (Compton's article *McCartney or Lennon?: Beatle Myths and the Composing of the Lennon-McCartney Songs* provides a wide range of quotations). George Martin describes the Lennon-McCartney collaboration as follows:

> *Well, they never really wrote songs together... John would write the germ of something and say, 'I'm having trouble with the middle eight, what do you think?' Paul would say, 'Try this'* (Compton 1988:118).

Contrasts between Lennon and McCartney on both a personal and musical level have been regularly noted within the literature. Compton, for example, describes McCartney as 'always more interested in music' and Lennon as 'always more interested in lyrics' (1988:123), while McCartney himself notes: 'John brought a biting wit. I brought commerciality and harmony' (Smith 1988:200). Given these contrasts, it is not surprising that these songwriters were able to make such effective contributions towards each others' work, and their partnership can be seen as ideally suited to the production of AABA songs which benefit greatly from strongly contrasting middle eight sections.

Some further observations can be made in relation to Lennon-McCartney's devotion to the AABA song form itself. At a time when many of the other successful pop writers clearly preferred the verse-chorus form (see Table 1), Lennon-McCartney's adherence to the AABA form can be seen as a link to the Tin Pan Alley tradition and to the teen pop songs of Goffin-King and Barry-Greenwich. However, although Lennon-McCartney's liking for songs by earlier professional pop composers is well-documented, the connection of the Beatles with previous mainstream pop is often overlooked or understated by pop music historians. Allan and Treadwell present a common view of early 1960s popular music history when they argue that:

> *The Beatles and those who followed them in Britain brought back much of the guts missing from American rock — and destroyed the careers of many teen idols in the process* (1993:103).

Other writers, while acknowledging the importance of the British invasion in breaking the monopoly held by US performers and writers on the US pop charts, have begun to question the validity of the criticism of earlier artists which is implicit in the type of statement quoted above. For example, Kelly regards the British invasion as but one of several important 'invasions' associated with early 1960s popular music, including what he describes as a 'twist invasion', a 'girl group invasion' and a 'surf and drag invasion' (1991:133). He provides chart information to support his proposal that these styles coexisted with the new British music, rather than being displaced by it, and argues that:

> *It is a terrible irony that so many American rock'n'roll fans and critics labor under the misconception, spread by many opinionated authors, that the American pre-invasion music was different from the invasion hits and relatively worthless* (1991: 93-94).

Keightley (1991:160) argues that the tendency of popular music historians to associate rock and roll with what he describes as 'rupture and rebellion' has meant that accounts of popular music evolution often focus on areas of difference rather than similarity. If rupture and rebellion are seen as central to rock and roll, then accounts of the British invasion will obviously tend to highlight those elements which are seen to contrast with previous teen pop traditions. By adhering to the classic AABA form Lennon-McCartney continued a long tradition within popular songwriting, suggesting that those accounts of the British invasion which view the Beatles as the saviours of rock, overstate the relationship of the new music with rhythm and blues, and understate its connection with previous mainstream pop.

The final form I wish to discuss, I describe as the 'gospel-pop' form, and it is particularly associated with Curtis Mayfield and the Motown songwriters (especially Holland-Dozier-Holland). As is already apparent, black songwriters made little use of the twelve bar form or the AABA form, preferring the verse-chorus form instead. In fact, Holland-Dozier-Holland, Motown's most successful songwriters make no use of the AABA form at all. In addition, it should be noted that when one considers the overall pattern of features present in the black pop crossover songs, it becomes apparent that the most closely related African-American musical tradition is gospel. Maultsby (1990:202) stresses the importance of the gospel tradition which, she says, 'for more than eighty years... has preserved and transmitted the aesthetic concepts fundamental to music-making in Africa and African-derived cultures'.

Gospel music almost invariably played an integral role in the development of the musical sensibilities of black musicians. Lamont Dozier (1992, pers. comm.) for example, says of the Motown writers and performers: 'We were all from the gospel church'. It is not surprising then, that elements of gospel style should be appropriated into the black pop crossover songs. Returning to the examination of musical form, it is apparent that gospel elements are strongly in evidence. Boyer (1992:280) discusses the predominance of verse-chorus forms in the gospel repertoire (with the addition of an occasional repeated refrain AAA form), and describes the different melodic styles normally applied to these song sections. The verse 'with its complex melodic line' is contrasted to the chorus, which is said to consist of 'a genuine sing-along refrain that the marginally sophisticated gospel ear can pick up after one hearing'. This type of scheme is ideally suited to the call-response between preacher or soloist (singing the verse) and congregation (singing the chorus). These verse-chorus forms predominate among the black pop crossover songs, and are increasingly evident in the songs by Mayfield, Robinson and Holland-Dozier-Holland respectively. The song forms employed by the latter writers occur in exactly the type of profile identified by Boyer: verse-chorus forms dominating, an occasional AAA form, and an absence of AABA forms.

In addition, many black pop crossover songs employ the type of short, sing-along chorus identified by Boyer as typical of the gospel song. Holland-Dozier-Holland are again at the forefront of this stylistic development within the popular mainstream, writing by far the greatest number of songs of this type ('How Sweet it is to be Loved by You', 'Stop in the Name of Love', 'Baby I Need Your Lovin''). They also compose a large number of songs which feature contrasting verse and chorus melodies similar to those described by Boyer. Another element assisting in the creation of a sense of communal, congregational involvement is the employment of backing voices to reinforce important lyric and melodic hooks. This technique is applied most frequently by Mayfield, Holland-Dozier-Holland and Holland-Whitfield, who use such lyric and melodic doubling for both short choruses and key words within verses. At times the backing vocals deviate slightly from the lead melody, singing notes of different pitch or rhythmic duration to create the effect of congregational singing.

Boyer (1992:285) has identified the gospel vamp as a 'short musical phrase of two, four, or eight measures that is repeated over and over' and describes it as 'the most important stylistic element in contemporary gospel'. The importance of riffs in the music of Mayfield and the Motown writers bears direct comparison to Boyer's assessment of the importance of the 'vamp' in gospel music. Musematic repetition, in the form of riffs, plays an important role in song structure. Holland-Dozier-Holland demonstrate a particular awareness of the structural possibilities of riffs, using them to help create variety in an otherwise highly repetitive framework, as well as to provide a foundation on which more free-flowing, irregular song forms can be constructed. Call-response dialogue between lead and backing vocals is also an integral part of Motown songs in particular. Contrapuntal interplay between these parts is a feature of four in five Motown songs on average, as opposed to one in two Mayfield songs and one in seven Cooke songs. Lyrics and melodies are often divided up between lead and backing voices.

In summary, Curtis Mayfield and the Motown songwriters demonstrated that black songwriters could achieve substantial success by adapting the musical language of gospel to create original gospel-based songforms. Given the extent of their success, these new songforms represent a radical new element within the pop mainstream. Although artists associated with gospel, such as Ray Charles and The Drifters, had already crossed over into the popular charts, the extent of this crossover was comparatively limited. In addition, it often involved the performance of songs written by white songwriters who had limited experience of gospel traditions. Holland-Dozier-Holland's songs were especially notable for the way in which they elevated rhythm to a position of major, if not primary, importance in song structure by aligning prominent riffs or particular rhythmic feels with specific song sections. Lamont Dozier explains that 'the feel is all important... people get comfortable with a groove and respond to that... then the groove is interrupted with another direction' (1992, pers. comm.).

In contrast, very few of the white songwriters employed rhythm in a structural way. In fact, many white writers appear to have treated rhythm as an element of minor importance. Brill Building songwriter, Jeff Barry (Smith 1988:144) does not even mention rhythm in an explanation of song construction: 'Ellie (Greenwich) would sit down at the piano, and basically there were three parts to the song — the words, the melody that the words were hung on, and the chord bed'.

Finally, when discussing the developments associated with songs by the Motown writers, the peculiar nature of the Motown recording process must be considered. A Motown recording session, particularly when directed by Holland-Dozier-Holland, was likely to be a very dynamic and communal process. Session players, often following minimal directions, would create grooves that became the building blocks for often undefined songs. Lamont Dozier (George 1985:117) recalls, 'We would have parts of songs, like hooks or maybe parts of a verse'. Earl Van Dyke (George 1985:115) says of Holland-Dozier-Holland: 'Yeah, they'd come in with about five chords and a feel'. This process can clearly be seen to provide a foretaste of what has since become a very standard practice within the contemporary recording studio, particularly in relation to technology-based song creation.

Notes

1 Ennis (1993:184) and Brackett (1994:31-32) argue persuasively that the machinations of the music industry also played an important role, in that music classified as 'R&B' was not promoted as heavily as 'pop', and did not have the same access to distribution networks.

2 Tin Pan Alley referred to a small section of Manhattan where, in the early part of the century, a range of activities relating to the popular music industry took place. The sound of songwriters composing on cheap pianos was said to resemble the clatter of tin pans. The term has been used to describe US popular song tradition in the early decades of the century.

3 The Brill Building has been described as an early 1960s version of Tin Pan Alley, and involved such well-known professional songwriters such as Leiber-Stoller, Goffin-King and Mann-Weil. Many of the Brill Building songwriters provided songs for the young teen soloists and girl groups who were extremely popular in the early part of the decade.

References

Allan, T. & Treadwell, F. 1993, *Save The Last Dance For Me: The Musical Legacy of the Drifters,* 1953-1992, Ann Arbor: Popular Culture.

Brackett, D. 1992, 'James Brown's 'Superbad' and the doubled-voiced utterance' in *Popular Music* 11, 3:309-324.

Brackett, D. 1994, 'The politics and practice of 'cross-over' in American popular music 1963 - 1965' in *Music Quarterly* 78, 4:774-797.

Boyer, H. 1992, 'Roberta Martin: Innovator of Modern Gospel Music' in Reagon, B. (ed) *We'll Understand It Better By and By: Pioneering African American Gospel Composers,* Washington: Smithsonian Institute.

Compton, T. 1988, 'McCartney or Lennon? Beatle myths and the composing of the Lennon-McCartney songs' in *Journal of Popular Culture* 22, 2:99-131.

Ennis, P. 1993, *The Seventh Stream: The Emergence of Rock 'n' Roll in American Popular Culture,* Hampshire: Universal Press of New England.

Fitzgerald, J. 1995, 'When the Brill Building met Lennon-McCartney: continuity and change in the early evolution of the mainstream pop song' in *Popular Music and Society* 19, 1: 59-78.

Fitzgerald, J. 1996, 'Lennon-McCartney and the middle eight' in *Popular Music and Society* 20, 4:41-52.

George, N. 1985, *Where Did Our Love Go?*, New York: St. Martin's.

Hoffmann, F. 1982, 'Popular music and its relationship to black social consciousness' in *Journal of Regional Cultures VIII,* 3 & 4:55-62.

Keightley, K. 1991, *The History of Exegesis of Pop: Reading 'All Summer Long', M.A.* dissertation, Montreal: McGill University.

Kelly, M. 1991, *The Beatle Myth: The British Invasion of American Popular Music, 1956 - 1969,* North Carolina: McFarland.

Martin, G. 1979, *All You Need Is Ears,* New York: St. Martin's.

Maultsby, P. 1990, 'Africanism in African-American Music' in Holloway, J. (ed) *Africanisms in American Culture,* Bloomington: Indiana University Press.

Middleton, R. 1990, *Studying Popular Music,* Milton Keynes: Open University Press.

Middleton, R. 1993, 'Popular music analysis and musicology: bridging the gap' in *Popular Music* 12, 2:177-190.

Moore, A. 1993, *Rock: the Primary Text: Developing a Musicology of Rock,* Buckingham: Open University Press.

Smith, J. 1988, *Off the Record: An Oral History of Popular Music,* New York: Warner.

Tamlyn, G. 1995, 'Rhythmic roots of rock'n'roll in rhythm and blues', paper presented to VII International Conference of the International Association for the Study of Popular Music (IASPM), Glasgow.

MARKETING AN (SO FAR) INDEPENDENT BAND

FRUIT

Adelaide band FRUIT was born in June 1995, from a merger of two groups of three booked to play an acoustic evening. To add to the flavour of the night the six rehearsed a few songs together with the outcome being six new songs. What was to be an encore became a set, and what is today a thriving 'indi' international touring band, FRUIT, and music company, FRUIT Music.

In the initial two years, FRUIT's style leaned towards acoustic folk, ballads and jazz. Since a line-up change in November 1997 the band has developed a more commercially powerful blend of funk, rock, pop and jazz whilst managing to maintain the writers' integrity and meet a range of markets both mainstream and niche.

Music markets globally, suffer from the commercial reality of being controlled by a powerful few and that powerful few being the power base of revenue within the industry.

In our experience the principal controllers are the record companies and radio networks. Record companies being:

First tier:	Majors (6)	Sony, Seagram, EMI etc
Second tier:	Major subsidiaries	Murmer, Universal, Polygram etc
Third tier:	Major indies	Arista, V2 etc
Fourth tier:	Indi subsidiaries	
Fifth tier:	Indi labels	Krell
Sixth tier:	Indi bands	Fruit Music

Radio networks follow a similar format starting with majors (including Austereo, ABC & Triple J), indi's, community networks and an ever-growing college (university) radio presence.

It stands to reason that the majors (record companies and radio networks) would work with majors and indies with indies, however this is not so. The majors in the record industry have significant influence over all tiers of the radio network. Essentially it comes down to who has the capital to pay.

So given the above power based scenario, how have FRUIT formulated a marketing strategy that defies the odds of indi success?

- Look outside the square
- Strategic planning
- Strategic partnerships
- Developing and projecting a professional image
- Being prepared for and taking opportunities
- Focus on the real issue — the music
- Create a performance not just another gig

In their first and second years, FRUIT developed a marketing package in the form of a diecut folio showing an image of the band and its audience plus incorporating quotes from media. They:

- Produced a CD for local release *Fruit* 1996;
- Played locally and interstate at booked and self produced concerts;
- Organised a mailing list;
- Developed press, radio and TV networks.

FRUIT'S first two years were similar to most bands, however there was one added ingredient — the desire to operate as a successful business. So a business structure was implemented:

- Registration of name;
- Formalization of accounts, business meetings;
- Sub-groups formed to handle marketing, production etc.
- Development of slick marketing materials, ie CD, press pack, photographs.

Fruit

By the middle of its second year, an offer to perform in the USA was becoming a reality, shows were selling well, as were CD's. Along with this rapid growth was the fact that the demands of management were consuming the musical creativeness of the group. In May 1997, on the eve of FRUIT's second release, *Skin,* Sue Arlidge joined the group as general manager.

Sue brought corporate management skills to the business and a small amount of music industry knowledge. She had a strong background in small business development, industry systems, marketing and strong networking skills. FRUIT's ability to reach not only the Australian, but the international market is largely due to the presence of the manager on tour with the band implementing these networking skills.

Following our first international tour to North America, Big World, a publicist/marketing company headed up by Jane Sloane, was employed with a brief to market the group across Australia.

By now the business was consuming more money than was being made. With a view to remaining independent, a sponsorship campaign was launched involving the development of a twelve page glossy booklet sent to prospective partnership companies with individualized cassettes. This project bore minimal success and in hindsight was premature: no one knew who FRUIT was, so why would they buy into an unknown product? However, the project was seen by the industry as an extreme marketing exercise and, in turn, increased the image of FRUIT within the industry.

The industry knew FRUIT were here and were not going to go away.

From this point all marketing materials followed a consistent image: posters, flyers, postcards, folios — all depicted a sense of success and professionalism.

This was further reinforced when FRUIT was invited to play at the Australian Performing Arts Market 1998, as a showcase to national and international performance art buyers.

With elevated profile and stronger promotional resources, FRUIT embarked upon its inaugural east coast tour. With two strong CDs and exceptional promotional materials, FRUIT secured shows in some of Australia's premier performance venues: Tilley's in Canberra, The Basement in Sydney, The Continental in Melbourne along with the Sydney Mardi Gras. FRUIT were continuing to gain momentum having confirmed the opening spot for the Adelaide Fringe Festival and the Adelaide Festival. As a consequence of a performance at The Basement, FRUIT were invited to perform at the Edinburgh Fringe Festival and gained interest in North American shows through the Arts Market performance.

In May 1998, having reviewed the position in the big picture and the future direction of the band, FRUIT and FRUIT Music decided to take a more mainstream marketing approach and employ the services of Michelle Buxton (Buxton-Walker). This company managed acts such as Men at Work, Colin Hay, Vika & Linda Bull and The Gadflys while running a publicity company, marketing these acts and working programmes such as 'Hey Hey it's Saturday'. Michelle ran the publicity campaign for FRUIT at the Edinburgh Fringe Festival and has become a strong partner in FRUIT Music.

With the ever evolving direction of the band, the vision and passion of Jane Sloane, the gritty determination of Sue Arlidge and the industry punch of Buxton-Walker, FRUIT are now seen as a strong force within the Australian music industry as a successful indi band and business. This is possibly more evident on the international front as this paper is completed whilst on tour in Sao Paulo, Brazil at the beginning of an 18 week international tour spanning five countries and some 100 confirmed shows.

FRUIT MUSIC

Independent Releases

Fruit 1996	All available at www.fruit.on.net
Skin 1997	or
Shift 1998	Niche Records ph: 1300 6559 66

OBSERVATIONS FROM A BI-CULTURAL PERSPECTIVE

NANCIA GUIVARRA

❖

Before I start I'd like to thank elders Lewis O'Brien and Georgina Williams and the Kaurna dancers for welcoming me onto their land. It's important to me: I would feel very uncomfortable if they hadn't. I have utmost respect for all our elders and it's because of their work I'm here today.

Thank you to Gerry and her team of organisers too. It's been one of the most interesting conferences I've ever been to.

I'm Nancia Guivarra and I'm the producer of 'Awaye!' on Radio National. 'Awaye!' is Radio National's only indigenous arts and culture show. I was very surprised when 'Awaye!' was invited to speak here. My executive producer commented that I would be a cat among the pigeons. I feel more like a pigeon among the cats.

One of the reasons I'm here today is because very rarely are indigenous people's knowledge and experience of the world and their contributions to Australian society valued. Being invited here is an acknowledgment that our opinions and points of view are valid. So thanks.

I've thought very long and hard over what I would say today and that's mainly because I wondered what I could possibly say to you about indigenous music and the media that you don't already know. Especially to those of you are anthropologists, ethnomusicologists, popular culture lecturers or people who just have a great interest in music. After all, there is not a large body of indigenous music out there in the mainstream media.

I was billed as a music journalist on the brochure. I'm not actually a music journalist. I am a journalist and I specialise in indigenous arts and culture issues. I have worked on 'Awaye!' for four months. I have a news and current affairs background in community radio and I've nearly completed my masters degree in journalism. So what could I possibly offer to you in the way of knowledge that you probably would not hear or read anywhere else? I pondered over this long and hard and came up with the paper title of 'Observations from a bi-cultural perspective'.

As I've said before, it's an issue to indigenous people that we do not have a voice, and our concerns are not often heard in the public arena. We often talk amongst ourselves but we do not give non-indigenous people the benefit of that knowledge. So as an indigenous person I thought I would give you the benefit of my experience and insights into how I see indigenous music in the media in Australia. So this needs some background.

I'm Aboriginal and Torres Strait Islander and I mean *both* Aboriginal and Torres Strait Islander. My mother is from Cherbourg and therefore we identify as Wakka Wakka people although we believe we were actually taken from somewhere else to Cherbourg.

My father is a Torres Strait Islander born in Cairns. We are Meriam people and I have direct traditional ties to Darnley and Mer Islands. I'm pretty proud of that. I have not actually found any

European heritage in my ancestry yet. So in Russell Morris's words, 'I am the real thing'. I say that purposely to rebut any misconceptions that people may have about my appearance and where I'm coming from, and also because the authenticity of indigenous people is so often under scrutiny. It is also more culturally appropriate for me to give you this sort of insight.

I live in a bi-cultural world whereas most Australians don't. Therefore I pay respects to my own culture and I also pay respect to the dominant Western culture. So in looking at indigenous music in the media I feel that I'm in a unique position to comment. Many of you who study music, particularly anthropologists and ethnomusicologists, need only look at our culture from your point of view. You may look at it or study it for a couple of weeks, a few years, or even a lifetime (like the Berndts), but you don't live it.

I've had a lifetime of black culture. I've also had a lifetime of Western culture. But I can't claim my experiences to be representative of all indigenous people. As you are probably aware, there are many different Aboriginal cultures in Australia. These are only my experiences and the influences that I've had from my contact with other indigenous peoples.

I feel that music is *very* important to us. I can't stress that enough. At just about every major event in my community there are songs and dances and music. I do not mean we put on a CD, I mean we made the music ourselves. I love singing with my family. Just about every black household I've been in has a guitar, and we all sing and dance.

To illustrate this as a community feeling: my father played in a band in Brisbane called The Opals in the 1960s. Our music is inherently political. The Opals were a band who played at the Opal functions or One People of Australia League dances in Brisbane. In that band was my Dad, Wally Guivarra, Darcy Cummins, Andy O'Chin and Ron Hurley. Out of that band spawned the younger popular musicians Andrew Beckett (the lead singer of Tribal Link) and Marlene Cummins, whose son Leroy played with Mixed Relations, among other bands. At that time The Opals were playing mostly covers for their community.

Although I never learnt any of the traditional Aboriginal songs or dances, I was privileged in my younger years to be shown traditional Islander ones by my grandfather. He also played steel guitar. There are other reasons why I know that music is a strong part of our culture. It is traditional and although it may have changed forms or styles, it's still a hugely significant aspect of indigenous peoples' lives in this modern world.

This is reinforced for me by the time I have spent with other indigenous peoples. I was part of an indigenous exchange program and I have spent time with the Cree people in Saskatchewan, Canada and the Kanaka Maoli in Hawaii. Music is integral to all of our lives if we still value our culture.

The value of music has also been confirmed to me at this conference through the CASM sessions. From my research for 'Awaye!', I have been learning more and more about the wealth of indigenous musicians out there. On most occasions when I meet with indigenous people, it is accompanied with songs and dance. That's another difference I have noted. In Western culture there are people who listen to music and have a great interest in music but do not dance, whereas music and dance always go together for us.

I also respect a lot of Western music. During my high school years I played clarinet in the school orchestra, so I have an appreciation of Western 'art' music. I bought my first record player in the 1970s, a groovy curvaceous one with these circles you see on the frames of sunglasses nowadays. I was a religious 'Countdown' watcher. I loved Sherbet. I was even a member of the short-lived Countdown Club. I bought 'Smash Hits'. In fact I started out in radio because of my great personal interest in most rock/pop music. I did an Australian music show at 2XX in Canberra for nearly two years before I moved to Sydney. I have subscribed to *Rolling Stone* and *Juice* on and off over the years and I'm a regular concert goer.

So I'm saying that I'm not out of touch with Western pop music and the media because it has been a part of my life. When I was given the topic of indigenous music and the media, my immediate thought was that it was a bit of an oxymoron. What indigenous music and the media?

A great illustration of this is the *Rolling Stone's* 'Twenty-five years of Australian rock' edition put out in early 1998 (this magazine is one of the largest music publications in Australia). I was pretty excited about it, being very respectful of both black and Western musicians, like INXS, Midnight Oil, the Saints, Nick Cave, Yothu Yindi and the Warumpi band. I thought I might see them all come together in a celebration of all of their contributions to Australian society and music.

There was not a single mention of indigenous musicians! The *Rolling Stone* featured twenty-five interviews with Australian rock/pop bands representing the 'state of Australian music, past, present and future'. I furiously looked to the interviews with Peter Garrett and Paul Kelly thinking they would mention us. While it may have been an editorial decision, we were not included in any of their interviews either.

I was absolutely disgusted! Particularly because some of the bands who were profiled could hardly be called uniquely Australian in their style of music.

So what makes Australian music uniquely Australian in the world's eyes? Let me put it another way. Who closed the Olympics at Atlanta? David Page's music and the Bangarra Dance Theatre. Recently at the Commonwealth Games in Kuala Lumpur, Australia selected the Coloured Stone Band to represent us. It is such a contradiction in values to promote us as uniquely Australian and then deny our contribution to society. Recently I was asked: 'What have Aborigines contributed to the economy of Australia?'. I said, 'You're standing in it!'. I thought that would have been obvious.

Toby Creswell and friends formed *Juice* with more of a social conscience. For example, there was a recent article by Biripi man, Grant Saunders, about Sydney's Koori Radio. *Juice*'s acknowledgment of our contributions does not go unnoticed.

In terms of mainstream radio, I guess Triple J is it for us. They're great: they play our music in NAIDOC week and on Sorry Day. I heard 'From Little Things Big Things Grow' by Kev Carmody and Paul Kelly on Sorry Day. Triple J initiated coverage of Stompem Ground, Meinmuk, Barunga and they unearthed Tribal Link. These initiatives have been instrumental in helping indigenous musicians overcome some of the obstacles they face in trying to forge a public profile. However, these are still only isolated events.

We're definitely not a part of the mainstream. I think it's inherently racist. Most indigenous people realise that we are marginalised within the rock industry and as our keynote speaker, Graeme Turner, said earlier, this is an industry that's increasingly becoming marginalised. So we are marginalised within that marginalised group.

So we develop our own networks, the National Indigenous Radio Services (twelve major stations), Imparja TV, one hundred and nine BRACS stations and some of our own shows ('Awaye!', 'Deadly Sounds', 'Arts Yarn Up') are broadcast on the CBAA network as well.

We love listening to our own music. Its inherently political messages are often very emotive and, unfortunately, hard for non-indigenous people to accept. Many commentators know it's our message that many Australians do not want to hear. There seems to be a denial of our existence, which is also a denial of Australia's true history. We are tolerated but we are not respected.

However, I do not believe that mainstream success is the measure of success for most indigenous bands. The CASM staff and students have reinforced that for me. As I've said before, we just play music because it's a part of our culture, therefore any mainstream success as a result of that is a bonus. To be respected in your own community is more important. To use non-indigenous indicators as a measure of success is inappropriate.

Graeme Turner's presentation about the declining state of new and emerging forms of pop music and the question from the opening session: 'Do we need a rock industry?' are insightful. Graeme said that people who listen to mainstream easy listening music (the majority of CD sales nowadays are reissues of older music) are probably people who do not really like music. All I can say is, while mainstream culture may not need music, I'm sure that it will always be within indigenous communities. I would like to leave you with this thought: Change is never initiated by the majority, 'cause they all think alike!

INTER-PLANETARY SOUNDCLASH: MUSIC, TECHNOLOGY AND TERRITORIALISATION IN MARS ATTACKS!

PHILIP HAYWARD

❖

Introduction

The title of this paper alludes to the tradition (first developed within reggae and now more broadly based) of setting up a contest between two DJs/producers and their sound systems, a contest where the outcome is measured in terms of the audiences' perceptions of the most 'deadly' — the most creative and effective/affective — sonic performance.[1] In its original context this practice takes forms such as successive live sets by DJs or where different producers/artists feature on opposite sides of vinyl albums (thereby inviting comparison with the other). In other spaces, other places, the soundclash is even more literally enacted. At London's annual Notting Hill Carnival for instance, sound systems are set up opposite each other, under the Westway flyover, in the same narrow, crowded streets. Here, their pumped-up bass outputs overlap, blurring with each other at a median point, transforming into sheer noise, destabilising normal social spaces and, on many occasions, sonically facilitating and accompanying actual clashes between audiences and the police (whose own sirens have often provided an eerily appropriate dub-style treble intrusion into the unearthly din generated by the sound systems). I cite this example at some length since the soundclash, an aural contest where combatants battle with sound, is literally enacted in *Mars Attacks!*

In this sense, the use of music in film — like the example of the use of music in London's Carnival discussed above — can be understood within the framework of what Murphie (1996) refers to as a 'popular music event'. Drawing on Deleuze and Guattari's radically original work of film theory, *A Thousand Plateaus* (in English translation, 1987), he describes these as phenomena which:

> *...do not only derive from certain abstract social formations (such as national states with their attendant State philosophies and State art). Such events also, in a very specific way, mark out and/or erase certain territories for social formations in the first place.*

Equally, drawing on another broader framework advanced by Deleuze and Guattari, the 'space opera' (to use a 1950s term) of *Mars Attacks!* can be considered as a 'veritable machinic opera', wherein the 'varying relations into which a color, sound, gesture, movement or position enters in the same species, and in different species, form so many machinic enunciations'. The-machinic ennunciations Deleuze and Guattari refer to here, may be understood as meta-processes involving the various animate species, hard technologies and the social-cultural matrices and discourses that constitute what might be termed 'the diegesis of existence'. While Deleuze and Guattari may not have had extra-terrestrials in mind when they produced this formation, it is singularly appropriate to the representation of (biologically) inter-special conflict and difference in *Mars Attacks!* and the particular role that sound plays in this.

Burtow/Elfman — Oeuvres

For those unfamiliar with the director and his oeuvre, Burton is a former Disney animator whose first feature film was *Pee Wee's Big Adventure* (1985). He followed this up with his highly original comedy-horror feature *Beetlejuice* (1988) before going on to direct the first, dark, stylish and heavily stylised *Batman* (1989); the cult Gothic teen angst drama *Edward Scissorhands* (1990); the animation feature *The Nightmare Before Christmas* (1993) and his eponymous tribute to 1950s B-Movie director Ed Wood (1994). All of these films have featured original and ambitious uses of film music and soundtrack. Burton's background in animation is significant here, since (free from the restraints of aural realism iconic to [visual] photo-realism), the animated feature film has a rich history of inventive soundtrack work and of colourful musical composition (exemplified by the work of composers such as Cari Stalling). Like *Beetlejuice* and *The Nightmare Before Christmas, Mars Attacks!* features music by the prolific Hollywood composer Danny Elfman. Elfman described in Adams (1997) working on the film as 'a special treat', which allowed him to revisit and rework a series of seminal 1950s sci-fi film scores. More specifically, Elfman's score for *Mars Attacks!* takes its cue(s) from Bernard Hermann's music for *The Day The Earth Stood Still* (Robert Wise, 1951), which Elfman (1998) has cited as the inspirational point for his career as a film composer. As subsequent sections of this paper will argue, Elfman does not simply imitate his inspiration in *Mars Attacks!* but rather reworks his source, producing a contemporary angle, modifying the affective aspect of Hermann's 1951 score in keeping with the distinctly contemporary tone of Burton's film.

Elfman described in Adams (1998) his general technique of reworking classic film scores in terms of a deconstruction[2]; of a 'dropping-back' through layers of film score conventions and histories to reconfigure styles derived from key Hollywood composers. Following the model set down by composers such as Erich Korngold in the 1930s[3], Elfman's scores often utilise prominent *leitmotifs,* musically illustrating and enhancing key characters and themes. One of the most obvious of these is their use to introduce (and emphasise/amplify) the narrative presence of the film's heroes. As Elfman has emphasised, *Mars Attacks!* — as a studiedly unheroic film — resists such a standard approach, since the most prominent 'characters' are the scandalously amoral, anti-heroic Martian hordes. For the Martians' signature sound, Elfman augmented an orchestral march sequence (composed in the style of mid-period Prokofiev[4]) with a prominent melodic line played on the theremin. As discussed in detail in Hayward (1997), the theremin was one of the earliest musical synthesisers. Its most novel attribute was its contact-free musical interface. The instrument was played by the performer moving their hands between two aerials and changing the pitch and volume of a signal. The instrument became a staple device in Hollywood cinema from the 1940s to early 1960s to signify a range of eerie and/or unearthly characters, events or moods. In this regard, Elfman's use of the theremin for the Martians' theme clearly draws on the earlier usage. Indeed Elfman has acknowledged that when writing the score for *Mars Attacks!* He frequently replayed Hermann's film music.[5]

As outlined in Adams (1998), in his attempts to produce a contemporary version of the original theremin and orchestral affect, Elfman restyled the original 1940s/1950s instrumental role and character of the theremin. Intent on producing a contemporary sonic 'high gloss' for his score, Elfman used the theremin — which he has characterised in terms of its trademark *rough-edged* sound — as a source of melodic lines and samples. The samples enabled him to get required theremin parts 'right in tune' with his orchestral score and, in the final version, these were combined with parts originated on the other notable early 20th century synthesiser, the ondes martenot.[6] As he characterised it, the ondes martenot 'could play any melody we wanted it to play really well... (but) the theremin had more *nastiness* (my emphasis) in the sound'. Despite Elfman's appreciation of the theremin's *nastiness,* the rough edges of the instrument's sound are largely smoothed over in his 'more perfect copy' (to cite a common definition of the simulacra) producing something with a significantly different musical/sonic affect.

The opening sequence of the film exemplifies this aspect of Elfman's revision of his reference sounds. Unlike the dissonant edge of the theremin as a sonic marker of 'other worldliness' in the opening sequence of *The Day the Earth Stood Still, Mars Attacks!* opens with images of a huge fleet of flying saucers, spread out across space, approaching the Earth. These images are accompanied by a lush, harmonically integrated score, where the theremin lines are a smooth melodic response to the choral melodies which precede it. This is immediately established as anthemic, by the juxtaposition of music and image (and the overt reference to previous sci-fi film conventions); the music operates and articulates a classic process identified by Deleuze and Guattari, whereby 'one ventures from home on the thread of a tune'. Despite this aspect, and the clear marking of the theremin featured passages as the Martian's specific anthem, it would not be 'over-reading' this to assume that the edginess of *The Day the Earth Stood Still's* opening orchestral and theremin sequence was appropriate to that film's nature as an (unselfconscious) sci-fi thriller — produced at a time of very real (earthly) Cold War. By contrast, the smooth stylishness of *Mars Attacks!* is threat free, reflecting a geopolitical climate where — for the West, at least — nothing of quite the same kind is at stake and no such pronounced unease necessary. In another sense, the opening might be seen to epitomise what Marjorie Perloff (1990:195) has described as a key aspect of contemporary Western culture (in its Postmodern phase) — its 'cool Futurism'.

Whitman — Indian Love Call

If Elfman's score exemplifies a cool Futurism, inscribed, albeit prominently, within the textual planes of the film score/underscore, the nemesis of both this musical approach and the Martian hordes it signifies, is another distinctly rough-edged 1950s sound, one significantly 'un-reworked' by the film, and directly appropriated and inserted into the narrative, soundtrack and score. The sound-presence in question — the source of the film's final climactic clash — is Slim Whitman's 1955 recording of the Broadway show tune 'Indian Love Call'. For all Elfman's (previously discussed) characterisation of the odd *nastiness* of the theremin, the instrument's lines are notably less musically distinctive and/or 'odd' in relation to *Mars Attacks!* orchestral score than the yodelling and steel guitar lines of Whitman's record. Indeed, it is the sonic oddness/otherness of the track, and its marked difference from the smooth dissonances of Elfman's score, which produces such a deadly impact on the Martians who encounter it; causing their invasion attempt to be foiled. In this regard, the score's theremin derived sounds are normal, stable and hegemonic, whereas Whitman's recording is aberrant.[7]

In both the absence of any other contender, and in terms of the dramatic effect of his intervention, Whitman — or, rather, the sound of his recording — is the principal heroic presence in *Mars Attacks!* The track enters the score and narrative in the final quarter of the film, when all seems lost, when the Martians are gleefully conquering and trashing the planet. It emerges as a significant voice and presence when a group of Martians burst into an old people's home and begin to terrorise and kill the inhabitants. Finding one elderly woman unaware of their presence, one Martian carefully lines up a ray-gun at her head and then pulls off her headphones as a prelude to blasting her away. However, his (?) intentions are immediately undermined. As soon as the sound of Whitman's record emerges from the discarded headphones, the Martian's brain starts to boil and then explodes. As the woman and her grandson discover, the recording has the same effect on all Martians.[8] After playing it through the streets, the duo finally arrive at a radio station and broadcast it repeatedly. Transmitted throughout the world, deterritorialising and reterritorialising, it finally obliterates the Martians and saves the planet... In the moment of the violation of the woman's private space, the uninvited disruption of her communion with a specific sound and sound text, the film does not simply present us with an invented absurdity, it resonates and loops back to various (pre-Christian) cultural practices of sound and sonic association. Most particularly, the sequence invites comparison to those Papua New Guinean societies for whom certain sounds are sacred to particular groups. In these contexts, it is taboo for outsiders to simply hear the sounds of ritual instruments such as ritual bullroarers[9], or particular chants. What is notable in *Mars Attacks!*, is that Burton does not attempt to provide us with any 'ancient' and/or (conventionally) holy sound to symbolise essential humanity, but rather a sound plucked from the era and cultural context from which he derives his inspiration.

Now largely forgotten by contemporary performers, 'Indian Love Call' was written by Oscar Hammerstein (music) and Rudolph Friml (lyrics) for the Broadway operetta *Rose Marie*, which premiered in 1924. The song drew upon well-established musical clichés for the representation of 'Indians' (indigenous North Americans) on stage and screen; and — 'oft-parodied, almost self-parodying' (as outlined by Pisani, 1998) — its popularity was influential in reinscribing these in 20th Century popular culture. These clichés — combined with a less specific exoticism — are exemplified in the song's opening (the sequence featured repeatedly in *Mars Attacks!*) where, as Graeme Smith has characterised it: 'the opening, descending, chromatic melody — reminiscent of the composition 'Bali Hi' (Roger and Hammerstein, *South Pacific*) — contrasts to the 'Red Indian' pentatonic style answer tune'.[10]

In its debut run, Mary Ellis and Dennis King's duet on the song rapidly established itself as a 'showstopper'.[11] The play's narrative is set in Quebec and concerns a famous opera singer performing in Montreal, who travels to a remote forest area to meet and assist her brother who is in hiding after killing a 'mountie' (mounted police officer). There she meets another mountie who — somewhat awkwardly — falls in love with her, despite his knowledge of her brother's crime. The song initially enters in the narrative as an intrusion into the Euro-Canadian milieu, as a melody, sung off-screen, echoing around the landscape they move through, by indigenous Canadians (the 'Indians' of its title). It is subsequently taken up by the heroine, and the mountie who rapidly falls in love with her, who perform it within the narrative as a love duet. This complex transaction and trans-identification of a musical-acoustic index of 'otherness', is, in Deleuze and Guattari's terms, 'inter-special'; not so much a sound*clash* here (in the narrative/diegesis) as a smooth, machinic, territorialistic acquisition.

The composition was recorded at least twice in 1925, with versions by the Paul Whiteman Orchestra and Leo Reisman. The tune also experienced a major revival in popularity following its appearance in the 1935 MGM musical version of *Rose Marie*, performed by the highly popular film musical performers Jeanette MacDonald and Nelson Eddy. This version was released as a successful single in 1936. Further versions followed, by Artie Shaw and his Orchestra (1938)[12] and by Ann Blyth and Fernando Lamas in the 1954 Hollywood remake.

The version recorded by Whitman in 1955 differed markedly from its predecessors by virtue of its particular sound and sonic spatiality.[13] As the work of Peter Doyle has revealed, American popular music between the 1930s and 1950s, and particularly that of the cowboy/hillbilly genre(s), produced a number of explorations of complex, pseudo-spatial soundscapes — monaural recordings where the use of echo and reverb, together with particular instrumentations and melodic ornamentation and emphasis, produced 'impossible spatialities' — virtual acoustic spaces, impossibly 'deep', echoic and reverberative. Despite being unusual in Whitman's repertoire by virtue of being a cover of a Broadway show tune[14], Whitman's recording of 'Indian Love Call', and particularly its introduction, exemplify this and provide a clear example of the sound qualities Doyle has identified, whereby:

> *...the voice, often used in the falsetto range (setting it apart from 'normal' vocal performances) is always being shadowed by ever more abstracted or rarefied echoes. The steel guitar, prominently used in the arrangements, is often both echoed and reverbed to produce multiple distortions, and often features heavy use of harmonies (which stands in a roughly similar relation to the usual sound of the steel guitar as the falsetto does to the standard voice).*[15]

Within the actual and virtual spaces of the recording studio, technologies of software, hardware and bodies are dedicated to intricate fabrications of sound, continually reterritorialising and deterritorialising in search of ideal acoustic refrains. In these actual and virtual spaces the complex cultural inscriptions of the original composition are further refracted and reconstituted. The music creates its own milieus within itself; its own eddies and becomings.

The combination of what might be considered the technological 'exotica' of the complex echoic and reverberative spaces; the Orientalist features of the original composition; and Whitman's melodramatic delivery, produce a highly idiosyncratic recorded sound. The track sounds all the more unusual in the late 1990s, since Whitman's oeuvre has remained undiscovered (and thereby unrevived) by popular cultural archaeologists and thus has no contemporary counterparts. Fixed in a remote moment, recorded on the historical cusp year of 1955, immediately prior to the moment of rock and roll, and the very different affective spatialities of Elvis Presley's early recordings at Sun Studios,[16] the sound remains the province of original aficionados, such as the grandmother featured in the film. Located there, it occupies a similar cultural era to the original alien encounter/invasion sci-fi movies that Burton spoofs in *Mars Attacks!* (such as *The Day The Earth Stood Still* [1951] and *It Came From Outer Space* [1953]) and the period during which the theremin stood as a prominent cinematic marker of aural otherness and weirdness (see Hayward 1997:28-53). Indeed, the use of Whitman's track and the theremin, which Burton territorialises in the film, offers a tantalising point of comparison between aspects of that previous era. While Whitman's work has often been considered as relatively isolated within the generic characteristics of hillbilly music (albeit mediated by its studio experimentation), his falsetto vocal sound and the wavering tones of the steel guitar bear more than a passing relation to the by-then well-established tradition of the theremin melody as screen score motif. Whitman's own recordings of tracks recently popularised in a hit Hollywood musical suggests a knowledge of film and film music on the part of either the artist or his producer. Interesting as the line of conjecture might be,[17] it is other factors which determine the use of the track in the film.

Machinic Enunciations & Weird Auralities

Reviews for *Mars Attacks!*, at the time of its original cinema release, were mixed (at best). Reviewers were, almost without exception, left somewhat puzzled by its tone. Unlike *Beatlejuice*, it was a comedy with few obvious jokes (successful or otherwise). Unlike *Edward Scissorhands*, it offered no sympathetic leading characters. Unlike *Batman*, it lacked dramatic impact or bite. In this sense it was essentially seen as self-indulgent, as a director's 'folly'. Burton's film is concerned with, and a prime example of, 'trash-culture' — contemporary, self-conscious, glossy, high-budget trash maybe, but trash all the same. It reinvigorates the B-movie by producing a homage that sparkles with allusion and special effects of such a different order of accomplishment to their inspiration that they inhabit a different plane of affectivity. The Martians exemplify this, the inhumanity of their appearance — obviously not performed by men in suits or paper mache mannequins — marks them out as different creations from the zero-budget improvisations of films such as Burton's favourite Ed Wood production *Plan 9 From Outer Space* (1956). With their gleeful, vicious amorality they are more than a match for all that Earth's military can muster.

As previously discussed, the Martians come undone as the result of a soundclash of epic proportions. Whitman's 'deeply weird, impossible spatiality' — and particularly his keening falsetto and steel guitar counterpoint — slices through the smoothly modulated theremin that (extra-diegetically) represents the Martians' threat and persona. They are 'outweirded' by a sonic spatiality premised on a cultural inner-space — the virtual spatiality of the mix — that is more powerful in its condensation of odd, intense, human and — arguably, above all — specifically white American subjectivity (in what Deleuze and Guattari would characterise as its moment of *becoming animal*) than the malice of Outer Space embodied by the Martian hordes. Just as decisively as in its (unreconstructed) contemporary retro-sci-fi counterpart *Independence Day* (1996), it is the USAnians who save the human race.

Whitman's track, and, by implication, the US hillbilly genre it derives from, are also identified within the film as the apogee of low, *declassé* taste; as 'white trash' culture within the film's high-gloss trash aesthetic. This form is shown to be as alien to Las Vegas glitz as it is to the prim family-orientated culture of Washington and Middle America (represented by the president and his family in the film).[18] Whatever its studio context, Whitman's ululating sonic assault is predicated on unfettered emotive expression, the free-fall and soar of vocal and slide guitar glissandi, echoed and refracted in the virtual space of the record's mix. In this manner the recording resonates with the emotive cries of a marginal cultural tradition unpasteurized by postmodernity. In terms of dominant tastes (even in the eclectically pluralist late 1990s), the track and the tradition are so ultra 'trashy' that they represent the 'wickedest', 'deadliest' sounds on offer. The trebles hit places where the bass does not even register...

In terms of the formation offered by Deleuze and Guattari (1987:348), Whitman's music, for the Martians at least, represents 'the cutting edge of deterritorialisation'. Indeed, in a phrase which could almost have been scribbled by a Martian invader into their space-ship's log as the full realisation of their imminent annihilation hit home, the music:

> *...invades us, impels us, drags us, transpierces us. It takes leave of the earth, as much in order to drop us into a black hole as to open us to a cosmos. It makes us want to die'.*

Set against Elfman's highly polished score, where even the (treated and combined) theremin and carefully crafted musical dissonance has an exemplarily contemporary sheen, the rawness and emotion of Whitman's track provides a musical and cultural noise that not only kills Martians within its fiction but also deterritorialises more broadly, unravelling the generic context into which it intrudes.

But despite the centrality of Whitman's recording to the narrative, it is another track, Tom Jones' evergreen MOR[19] standard 'It's Not Unusual' (originally recorded in 1965), which precedes the narrative's transformation into a dual of musical/metaphoric oppositions. In many ways the appearance of the track in the film is almost classically Shakespearian, akin to the gatekeeper 'sketch' in Macbeth, which presages violence and upheaval. In a series of sequences depicting Martian attacks, the film shows us Jones on stage in Las Vegas, providing a spirited rendition of the Vegas 'anthem'. As the song's title and lyrical refrain constantly re-states — 'It's not unusual'. Within the film, the song and its sounds represent normality. On a deeper level, that of musical-historical association, it also represents another stability, that of the pop music mainstream. Bursting on-stage, the Martians stop the number in mid-flow and shoot-up the club, unmoved and unaffected by Jones and his bands performance.

Established and inscribed within the film as an exemplar of musical normality, the song is positioned in polar opposition to Whitman's tune, which enters minutes later. What Burton's film offers here is a set of musical refrains and territorialisations. The Martian's refrain(s), territorialisations and deterritorialisms are signified in the (extra-diegetical) musical score and, specifically, in the theremin themes. These work off an identifiable tradition, laden with the affect and significance of *The Day the Earth Stood Still* (et cetera) and are, in a sense, given and unproblematic — clearly understood as aurally emblematic of alienness. Jones's track — hoary, respectable and even rehabilitated as acceptable kitsch through its 1987 reworking and re-release[20] — represents the territory invaded by the Martians. This is a territory marked by a refrain which is weak; its lyrical hook, even when sung with Jones's deep-throated passion, simply emphasises terrestrial normality. Jones, in Murphie's (1996:19) terms, represents the perception of the pop star as ideal 'despotic' subject, occupying a 'smooth space', transcending the time/spaces of 1965 to 1995, consistent and virtually unchanged.

With the arrival of the (necessarily extra-terrestrial) Martians, the certainties destabilise. Previously inscribed and maintained territories are contested anew. In terms of the film's sequential flow, the soundclash between Whitman and the Martian invaders skews away from the (up-to-then) linear narrative, moving into a battle of musical and associative refrains which struggle to impose their territories, their orders of affectivity, upon the film's plot (and the USA, as represented). To mix genre references, Whitman's music bursts into the narrative like an aural cavalry emerging over the horizon. It also recalls a motif from the fantasy/horror genre, that of a hidden, primeval force unleashed from its confines to combat evil and save the day. In this sense, Whitman's recording and its trademark sonic spatialities are mythic; as deeply historical, within the surface of 1990s late-period postmodernism, as they are deeply weird. In this way, Burton's flatly hysterical film twists into the mythic and lifts its narrative into a more complex self-reflexive text, cued by and premised on a sonic soundclash framed within histories and discourses of sound technologies, their musical application and their affectivity.

The difficulty with this of course is that this aspect is 'unreadable' on the purely narrative level, invisible in terms of mis-en-scene, but clearly apparent in its audio track. Burton and Elfman's collaboration on *Mars Attacks!* produces a film whose impact and complexity require *to be heard.* Its critical under-recognition reflects the manner in which, even in the age of spectral-mixing, THX sound and film composer-as-celebrity, soundtracks are predominantly under-listened to and under-engaged with. Being Hollywood, rather than the avant garde, the film's sonic accomplishment has a particular enablement, permitted and facilitated by the film's nature as a big-budget, idiosyncratic spoof and premised on Burton's prior bankability. In this, the film offers a notable example of innovative contemporary postmodernism and emphasises one of Attali's premises; that sound and noise have a constant ability to destabilise and deterritorialise and reterritorialise. In this manner, the film's conclusion — apparently facile in terms of the *sturm und drang* of the conflict which dominates the film — can be read as a clear aural resolution, a gleeful attempt to (globally) reterritorialise. Having performed its function, with all the Martians apparently dead, 'Indian Love Call' disappears from the film's diegesis and soundtrack. The final act of reconsecration of space, normality and stable musical aurality is provided by Jones who, off-stage in the natural landscape, launches into 'It's Not Unusual' anew, accompanied — in classic musical film fashion — by off-screen accompaniment. The star-as-despot — and with him, all other normality — is reinstated. The film thereby performs a classic narrative closure which, as in many Hollywood genres, only just manages to cram its genies back into their box.[21] Its sounds echo, re-sound and, in the context of 1990s multi-product packaging, re-group and resignify on the soundtrack CD. Here, sheered from their visual and dialogic narrative, their soundclashes can be eternally replayed; eternally evocative of the 'forces of chaos' (Delueze and Guattari, 1987:312) — terrestrial or otherwise — which provided the big dimension to the human condition. It is precisely this quality that Jones's reassuring refrain tries to banish to the dark edge of existence so playfully enacted and defeated in Burton's film.

Thanks to members of the IASPM e-mail list, especially Peter Doyle, David Horn and Graeme Smith, for their assistance with research for this piece. Also thanks to Andrew Murphie for his perceptive comments on the final draft and Rebeeca Coyle for various assistances.

Notes

1 While this article discusses musical passages in the film version, the musical sequences referred to are included on the (eponymous) CD soundtrack album, released on Atlantic Records in 1997. It has been gratefully acknowledged that *Conversions, The Journal of Research into New Media Technologies, Spring 1999, 5 : 1* have kindly granted permission for this version of the paper to be published here.

2 Understood in the conventional rather than Derridean sense.

3 For a discussion of Korngold' and the Classic Hollywood film score in the 1930s see Kalinak, K. 1992, *'Settling The Score'* Madison: University of Wisconsin Press: 66-110.

4 Prokofiev wrote one of the first symphonic-style film scores in 1934 for the film Lieutenant Kije.

5 Elfman has stated that [with] 'the theremin thing… I went and listened to *The Day the Earth Stood Still* to make sure. Sometimes I do something and I need to hear the source and go, 'God, have I just done that?' And it's really tricky, especially when you are dealing with the theremin. You start doing an octave [slide] on a theremin and it's like, 'Whoa! I better put on *The Lost Weekend* and then go quick [and check]' (cited in Adams, D. 1997).

6 Although unconfirmed at time of writing, Elfman appears to have followed the lead of composer Howard Shore in this regard; since Shore employed Lydia Kavina on theremin and Cynthia Miller on ondes martenot in his soundtrack to Tim Burton's film *Ed Wood* (1994).

7 This is a curious twist, in many ways, since 'Indian Love Call's opening yodeling sequence is more akin to classic uses of the theremin in its melodic leaps and oddness than Elfman's smooth 1990s substitution.

8 As Peter Doyle has pointed out, there is a 'metaphysical' precedent for this in the 1980s radio series 'Riders Radio theatre', produced by the group Riders in the Sky, as a homage to 1930s cowboy radio shows. Ranger Doug used to defeat the baddies with a 'yodelling secret weapon'. (Peter Doyle, e-mail communication to the author, 12/9/97).

9 An instrumental device which, when whirled round the head on a string, produces a deep roaring noise.

10 Smith, G. 1997— e-mail to the author, September.

11. ibid.

12 With Tony Pastor on vocals.
13 Recalling the echoic rendition of the melody, heard from off-screen, in the 1935 film version.
14 Although Whitman also recorded a version of Rose Maile's title song and released it as a single in the same year as 'Indian Love Song'.
15 Email communication to the author, 8/9/97.
16 Such as the immense, dramatic spatialities of Heartbreak Hotel (1956) which marked both something of a zenith of such sound explorations and the end of an era, with rock music overwhelming eschewing such approaches from then on.
17 Research and documentation on this area is scant and, in this sense, unproven.
18 The film pointedly features Jones exclaiming 'What the Hell's that ?" when he hears it broadcast over the radio for the first time.
19 MOR - Middle of the Road - a term which refers to mainstream music tastes.
20 Which marked Jones's return to the UK/USA singles charts after a ten- year absence.
21 It has often been observed for instance, with regard to film noirs, that it is not the femme fatale's eventual submission to patriarchy/marriage, or alternatively her demise, which we remember; rather her power and glamour within the (temporarily) 'suspended solution' of the narrative.

References

'An Interview with Danny Elfman' on the Film Score Monthly website <http://www.filmscoremonthly.com/ar-ficiesl /elfman.html.> in Adams, D. 1997, *Tales from the Black Side.*

Deleuze, G & Guattari, F. 1987, *A Thousand Plateaux,* Minneapolls: University of Minnesota Press.

Doyle, P. *Spatiality in Pre-Stereo Popular Music Recording.* PhD-In-progress — Macquarie University, Sydney.

Elfman, D. 1998, 'Foreword', *Gramophone Film Music Good CD Guide,* London: Gramophone Publications, (Third Edition).

Hayward, P. 1997, 'Danger Retro-Affectivity! The Cultural Career of the Theremin', *Convergence* 3:4, Winter.

Murphie, A. 1996, 'Sound at the end of the world as we know it – Nick Cave, Wim Wenders' Wings of Desire and a Deleuze-Guattarian Ecology of Popular Music' in *Perfect Beat* 2:4, January.

Perloff, M. 1990, *The Futurist Moment,* Chicago: University of Chicago Press.

Pisani, M. 1998 'I'm an Indian Too', in Bellman, J. (ed) *The Exotic in Western Music,* Boston: Northeastern University Press.

Discography

Music From the Motion Picture Soundtrack *'Mars Attacks!'* — Music by Danny Elfman, Atlantic Records

DISPLACED RHYTHMS: EVICTING ROCK AND ROLL

SHANE HOMAN

❖

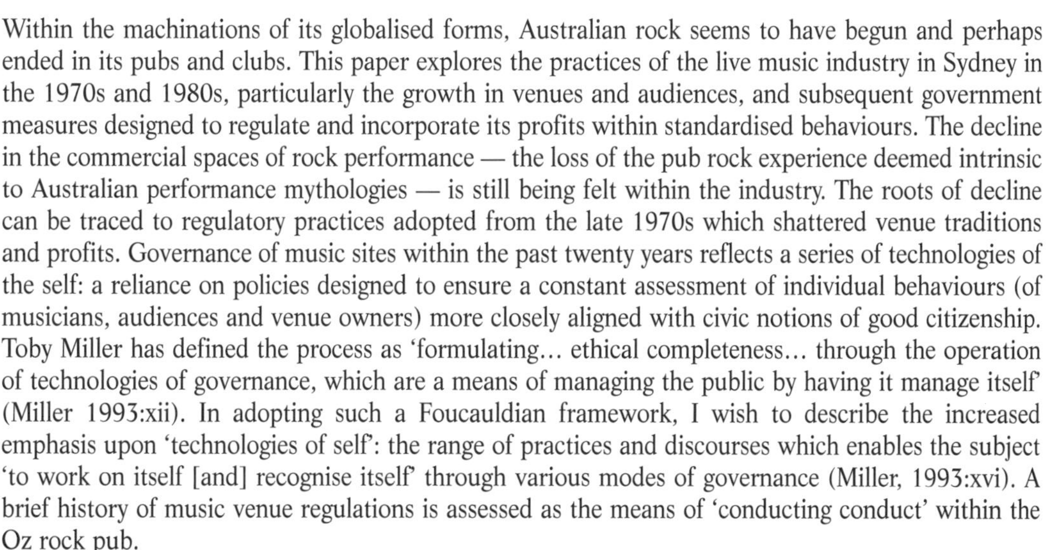

Within the machinations of its globalised forms, Australian rock seems to have begun and perhaps ended in its pubs and clubs. This paper explores the practices of the live music industry in Sydney in the 1970s and 1980s, particularly the growth in venues and audiences, and subsequent government measures designed to regulate and incorporate its profits within standardised behaviours. The decline in the commercial spaces of rock performance — the loss of the pub rock experience deemed intrinsic to Australian performance mythologies — is still being felt within the industry. The roots of decline can be traced to regulatory practices adopted from the late 1970s which shattered venue traditions and profits. Governance of music sites within the past twenty years reflects a series of technologies of the self: a reliance on policies designed to ensure a constant assessment of individual behaviours (of musicians, audiences and venue owners) more closely aligned with civic notions of good citizenship. Toby Miller has defined the process as 'formulating... ethical completeness... through the operation of technologies of governance, which are a means of managing the public by having it manage itself' (Miller 1993:xii). In adopting such a Foucauldian framework, I wish to describe the increased emphasis upon 'technologies of self': the range of practices and discourses which enables the subject 'to work on itself [and] recognise itself' through various modes of governance (Miller, 1993:xvi). A brief history of music venue regulations is assessed as the means of 'conducting conduct' within the Oz rock pub.

The practical and indeed, mythological, value of the pub circuit resided in the initial and sometimes desperate attempts involved in securing audiences' approval, and in the basic conditions of performance which supposedly created enhanced endurance and musicianship. From the late 1970s the Australian music industry benefited from sustained media networks prepared to air local product on television and radio, and the willingness of venue owners to hire rock bands to mutual profit. The larger well known venues on the national rock circuit operated within a landscape of blatant licensing and building law ignorance, corruption, and lax policing. The extent to which bands in Sydney 'could walk into a pub and say, 'we can double the amount of people you've got in here now'' (Coupe, S. 1996, pers. comm., 25 Jan) is confirmed by the growth in small and large pub venues catering to a spectrum of commercial and alternative tastes. Suburban venues, in particular from the late 1970s, exploited their larger lounges and auditoriums in purpose-built entertainment areas. Some of the venues involved were the Royal Antler Hotel at Narabeen, Selina's (the Coogee Bay Hotel), the Manly Vale Hotel, the Bexley North Hotel, the Caringbah Inn, the Dee Why Hotel, the Family Inn at Rydalmere, and the Comb and Cutter Hotel in Blacktown. These venues, fondly remembered by older promoters, can all be connected to the formative experiences of successful bands. Midnight Oil's early audiences were to be found at the Royal Antler; Flowers (Icehouse) and Mental As Anything gained wider recognition at the Civic

Hotel; Rose Tattoo found their early Sydney audiences at the Bondi Lifesaver, and so on. The promoter of the Civic Hotel and Stagedoor Tavern, Bob Yates (who later managed Mi-Sex) reflected upon the necessary illegality of the circuit's black market economy:

> *By the end of the 1970s there was a fantastic circuit... I think most people were (making payments to licensing squad police), because most venues were so obviously flouting the law... we had guys turning up to inspect the Civic Hotel and turning a blind eye. The Stagedoor had a tavern licence, which meant they weren't supposed to open on Sundays, but I can show you a million posters where it was open with massive bands... I can remember one night with Mi-Sex at the Tavern, we must have had 1500 people in there at $4 a head, so it was considered big money... Everyone used to boast 'we played the Stagedoor with 1600 people'. It was more than just greed, it was an ego thing on the part of the bands* (Yates 1995, pers. comm. 10 Aug. The Stagedoor was licensed for a capacity of 128 people).

The event that was to transform the regulatory landscape for venues was the fire that led to seven deaths at the amusement centre of Luna Park on Sydney's foreshore in June 1979. All places of assembly were reviewed, with an emphasis on venue capacities and site exits. Hotels were a primary focus of concern. If not the sole determinant of regulatory change upon the State's venues, the extent of non-observance of fire laws within leisure sites, evident in the Luna Park coroner's inquest, could no longer be ignored by the government following the minor panic constructed after the Luna Park deaths. The eventual legislative response did not occur until the transfer of public entertainment regulation from local councils to the Liquor Administration Board, within the *Liquor Act 1985* (NSW).

With the desire to reform the safety of all entertainment premises, the amended Liquor Act provided stronger fire safety laws for entertainment premises, with new audience capacities based on venue size and safety structures. Administered by the Liquor Administration Board, audience capacities were governed not from the Oz rock principle of the greatest number a room could uncomfortably hold, but by the extent to which owners had implemented fire safety precautions. The 1985 amendments compelled venue owners to examine what had been conveniently overlooked throughout the extremely profitable Oz rock scene: the specific numbers of people attending performances, their entrance and exit to the site, and the type of performers within the venue. Tightening of laws governing internal décor like paint fire ratings and fire-retardant furniture further questioned the appropriateness of some sites as entertainment venues. The Manly Vale Hotel in northern Sydney's beach circuit presents an example of the conflicts in operating a venue of Oz rock principles within the changing environmental climate of the 1980s. The Manly Vale, as one of the northern suburbs 'surf-rock' sites, exemplified the youth-alcohol nexus of the circuit, as performer Richard Clapton remembers:

> *My audiences, when I say rioting, it wasn't ugly violence. At the Manly Vale, it always used to amuse us — the whole audience used to go out into the carpark and there'd be hundreds of cars with a marijuana cloud over the whole area. It was sort of like this ritual. My punters would sit out there and get stoned out of their brains, and blatantly so too. Then they'd come in and start drinking on top of that. I didn't get the more ugly violence that some of the bands attracted. It wasn't violence, it was really people having a good time, more, 'fuck off and let us have a good time'. The Manly Vale probably ended up [being] my favourite gig* (1997, pers. comm. 5 Feb).

Built in 1964, the Manly Vale remains a good example of the labyrinth of regulations venues endured throughout the 1980s. In the initial years as a rock room, its auditorium operated with an official capacity from the Licensing Court of 1058 people, although the hotel had been known to have 1500 - 1700 people on popular band nights. Yet the local council stated that under the *Theatres and Public Halls Act 1908* (NSW), the capacity of the International Room was 1048 people. The council also noted that under the provisions of *Ordinance 70* within the *Local Government Act 1919* (NSW), the venue had serious shortcomings regarding the number of exits and exit widths, and would be suitable for no more than 400 people. A Supreme Court judgement in December 1984 found the venue to be highly deficient in complying with Ordinance 70 provisions, based upon a Board of Fire Commissioners report. Previous legal battles with the Council paled beside the orders relating to fire upgrading required throughout the entire building. There were few sections of the building that did not require structural amendment. The council required inflammability of decor interiors; upgrading of fire equipment (hose reels, fire blankets, alarms); the installation of fire-rated partitioning, and increased width and number of exits. Any future increases in the venue's capacity required a further three exits from the auditorium. Much of the hotel's problems in this area derived from the auditorium being situated on the first floor: entertainment areas above ground level were required to observe more rigid compliance codes. Leaseholder Graham Francis clearly believed the 408 capacity limit to be unworkable in terms of rock bands. Apart from the costs of installing a further three exit doors, he also faced the additional costs of adapting existing 1960s exits to the current 1980s standard: this required attaching panic bolt latches and ensuring all doors swung outwards. Authorisations regarding venue capacity were confused further: in April 1983 a police report on the venue calculated that 737 patrons could be allowed in the auditorium. A final Liquor Administration Board assessment of the hotel's lounge bar revealed the absurd realities of compliance:

> *The minimum aggregate width of exits required for the population you are seeking in the Lounge Bar under Schedule Two is 3570 mm. From the plans provided it appears the total aggregate width of exits from the Lounge Bar is 3350 mm* (Liquor Administration Board 'Entertainment Authorisation' letter to Manly Vale Hotel, 16/2/88).

In this instance, a shortfall of 220 mm in regard to door widths rendered the Lounge Bar's current capacity inoperative, requiring a further exit to be installed, or existing exits renovated. The venue's front stairs were also found to be inadequate. As lease holders faced $500 000 costs to meet structural changes, the management had little incentive to upgrade to continue its rock format. The Manly Vale's history characterised the confusing array of authorisations that confronted venues from the late 1970s: Warringah Council, local police and the Liquor Administration Board often presented different compliance standards. The site was eventually redeveloped for local housing.

The new fire regulations placed all venue owners on notice that inspections would eventually be made on their premises; the simple threat of observation was sufficient in an industry proud of its unregulated profits. While commendable in abolishing the more dangerous practices of venues (band equipment blocking exits, lack of fire fighting equipment and exit signs), the regulations had significant flaws. The Chairman of the Liquor Administration Board believed that the typical street corner pub 'with four or five doors' need not worry about the new fire laws (Smith 1983:16). Yet the aggregate widths of exits, not the total number of exits, was often a prime concern. Older street corner pubs, often constructed before the abolition of six o'clock closing, may have possessed several exits on different street fronts, yet still failed to comply with increased maximum *aggregate* widths, due to the thinness of doorways constructed in earlier times. The industry also had a reasonable complaint in regard to the specification of entertainment premises constituting the major source of concern regarding fire safety. Many within the industry argued that regulations discriminated against sites with entertainment. Other pubs with equally large assemblies of people which did not charge admission to enter the venue, for example the well populated hotels in the Rocks area, or those which attracted large crowds to watch rugby matches or title fights, were not subject to similar laws.

The live industry's perception of state conspiracies of discrimination also extended to noise law changes governing licensed premises. One music journalist branded the new public entertainment laws as Orwellian, and likened the Licensing Squad to the Thought Police (Stafford 1984:4). Hotels located on main streets and zoned as business sites often bisect residential streets. In accordance with a decreasing tolerance towards commercial uses within or near private housing, a series of 1980s and 1990s legislation was established to safeguard, in the words of the Liquor Act, the 'quiet and good order of the neighbourhood'. A premise's noise level could now not exceed the background noise level (the surrounding noise within the area) by more than five decibels before midnight. Further, levels after midnight could not exceed the background level. Measurements of noise levels were to be conducted at the boundary of the nearest residence. The ability of hotels or clubs to provide rock bands after midnight was made increasingly difficult, given the need to ensure band PA levels heard in the street did not exceed the ambient levels of the venue's surroundings: a particularly difficult exercise as traffic and other noises recede throughout the night. Further changes in 1989 enabled a single resident to bring a complaint before the Liquor Administration Board in regard to premises' noise levels (three complainants were previously required before action could be taken against a venue). Venue managers regarded the change as further evidence of local and State governments' determination to dampen trading rights and the longer term profitability of hotels, restaurants and clubs. It was argued that the onus of proof in the complaints procedure lay with the venue, and not the complainant, which encouraged frivolous and unsubstantiated claims of noise disturbance.

Such changes to entertainment authorisations from the late 1970s were a significant shock to an industry more familiar with the corrupting practices of unregulated expansion. Increased regulation of liquor consumption presented another significant factor for venues, in the introduction of Random Breath Testing (RBT) by the Wran Labor government in December 1982 to curb drink-drive deaths. The live music sector (both its performers and audiences) was historically reliant upon the car as both a symbolic and practical means of transport. From the beginnings of a national circuit by acts such as Johnny O'Keefe and Col Joye in the late 1950s, the ability to travel long distances between performances has been part of performers' masochistic/machoistic tendencies: touring distances have been employed as part of a performer's mythological status. A survey conducted just ten weeks after the introduction of RBT highlighted the specific relevance of the new law to rock venue audiences who drove. The survey found young, male, unskilled blue collar workers experienced the highest exposure to increased policing of drink-driving behaviour (Homel 1983:9). This group represented the core audiences of those bands which can be placed within the Oz rock tradition: Cold Chisel, Australian Crawl, Midnight Oil, Rose Tattoo, Hunters and Collectors and so on. A significant part of the RBT strategy involved the visible presence of increased monitoring of behaviours; the extent of RBT patrols apparent to motorists was instrumental in effecting behavioural changes. Unsurprisingly, the hotel and club industries believed the new law to be the greatest threat since the introduction of six o'clock closing, representing a contemporary version of previous archaic temperance policies.

Increased governance of drinking behaviours and venue uses have compelled pubs and clubs to pursue other leisure attractions. Notwithstanding the revenue potential of the new gaming culture within hotels, the influx of poker machines has been preferable to publicans in various respects. Increasing local council sensitivity to live music sites has resulted in venue owners having to satisfy an increasing number of various conditions pertaining to live entertainment: extra security staff, venue sound absorption, reduced trading hours and so on. The removal of live music and the transformation of the lounge bar into the hotel casino requires minor internal alterations to accommodate the gaming room provisions of the Liquor Act, with ongoing costs regarding machine rental, supervision and administration. Hoteliers can realistically obtain twenty-four hour licences for their gaming rooms without the additional licence conditions required with live music. This has resulted in a strange division of hotel uses and trading, where the public bar can close at eleven pm, while the gaming room operates throughout the night. The behavioural patterns of gambling clientele, entering and leaving the premises in small groups at various times, are more favourable to councils and residents than the noise problems associated with the singularly noisy exits of live rock audiences. Gaming thus provides the potential for twenty-four hour use of the site, in comparison to the shorter periods maximised by live music.

The changing attitude to rock performance sites is intimately connected to the historic dialectic of public and private leisure, family and work responsibilities which have influenced leisure policy narratives. In their ideal forms, zoning practices strive to frame homogenous areas of interests and activities while eliminating other land uses. The rock pub or club represents a site where residential, leisure and commercial zoning provisions collide. One of the central objectives underpinning the history of NSW liquor laws is the safeguarding of the family unit, and restricting the male breadwinner's capacity for pub and club life. Recent encouragements emphasising family life above drinking and associated entertainments have encompassed three areas. Firstly, hotels are undergoing a transformation similar in scope to the 1950s lounge bar and auditorium extensions. Recent investments in hotel renovations underline a return to the 'family' hotel, emphasising restaurant/bistro facilities and 'respectable' consumption denoting improved surroundings. Secondly, the emergence of intoxication laws and associated regulations increasing the responsibilities of hoteliers in regard to responsible consumption denote governments' determination to combat binge drinking behaviour. Thirdly, noise laws have reinforced residential rights when in contestation with other land uses. The most explicit element of the public/private dialectic in this respect is evident in the insertion of 'public benefit' tests in the consideration of new venues and the operation of existing ones. Legislative trends indicate a concerted effort to consolidate private amenity within public laws. The strengthening of section 104 within the Liquor Act, the establishment of public benefit tests for venues, councils' increasing adoption of late night trading policies, more stringent noise measurement policies and reduced trading hours reveal the triumph of residential amenity over commercial concerns for the greater common good. As the smoke clears from the legislative and public relations battles within neighbourhoods, it is clear that residents have reclaimed their rights to influence the uses of public spaces.

New forms of cultural identity, capital accumulation and leisure consumption have emerged. As an 'uncontrolled Other' (Huxley 1994:160) within utopian suburban peace and quiet, music venues have been increasingly subject to laws to regain suburban order. Within the multiple 'publics' considered by local councils, state governments and the courts, the reinforcement of noise laws reveal the binding of property ownership to amenity debates. Noise laws in regard to entertainment sites embody implicit values of suburban life: the stability of property values and perpetuation of compatible low density housing. In the contestation of public and private space in the gentrification processes evident since the late 1960s in inner city areas, property owners have sought to maintain or 'improve' the ambience of their investments. This shift is best reflected in an observation from The Whitlams' lead singer/keyboard player Tim Freedman:

> *We put the 'The Whitlams live in Newtown, Australia' on the back of all our albums. Except for our live album, which had 'The Whitlams can no longer afford to live in Newtown'* (Eagles 1996:32).

In directing venue practices to conform to broader discourses of public health and amenity, local and state governments increasingly tied formerly ignored commercial practices to private (property) and public (health) spheres of interest and societal norms. Within the period discussed, liquor regulations emphasised venue management responsibilities, rather than limited trading hours, as a means to modifying consumption patterns. This shift to self-regulation replicated other strategies in harnessing live rock within acceptable commercial operations. Such 'technologies of the self' embody the principles of random breath testing in policing strategies employed to denote unpredictable and comprehensive state surveillance. The success in changing audience (and performer) drink-driving behaviours marked an important rupture in the intimate relationship between alcohol sales and live rock which had enabled the spectacular growth in venues from the late 1970s. Containment of excessive drinking cultures also began to be established within the venues themselves. The assembly of harm minimisation strategies codified in liquor laws from the mid-1980s firmly placed the responsibility on venues for their patrons' behaviour, in emphasising micro-management practices subject to punitive state measures. These regulatory shifts placed in question the seemingly innate practices of Oz rock venues which prefigured the hiring of Australian rock bands: the 'dionysic excess(es)' (Fiske, Hodge & Turner 1987:18) brought about, and reliant upon, large bar sales.

Building regulations as a means of 'conducting conduct', in imposing restrictions upon behaviours in and outside venues, also shaped the forms of entertainment choices made by venue owners. This is most evident in the shift in the public health assessment of venues, increasingly regarded merely as places of public assembly, rather than a variety of discrete sites with a mixture of entertainment uses. While a noisy boutique beer pub signals healthy consumption, a noisy rock pub correlates with unhealthy noise. More importantly, the rock pub, by virtue of providing live entertainment, becomes subject to the scope of public assembly laws (exit numbers, furniture fireproofing, door changes, exit widths) and noise laws (acoustic reports, soundproofing, PA limiters, double glazing) which are not applicable to other sites.

While denoting a significant shift in regulatory strategies, events of the 1980s can be placed within the historic reluctance by state governments, local councils and residents to acknowledge live rock music as music. Instead, rock music comes to be understood as noise, a by-product of industry rather than producing meanings for its audiences. To older jazz musicians and audiences and local councils in the 1950s, amplification signified as much about the new rock and roll as the music itself. Equally, the numbing performances of Billy Thorpe and the Aztecs in the 1970s intending to render competing band sound productions 'thin and lifeless' (Nimmervoll 1972:5) was an important part of performance meanings (and in constructing industry mythologies). The Angels, Rose Tattoo and AC/DC in the 1980s continued the strategy of sonic attack as fundamental to the live experience, where the music was felt as well as heard. Rock's place within the Australian pub was tolerated on the provision of mutual benefits to publicans, promoters and the State from alcohol sales. The excessive profits and practices of Oz rock continue to resonate as the mythological core within a local recording industry dependent upon transnational capital. Yet the fragile commercial contract of its live traditions has been fractured. The implications have yet to be fully realised by an industry still grappling with the end of the notion of the 'pub rock apprenticeship', and the contemporary view of rock as a loud, unwanted tenant who no longer pays 'his' way.

References

Eagles, J. 1996, 'Good Goff, it's a Whitlam' in *The Bridge*, Newtown, Sydney.

Fiske, J., Hodge, B. & Turner, G. 1987, 'The Pub' in *Myths of Oz*, Sydney: Allen & Unwin.

Homel, R. 1983, *The Impact of Random Breath Testing*, Sydney: NSW Drug and Alcohol Authority, Research Grant Report Series.

Huxley, M. 1994, 'Planning as a Framework of Power: Utilitarian Reform, Enlightenment Logic and the Control of Space' in Ferber, S.; Healy, C. and McAuliffe, C. (eds) *Beasts of Suburbia: Reinterpreting Cultures in Australian Suburbs*, Melbourne: Melbourne University Press.

Miller, T. 1993, *The Well Tempered Self: Citizenship, Culture and the Postmodern Subject*, Baltimore: John Hopkins Press.

Nimmervoll, E. 1972, 'Billy Thorpe Attacks Volume Critics and Gutless bands' in *Go-Set*, 29 January:5.

Smith, P. 1983, Untitled column in *On The Street*, 14 December:16.

Stafford, P. 1984, 'Larg Revisited' in *On The Street*, 1 January:4.

Warringah Council 1979-1990 Files obtained under the Freedom of Information legislation.

EXPERIENCES OF PERSONAL AND SOCIAL CHANGE IN THE PERFORMANCE OF REBETIKA IN MELBOURNE

KIPPS HORN

Rebetika music is a form of Greek popular urban music which, in its early stages of evolution, reflected life-style aspects of the lower classes, particularly in the port areas of Athens, Piraeus and Thessalonika. The music's assimilation by broader social groups led to transformations of its musical style and related attitudinal values embodied in its performance and composition. Despite these changes it is still performed in Greece and throughout the Greek diaspora including Melbourne, which is still home to the third largest Greek community outside of mainland Greece.

How and why it has remained alive in Melbourne (or any other part of Australia for that matter) and what role it plays in the lives of its performers and audience, are central questions in my current doctoral research.

Rebetika is a significant aspect of Greek-Australian migrant culture. The music has travelled with the people, its musical style signifying the meeting of a number of cultures and as such, its performance (along with other forms of Greek music) links us to issues of identity in terms of what it means to be a Greek-Australian. An important part of my work will be to ascertain to what extent changes in rebetic music performance in Melbourne reflects wider cultural changes associated with the Greek-Australian community during the past fifty years.

It is not possible in this paper to describe the entire stylistic evolution of rebetic music, however, it is useful to note that whilst the origins of rebetika are obscure, there is a case to be made for linking it with the urbanisation of Greece's population: a development begun after the Greek War of Independence (1821-1829). As in the rest of Europe, the urbanisation of Greece's population increased rapidly in the 20th century. Athens, the port of Piraeus, and Thessalonika were the main areas of urban development and, as mentioned, the evolution of rebetika music.

In the conference presentation of this paper, delegates listened to two recordings involving rebetika. The first featured improvised bouzouki music recorded in a Greek hash den in the 1930's whilst customers partook of the narghile — the hash pipe. The second involved a group of Greek-Australian, Turkish-Australian and mainland Greek musicians and their audience involved in a performance of a vocal improvisation with instrumental accompaniment, recorded in Melbourne 1997.

Both examples included aspects of rebetika music but, more importantly for this paper, the performances evidenced the living experience of the music over a span of sixty years and huge geographic and social distances.

The performers and audience in both recordings manifested not just an enjoyment in melodic, rhythmic and instrumental techniques, but their living experience and knowledge of the music and its performance. It is clear from their responses that they knew and shared the music and the ambience of the occasion. It is highly likely in the first recording and certain in the second, that musicians and audience shared *migratory* experience as they listened to *spontaneous music-making* embedded in *traditions* evolved and still experienced in Greece, Turkey, other Arabic regions, and now in Australia.

I do not intend to dwell on the fact that hash and cocaine usage was often associated with the rebetic music scene in pre-World War Two Greece, but to bring the discussion closer to contemporary Australian times, it might be illuminating to tell the following story.

A few weeks ago, one of the main centres of rebetika song in Melbourne was raided by the police and quite a number of older Greek/Australian regulars at the pub were found to have been growing marijuana between the tomato plants for sale in the pub. Coincidentally, at the same time the regular ensemble of Greek-Australian musicians disbanded due to a mixture of stylistic disagreements and the migration of a key member to mainland Greece. It is a story which resonates with the evolution of rebetika.

It does not give a description of the current rebetika music scene in Melbourne, but it does give a snap-shot of a particular moment in its evolution: a story with narrative elements touching on a transplanted traditional urban music, stylistic mores, the relationship between a group of musicians and their audience, and inter-generational contact with a traditional music genre — all elements to do with the study and experience of a musical form that is a part of Melbourne's (Australia's?) musical scene.

I must acknowledge that the threads of musical and non-musical tradition, improvisation and migration (key notions in this paper) are woven into my experience and bind me to my subject. How else does an English migrant with a background in so-called 'art' music come to be making connections with the popular music of someone else's culture?

In retrospect the weaving of the threads began twenty years ago during my first visit to Greece. It was a time in Europe (and, I have since learned, also in Melbourne) when there was a renaissance of interest in traditional Celtic music. Celtic music, with its joyous dance rhythms and searing laments relatively free of Western diatonic harmonies, has always enlivened me. In Greece, with each hearing of fragments of popular music seeping from taxis, bars, tavernas, shops and radios, I found that the music touched me in a similar way. Later, I was to learn of social, historical and musicological reasons for this, but at the time I was particularly aware of a sense of aliveness and renewal in spontaneous (improvised) elements in live performances. (To digress briefly, there has been a fruitful contact between Greek-Australian and Irish musicians in Melbourne which has played a significant role in the wide-spread introduction of the bouzouki in the folk and popular music of Eire).

These experiences, together with a conscious effort to explore spontaneous music-theatre experience in contemporary composition and performance to free myself from a heavily biased exposure to 19th century Western European 'art' music, focused my thinking around notions of tradition, improvisation and migration; the latter element, migration, becoming part of my personal experience when I came to Australia eight years ago, soon to find myself experiencing what the Greeks call ο πονοσ, (the pain) of migration.

These anecdotal credentials do not ameliorate a potential experiential gap between the outsider (me) looking in on a musical genre and those inside performing the music, but what I hope to establish is the idea that there might be commonalties in the experience of tradition, improvisation and migration (T.I.M.) for many musicians and audiences and that an exploration of T.I.M. as it relates to the experience of rebetika in Melbourne will be a worthwhile focus.

Before proposing what these commonalties might be, I must define my use of the terms tradition, improvisation and migration (see Figure 1).

Tradition is a term much used by conservatives and radicals alike. I use it in the radical sense in that, in the repetition of a custom or belief, the practitioners allow for adaptations and changes appropriate to their needs and context, and thus continually revitalise the tradition rather than merely repeating it in a meaningless habitual manner.

The use of the term migration is broad and not controversial. It embraces regional, international, internal and external population movements involving *personal and social change.*

Figure 1

Tradition	Improvisation	Migration
Beliefs or customs handed down form ancestors to posterity. Their practice involving their revitalisation.	Spontaneous creation of ideas and practices or re-organisation of received ideas and practices in performance.	Movement of people either temporarily or permanently from one location to another.

Improvisation is currently a 'hot' topic and has been subject to a wide spectrum of analysis. On one end of the spectrum it has been argued that no such thing exists and on the other, it somehow involves spontaneous, 'original' and free-forming composition. The above definition is applicable to improvisation in many fields, although in this research I limit discussion to musical improvisation. It takes into account a broad spectrum of ideas on the subject, focussing on *change brought about by the creation and re-organisation of musical ideas during a performance.*

Thus I have named a pivotal aspect of commonality found in the experience of tradition, improvisation and migration: that is, a cultural practice is recontextualised through experiences of tradition, improvisation and migration, often (but perhaps not always) with resultant changes to the practice. Figure 2 shows this and indicates relational aspects between customs, practices and beliefs, spontaneous performance events, population location and associated values and attitudes.

Figure 2

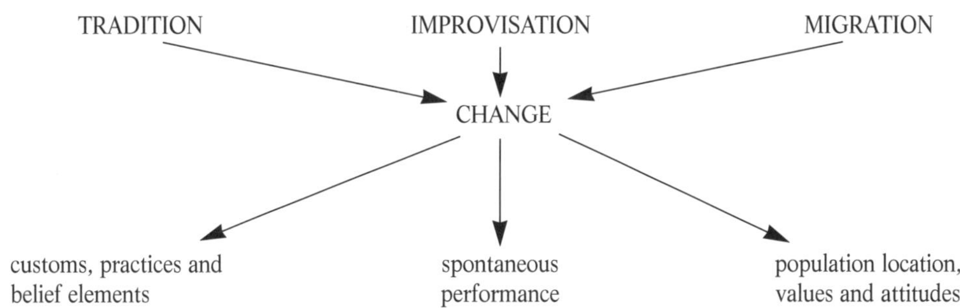

Figure 3 zooms in closer to the issues as they relate to rebetika performance in Melbourne. (It should be noted at this point that characteristics listed in figures 3-6 are not definitive. They indicate broader areas for inclusion in more detailed work). I am looking at how Melbourne musicians and audiences bring their past, present and potential future experience into the performance of a traditional urban music; how adaptable and flexible they are in recreating the music in a new or changed context. The figure also implies research questions such as — how do musicians and audiences experience improvisation? What does it mean to them? How does improvisational practice in terms of rhythmic and melodic modality occur? What meanings do terminologies associated with instrumental and vocal improvisation (such as taxim, tsakimata, amanes, figures, strophes, chromata, solo, text extension) have?

The Greek-Australian community in Melbourne now consists of three generations. What are first, second and third generational attitudes and values towards rebetika music? What do these attitudes and values tell us of inter, intra and trans-cultural issues and how do they relate to issues of Greek-Australian identity?

Figure 3

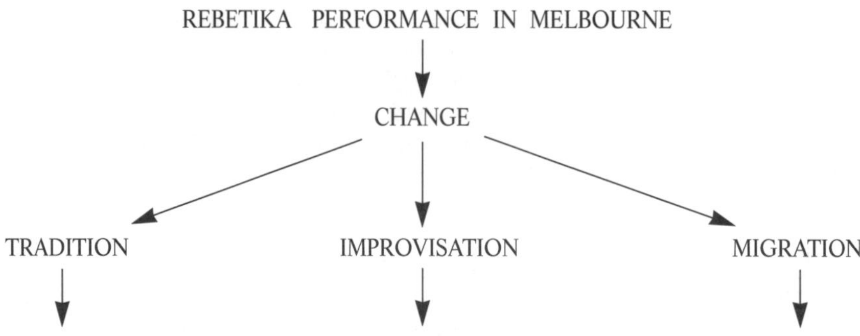

Rebetika is a traditional Greek urban music and a part of the lived and changing culture of Melbourne Greek-Australians. Its contemporary performance involves a revitalisation and to some extent, changing, of traditional experience. Its performance in Melbourne involves an integration of past, present and potential future experience for performers and audience. Traditional practises and beliefs are combined with new: possibly because of a perceived adapability of the performers and audience, and fluidity of the musical form. An ability to adapt and work within fluid forms relates closely to experiences of change.	Improvisation is a key channel of change in the performance of rebetika. Melodic and rhythmic elements are the main areas which feature improvisation. A musical and social examination of the improvisatory processes may be linked to experiences of tradition and migration.	Migration is a catalyst for change of personal and social values and attitudes. Generational differences and similarities of attitudes and values towards rebetika music in Melbourne may indicate broader cultural issues. Migratory experience may also be the catalyst for changes in performance style, playing techniques and techniques of making instruments.

Whilst I aim to use the T.I.M. focus to examine different aspects of rebetic music performance in Melbourne including, most importantly, how Melbourne musicians and audiences perceive rebetika, there are three key areas which I am looking at in particular: the melodic and rhythmic modal elements, and the musical instruments. Figures 4, 5 and 6 outline some of the issues involved in each area.

Instruments used in Melbourne rebetika music have been either imported, made by local instrument-makers, handed down as family heirlooms or found in op shops. An examination of their origins, physical characteristics and classification may tell us more about rebetika playing practices (including improvisation) and cultural meanings derived from the instruments.

My research interviews include a rich seam of stories and experiences associated with the making and acquisition of instruments in Melbourne. It is fascinating to spend time with Greek-Australian instrument-makers in their sheds as they relate experiences of tradition and migration to their craft. A keen transcultural exchange has been established between mainland Greek and Greek-Australian instrument makers. I know of at least three Melbourne Greek-Australian musicians now living in Athens who export their instruments to Australia.

Figure 4

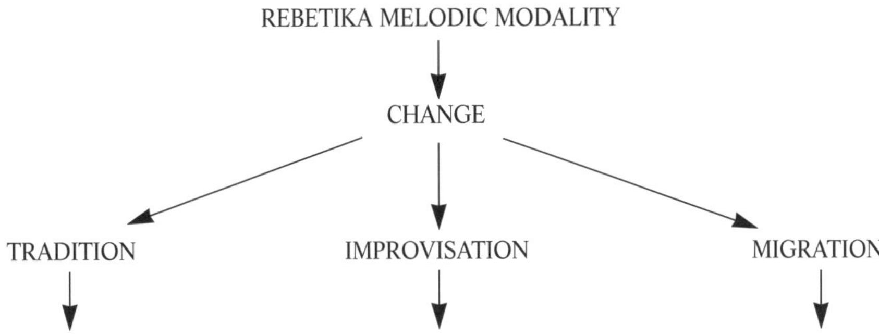

The makam system is a traditional Middle Eastern modal system adapted by the Greeks. Some Greeks argue that it has its roots in the older modal traditions of Byzantium. How is the traditional system, referred to by the Greeks as drokoi (roads), used and modified in the performance of rebetika music during the 1960s-1990s in Melbourne?	What do different aspects of improvisation in Melbourne's rebetic music tell us about changes in attitudes and values relating to the use of the *roads?* Assuming a close correlation between the use of traditional modes and an increased likelihood of improvised music, to what extent does Melbourne rebetika evidence use of traditional modes and how does the music reflect Western diatonic influences? How does improvisation practice in Melbourne compare with current and older mainland Greek practices?	There is a close relationship between many Melbourne Greek, Turkish, Arabic and Irish musicians in Melbourne and a consequent interchange and learning particularly in modal matters. How does this affect, if at all, changes in rebetic performance practice? How are generational attitudes towards modality reflected in Melbourne's rebetic music?

Figure 5

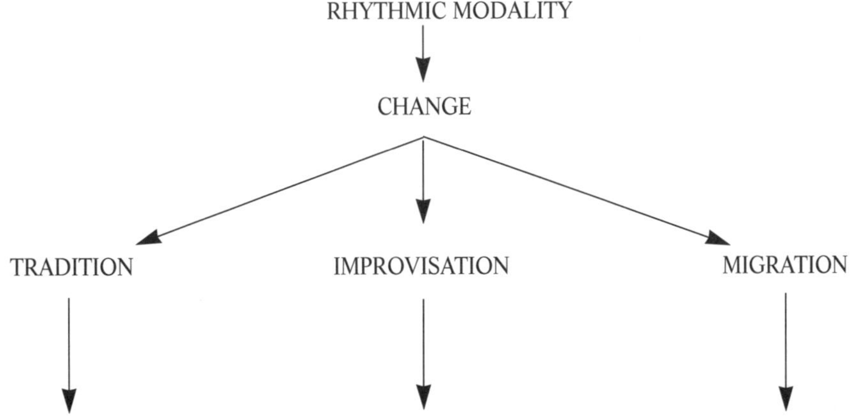

The main dance rhythms used in rebetic music, the zebekiko, hasapiko, hasapikoserviko and tsifeteli, have long Asia Minor/Greek/Turkish lineage. In mainland Greece, many variations of these rebetic rhythms have been discontinued or modified by Western popular music practices. What changes in traditional rhythmic practices can be heard in Melbourne's rebetika?	Specific instruments in rebetika ensembles are given rhythmic roles. Basic rhythmic patterns are decorated to varying degrees depending on the mood and skill of performers. Are the basic rebetika rhythms intact or have they been modifed? What do spontaneous rhythmic performance practices in Melbourne tell us about broader rebetika performance issues?	Greek migrants in the 1950s and 1960s were largely rural people who brought with them demotic (rural) dances performed within Greek social gatherings. Second and third generation children, have re-embraced urban dances, but there is a merging of the two — young Greek-Australians often perform rural dance steps to rebetika urban music. The evolution of rebetika has involved the 'migration' of dance rhythms from Greek Islands Greek diasporic communities across the world. To what extent do rebetika rhythms heard in Melbourne's night clubs, pubs and clubs reflect the evolution of rebetika amongst the diaspora?

Figure 6

REBETIKO INSTRUMENTS
↓
CHANGE
↓

TRADITION ↓	IMPROVISATION ↓	MIGRATION ↓
Rebetika style is generally perceived in four chronological divisions: 1900-1930, 1930-1940, 1950 – 1974, 1974-present day. Rebetika music before 1940 is often referred to as traditional rebetika. Rebetika post WW2 brought about a popularisation, demise and re-birth of the music. Stylistic division featured changes in instrumental and ensemble elements. 1960-1990s Melbourne rebetika features all these instrumental and ensemble variations. There is a lively discourse amongst Melbourne musicians about what constitutes a 'traditional' ensemble, what is a 'traditional' performance practice, and whether these considerations matter at all.	There are two main makers of rebetika instruments in Melbourne and a number of performers who also make instruments. The processes of their craft, solutions to technical problems and invention of new forms of rebetika instruments involve spontaneous crafting decisions. The instrument makers' work involves making changes and adaptations whilst engaged in traditional instrument making practices.	Rebetic instruments evidence Greek-Turkish and Arabic culture contact. A forced mass migration of Orthodox Greeks from Asia Minor to mainland Greece in 1922 marked a key point of entry for musicians and instruments to Greece. There is still much research to be done regarding the evolution of the bouzouki, the instrument most associated with rebetika. An organological study of rebetika instruments in Melbourne may help disclose the relationship between migratory patterns of local musicians and the evolution of their instruments.

To conclude, I want to note that my research does not set out to ask the question 'what is rebetika music practice in Melbourne?', but, 'how do Melbourne Greek-Australians perceive rebetika music in their lives?'. It is from this question that the three areas of tradition, improvisation and migration have emerged.

Greeks who came to Australia in the 1950s, mainly from rural areas, kept contact with their music traditions much of which, as has been noted, involved improvisatory practice. And whilst the idea of rebetika music in Melbourne in the 1950s was once described as 'absurd', it is now an established part of Greek urban culture in Australia and mainland Greece — to some extent there have been parallel developments in the interest in rebetic music in both countries.

In Australia, the telling of the rebetika story: the changes it has undergone and the changes its players and audience have undergone, may tell us more of the continuing encounter with evolving traditional practices, the role of improvisation and migration experience in the renewal of these practices and the nature, strength and renewal of Greek–Australian identity, particularly amongst the second and third generations.

Glossary

Amanes	A style of vocal improvisation common to the Asia Minor area
αυτοσκεδιασμοσ/aftoskethiasmos	Greek for 'improvsiation', literally translated as 'self directed'
Chromata	'Colour', timbre, nuances of performance
Demotik/demotika/δεμοτικα	Generic term for Greek rural traditional music
Figures/φιγουρα	A music or dance figure, often improvised
Makams	Anglicized term for the modal system common to Arabic and Turkish music, each makam has its own interval characteristics
Solo	Used by some Melbourne musicians to describe an improvised section performed by a musician in an ensemble who 'goes off and does his own thing'
Strophes/strofh	A turn or change of direction, as well as the more common reference to a stanza. Has been used in Melbourne to describe improvised vocal or instrumental decoration in the movement between two adjacent notes
Taxim	An improvised instrumental introduction or interpolation based on a makam
Tsakimata	Vocal exclamations interpolated into a performance
Roads/dromoi	Greek terminology for the makam system

THE AMBIGUOUS FLAPPER

BRUCE JOHNSON

This paper is adapted from a chapter of a book soon to be published by Currency Press,[1] examining Australia's transition to modernity and the relationship to Modernism. This debate has proceeded far enough now for us to know that the two are not the same, and that Modernism was actually concerned with taking control of the meaning of the modern by excluding all that was threatening to the custodians of cultural value in a masculinist society. The discourse of Modernism reviled mass culture as overdetermined trash peddled to passive consumers.

My purpose here is to suggest ways in which, on the contrary, women were able to use examples of low culture — specifically jazz and film — to become active and significant producers of modernity in their negotiations with more conservative social forces.

There are two stages in this paper:

1. An argument that the character of both jazz and silent film in the 1920s enabled women to interact with them as producers rather than just consumers;
2. A case study in which this convergence is articulated.

At first glance, the above argument, that women were producers of jazz in the 1920s, might appear to be an unlikely proposition, given the subsequent masculinisation of jazz performance, in which the stereotypical role of women has been as feminine adornments singing about their victimisation and subordination in love.

There are two senses, however, in which Australian jazz in the 1920s was much more feminised.

In the first place, more women led and played in jazz bands than at any time since, until perhaps the 1990s, and far from being a cause for remark, the image of the woman jazz musician was something of a stereotype.

The cover illustration of the sheet music of *Flappers in the Sky* depicts a biplane bearing the transgressive name 'Sky Pirate', with a group of flappers aboard. The currency of the female aviator as one of the popular images of the modern emancipated woman, is indicated in the song's lyric, with its references to modern girls' 'ambitions soaring', while 'man, mere man it seems will have to risk his very life, By planeing [sic] right out through the clouds, When he wants to find a wife'.

The same emancipative message is proclaimed on the cover, portraying the conduct of the women. One is flying while others, dressed in men's flying suits are insouciantly drinking, smoking, applying make-up, and one strums a poorly drawn guitar or banjo. That a woman would be playing an instrument associated with 1920s popular music is thus as much a part of the emancipated repertoire as all the other activities depicted. When seasoned theatre entrepreneur Ben Fuller formed the country's first 'jazz band' for his theatre circuit, it is unlikely that his shrewd show-biz instinct was dormant when he picked a woman, the singer Belle Sylvia, to lead it, and later replaced her when she left by another woman, Maybelle Morgan.

In particular, women were prominent in early improvisational practices, which also draws them into the production of silent film. John Whiteoak has studied the importance of women and the domestic piano in the early history of improvisation in Australia. The silent cinema, in the pre-jazz era, held the highest level of improvisatory practice, and the greater proportion of improvisational cinema pianists and organists were women. This is a provocative statistic, given that cinema attendance in Australia outstripped church attendance by 1919 and in NSW, by 1921 there were more cinema attendances than all other forms of theatre combined. By 1928, as the silent era drew to a close, annual cinema attendances in Australia had reached in excess of 110 million. Furthermore, there was an overwhelming gender bias among the early cinema audience. A royal commission into the moving picture industry in 1927 received evidence that about seventy per cent of Australian film audiences were women.

The 'sound track' of this predominantly female entertainment was the musical accompaniment. The accompanist was the commentator upon, participant in, and mediator of a message whose formal content was in other ways closed and fixed, so that the cinema pianist co-produced the film as a public practice. And this improvisational rearticulation of the product to local conditions was most likely to be conducted by a woman.

I am not trying to make the demonstrably absurd suggestion that women dominated in the male preserve of professional music. But in the earliest history of jazz in Australia, there were surprising numbers of women active as performers.

There is a further dimension to this which has disappeared as the meaning of the word 'jazz' has altered. In the 1920s the word referred not exclusively to instrumental and singing performance, but to a particular kind of dance.

First, it is useful to remember that of all public expressive practices, dancing is perhaps one of the two most democratic, and potentially the most unruly in that it needs no expensive equipment or hard won competencies — only a body that will do as its owner tells it, or that tells its 'owner' what to do. The other is vocalising. In the dance, cognitive discipline is threatened by corporeal abandonment. The pure physicality of dance provides the possibility for the most unmediated, unregulated display of subjectivity. The dancer is the dance.

Now, we must imagine these politics of the dance also framing jazz in the 1920s. 'Jazz' has been so securely categorised as a musical product or genre, that it is puzzling to encounter its Australian usage in the twenties.

It is only when we realise that jazz was understood to be interchangeably a musical form (noun) and a dance (verb), that these odd grammatical constructions become explicable.

'The jazz is a dance', reported *Table Talk* in August 1919. 'The jazz' - like 'the waltz', 'the tango', 'the quickstep'. A woman 'jazzes', as she also waltzes and foxtrots. The word 'jazz' carried with it all the semantic and ideological luggage of 'dancing'.

'The Jazz' was imagined and practised as a dance — a process in which active participation is the actual condition of its consumption. To a greater extent than is already the case in improvised music in performance, 'the jazz' was seen to be something done by what we would now think of primarily as its audience. You didn't dance to jazz that was being made exclusively by people who were separate by virtue of instrumental ownership, competence and the space defined by a stage. You 'jazzed'.

Dancing, and specifically 'producing' jazz in the 1920s was thus not only a more active and democratic experience than other embodiments of mass culture such as film, (the object of relatively passive spectacle), but it was especially open to women. The archetypal jazz identity of the period was female, described in London's *Daily Mail* in 1920 as 'the frivolous, scantily clad 'jazzing flapper', irresponsible and undisciplined' (Melman, 1988: 19). And the posture in which she is most immediately recognisable is the abandoned expansiveness of the quintessential dance of 'The Jazz Age', the Charleston.

Jazzing was a site for the reinvention of women throughout the 1920s in ways that sought to expand the possibilities available to them. In this decade, jazz was feminised in important ways.

Of course, the practice and discourse of jazz were framed by a larger patriarchal control and I now wish to turn to a case study which discloses the ambiguities in the relationships between such forces as gender, mass culture, technology, and modernisation.

Greenhide belongs to a film genre which reflects a growing interest in the changing position of women in postwar Australia. A general structural formula in these films is to place a young woman at a point of tension between traditional roles and contemporary possibilities. *Greenhide* was directed by Charles Chauvel in 1926, it is his second feature, following *The Moth of Moonbi* in the same year. It exemplifies again the contemporary fixation on the complicit themes of modernity, gender, and country/city, that the two films deal with mirror images of these issues.

Moombi is about an innocent young country girl drawn like a moth to the city. *Greenhide* reverses the dynamic, through the story of Margery, the daughter of Sam Paton, who lives in urban splendour in Brisbane and owns a cattle station called Walloon 'out west' in Queensland's Dawson Valley. The station manager is Gavin, nicknamed Greenhide for his toughness. By writing to Gavin and signing her father's name, Margery initiates an indefinite visit to the station. When Gavin's reply to her father alerts the latter to the scheme, he reprimands her for going behind his back, but decides that the best way to teach her a lesson is to agree to her proposal. The film then explores the consequences of Margery's transgressive gesture.

Following eleven minutes of *mise-en-scene* sequences, the audience is presented with a scene located in the extensive grounds of the Paton Brisbane home, where Margery is hosting a party for a large number of her female friends. Chauvel has to address the challenge of constructing her as a liberated young modern woman exclusively through visual images and subtitles. During footage of Margery sitting at a table talking gaily to her friends, the subtitles indicate an interest in horse racing, and suggest that she has recently lost money on a horse that was beaten by a nose. As the guests talk, they smoke with a staged obviousness that shouts 'Modern Women'. The stereotype is then reinforced in a sequence that now seems structurally clumsy and even formally grotesque, but which has very dense signification. It involves what I believe, is the earliest surviving movie footage of an Australian jazz band. Apart from its importance in setting the atmosphere of chic twenties socialising, this band is then used to provide a significant frame for the further definition of Margery's character.

The party footage is intercut with material that sets the narrative in motion, as Sam receives the telegram from Gavin from which he deduces his daughter's stratagem. In the meantime the intercut scenes continue to set the party atmosphere and in particular to define Margery's character.

Of all the cues provided by Chauvel in this party scene, Margery's 'jazzing' is the most sustained signal of her standing as a liberating imaginary for the modern woman in the cinema audience. Margery is a model for the visualisation of emancipative female social roles and practices. Her actions constitute an entry into male spaces: smoking, horse racing, and the rebellious plan to move from the decadent, feminised city, to the masculine 'elemental' bush. In a silent medium, her jazzing is more eloquent than any other visual signal. She literally enters the frame of the all-male band in a figure/ground configuration in which a woman becomes the jazz 'soloist'.[2] And as a dance, that solo is a transgression of the male leader/female follower paradigm of couple dancing that, since the waltz in the early nineteenth century had so powerfully modelled the bourgeois Romantic conception of the molecular social unit. Margery's jazzing is both significantly female and non-feminine: a dance, but one that is improvised, solo, abjuring nineteenth century notions of womanly lightness, modesty, grace and sexual dependency.

It would be a simplistic argumentative achievement however, to leave the discussion of *Greenhide* at that point. The image of the Flapper triumphantly dragging Australia out of the nineteenth century is no more accurate than any other simplistic popular culture mythology. The 'picture' is both less schematic and more interesting if we therefore take this examination a little further.

As the scene continues, Margery fantasises rural life during her coming visit, as being swept into the arms of a station-rider during a cattle stampede, or being 'sheiked' by a bushranger.

The image of 'The Sheik' climaxes (yes, I know) her erotic inventory, producing a further ambiguation of the narrative. I mentioned above that Margery's dance is both female and non-feminine. The flapper is already a complex figure, simultaneously gendered yet androgynous. This ambiguity is compounded when coupled with the 'Sheik' mythology, based on the bestselling novel and the resultant film, starring Rudolf Valentino. That scenario situates a woman in a sexually submissive role, but it was also a fantasy of uninhibited eroticism, hardly likely to increase her level of satisfaction with the traditional role of Edwardian wife whose only approved locus is the home. The image of the Sheik here assumes on the part of the young Australian female audience an easy familiarity with contemporary mass culture. That the young women in the audience would have immediately recognised the cinematic reference is a reasonable assumption given that the film's six month run at the Sydney Globe in 1922 was a world record.

What these two tropes — bushranger and Sheik — signify is an ambiguous dislocation of the position of women, a heightened awareness of sexual and erotic possibilities, and the consequent sense of the destabilisation of Anglo-European patriarchy.

Margery's invocation of musical and cinematic texts reminds us of ambiguities in the constellation of mass culture, gender politics, and jazz. Mass and popular culture like film and jazz are significant sites for the articulation of emancipated modernity in Australia. But in Chauvel's film the flapper is recuperated into the enfolding masculinist discourse, and it is important not to replace one simplistic essentialism with its opposite. It remains true, however, that in the negotiations between women's emancipation and a conservative patriarchy, mass culture, jazz music and jazz dance are the sites of modernity, the means through which a liberated future is imagined and acted out. When she goes to the west, the semi-private talisman of her potentiality as a liberated young woman that she takes with her is a 'jazz garter'. Whatever the conflicting ideological forces eddying around Margery during the film, she seems to come closest to breaking free into a liberated imaginary of modernity through 'jazzing'.

Notes

1 An extensively amplified and illustrated treatment of this topic may be found in the author's *The Inaudible Music,* to be published in 1999 by Sydney's Currency Press, from whom permission was kindly given to publish this version here.

2 The 'figure/ ground configuration' refers to a composition in which there is a clear distinction between a figure of central interest and a background of secondary interest.

References

Melman, B. 1988, *Women and the popular imagination in the twenties: flappers and nymphs,* London: Macmillan.

NEW AND EMERGING FORMS OF INDIGENOUS MUSIC

JARDINE KIWAT

In addressing what are called new and emerging forms of Indigenous music, we must start with the past. Because within the past there are essential tools that every Indigenous person, no matter what area they come from, will draw upon at one point or another in their lives. The day I met other Indigenous musicians in Adelaide was the day I joined the Centre for Aboriginal Studies in Music, known as CASM.

I would have to say that my life hasn't been an easy road. After what seemed an unusual amount of misfortunes I found myself outside the door of CASM at 77 Finnis Street to sign on as a part-time student in late 1981 and to eventually go full-time in 1982.

My parents were extremely proud that I was going back to study. I left high school in Year 10 after what could only be described as a dismal attempt at academia. One teacher I had was constantly telling me I would never amount to anything in life and constantly pronounced my name wrong to get a reaction. He received his reaction, and in those days four canings on each hand were considered appropriate educational counselling. I failed metalwork and woodwork in my last attempt to achieve something at school, but strangely enough went on to complete a four-year apprenticeship in boilermaking after leaving school. During these years my mother had a habit of playing Tahitian music every time she wanted to feel happy and, in particular, at Christmas time every year. This wasn't because we were Tahitian: it was a music my mother felt close to, a music my mother identified with, even though she was of South Sea Island descent — a mix of Aoba Island and Levuka Fiji. This music was from a community that sang and danced together, happy and content with many of their traditions alive and intact despite French colonisation.

My mother's people were blackbirded to Mackay on the Queensland coastline in the early 1930s and 1940s as slaves, to cut canefields and clear the Queensland coastline for development. All of their traditional language, music, dance and customs were forbidden to be practiced after arriving on the shores of Queensland. My father is of Torres Strait Islander descent and he was instrumental in terms of our family's identity and in terms of my mother's identity. My mother is highly respected in both South Sea and Torres Strait Islander communities and quite often finds herself the voice for many community issues in Mackay, even though she has limited knowledge of traditional ways.

I grew up in this small country town in the 1960s without even knowing what the word cross-cultural meant and not knowing what an important role it would play in my future. I was influenced by older sisters, cousins, aunties, uncles, and by my mother and my father. I was also influenced by a mixture of jazz and country from Mum, traditional Torres Strait Islander music/dance and original songs from Dad and by an odd assortment of David Bowie, The Beatles, Janis Joplin, Brook Benton, Jim Reeves, The Doors, Isley Brothers, Deep Purple, Daddy Cool, Neil Diamond, Skyhooks, Wild Cherry, Little River Band, Chain and, of course, lashings of Tahitian music at Christmas time.

As in most cases, our lives, family, culture, ideas and influences are kept in our minds somewhere. Once we have developed and are able to understand, this information can be transferred into a song, painting, theatre production, poem, or even into work in which life experiences are more relevant than a formal qualification. When you think about it, quite often the formal qualification doesn't match the position in question or vice versa. There is a real need in most university or TAFE courses to keep in line with the never ending changes in community music making. Particularly when high school students are looking towards careers as musicians, music educators and/or trainers.

The first time I became aware of cross-cultural music was when I enrolled in the Centre for Aboriginal Studies in Music (CASM) in late 1981. I had unwittingly joined at a time when CASM was riding on a wave of musical achievements and course developments and was fighting for recognition as the first Indigenous musical department of a university in Australia. It was also the first time I had contact with ethnomusicologists. They were students from an Adelaide University music program at the Conservatorium. I was asked one day if I would talk to these students to help them understand about Indigenous people. Hours and hours of my personal family information were documented on tape to be later transcribed into someone's thesis. It seemed a very one sided process (I talk, you take).

When I think about that experience today, I realise the need for Indigenous people to fulfil this role, to research and document their own histories, to provide easy access to cultural information for their communities and to retain what aural traditions still exist today, particularly within our older generations. At some time, particularly when working on large projects, there will come that moment when you need access to this information. It would be kept within your own family area or you would need to ask for permission to use certain songs/dances from those composers or elders that may be the keepers of such traditional music. There is a real danger this information will be lost unless younger Indigenous generations become responsible for the preservation of this knowledge and take an active and responsible role in ensuring aural traditions remain in tact.

I have plenty of respect for the functions of libraries but in terms of accessing particular and sensitive cultural information you have to go to the source (the people). In this situation, video and audio taping of this information becomes essential and the tapes should be kept in appropriate holding places within the community. Elders from this community would then decide what information can be accessed by anyone and what is privy to that particular Indigenous community.

In March this year at the Adelaide Festival we premiered a major work, 'Music is our Culture' by Indigenous composers including myself, Grayson Rotumah, Kerry McKenzie, Jensen Warusam, local composer Chester Schultz and the Adelaide Symphony Orchestra. Historically, it is the first major work of its kind in Australia and was a remarkable achievement for the Indigenous composers involved who, until now, didn't have any substantial contact with or inside working knowledge of an orchestra. Initial meetings for the project started in May 1996 and within a couple of days musical passages, poetry, and a few riffs were starting to filter through our minds and onto paper. There was a strong feeling at this initial meeting towards the necessity to have a strong traditional Aboriginal/Islander, music/dance focus in the project. In many ways, our knowledge in this area had a myriad of limitations. The outcome of the project was to reflect a true collaboration of Indigenous musicians with orchestral musicians. During the process I found on many occasions that we were leaning towards the orchestra routines and rehearsals more than we anticipated. This was quite often dictated by the need to justify the expenditure for the costly orchestra calls. The calls, spaced at three to four months apart, gave us little time to discuss each session we had with the players and automatically placed time constraints on a process that needed hours of discussion to keep us on track and focussed on including all our ideas. What we were developing were feelings, stories, cultural identity, memories of years of family issues and hardships and trying to squeeze them into a half hour piece of music.

In discussions with Symphony Australia, the need to include Indigenous music/dance/stories, the didgeridoo, and clapsticks throughout the project was made obvious. The project's purpose and authenticity were justified by the content that was distinctly 'Indigenous'.

Is it not enough to be Indigenous? Is it not enough just to know your family tree? What are the prerequisites for being Indigenous? How much information must an Indigenous person carry with them to justify who they are? Who or what determines what is Indigenous or not? However good the intentions are for whatever project you work on, these questions arise in the back of your mind, jumbled together with all the information you have been storing away for years.

As a facilitator in this area, you must be able to transfer this information into an understandable working process which enables the participant to achieve personal goals, as well as the goals of the collaborative team. The process then has to go through other musical changes to enable the ideas (particularly traditional) to be transferred into orchestral language. Normally, when writing music for yourself the only person you consult is yourself and if someone does criticise your work you go ahead with your idea anyway. However, when working as a collaborative team there are hours and hours of discussion before embarking on musical ideas, patterns, phrases and words. We had to talk in depth about how we wanted the project to unfold, to incorporate all our ideas and feelings, social and community issues, political decisions that have affected Indigenous peoples and the loss and separation of cultural practices in our own areas.

When we talk about new and emerging forms of Indigenous music, what are we saying exactly? To me this music has many faces. It takes on a personality of its own by evolving as a true representation of everyone's ideas and expressions. It is about the sharing of information; be it language, customs, songs or music. No matter what process you go through you have to move outside of the comfort zone that has been nurturing you, making you feel safe with all this knowledge you have stored away.

In many ways, when we start to analyse this music there is a danger that we tend to lose the simplicity of its evolution, and by doing so we are setting guidelines for what is traditional/non-traditional and Indigenous/non-Indigenous. How much more Indigenous can you be if you are already Indigenous? Do you need to play the didgeridoo to be Aboriginal or wear a zuzzi to be an Islander? Is it really necessary to have a complete knowledge of your traditions to be able to create a cross-cultural or new and emerging form of Indigenous music, song or major works?

In criticising what little information Indigenous musicians may have towards their cultural identity, are we not undermining the respect for their knowledge, however limited? And are we not judging them with a values system that doesn't recognise the fact that most of these musicians today, living either in the city or in remote areas, are living an emerging tradition influenced by country, reggae and rock styles? They can't go back and their forward passage is a never-ending corridor of criticisms.

In creating this music, you aren't required to change who you are to complete the process. It requires you to absorb, accept, interpret, and infuse all ideas that have influenced you throughout your life. This then allows the music to take a voice of its own. A voice that represents new and emerging Indigenous musicians all over Australia.

THE SIGNIFICANCE OF AN INDIGENOUS-OWNED RECORDING AND PUBLISHING COMPANY IN AUSTRALIA

ADÉ KUKOYI

❖

Background

I thought it is very important that I give you some insight into the background of Daki Budtcha Records: where it came from, why it was established and some of our experiences over the years.

During the 1980s, while I was living in Sydney, Maroochy Barambah was approached by one of the large recording organisations (for the sake of this paper I shall refer to this entity as 'X') to participate in a project about Indigenous Australian songs and stories. After the completion of this project, Maroochy received a lengthy contract in the mail in which the stated terms sought the transfer of the ownership of these indigenous materials to X. Maroochy and I pondered over this matter for a long time. We assessed the terms of this agreement and they did not impress us. We made enquiries with some reputable legal organisations in Sydney at the time, all with no satisfactory outcome. Finally, we decided not to proceed, as to my mind it breached traditional *Aboriginal Customary Law.* X hounded us for about two years or so, still we stood our ground. You could almost say, we were 'threatened' by X in some instances with numerous telephone calls and correspondence, yet we were unmoved. I could remember the day that a telephone call came through to inform me that the other person involved in the project (sadly, an indigenous Australian whose name you all may know, who I shall refer to as 'Y') had signed his/her contract. This brought us under enormous strain and pressure from X. Thankfully we did not cave in. Maroochy's role was inspirational in this whole matter. Along with me, she was prepared to fight fire with fire. Mind you, this was at a time when issues of ownership and copyright on cultural materials was hardly heard of, if at all, in the public arena. It was a relatively new concept to all the legal experts that we had spoken to in this regard. Personally, Maroochy and I felt strongly that something had to be done in order to educate and enlighten the broader society about important aspects of Aboriginal Customary Law; in songs, stories and dances.

It was against this background that we established Daki Budtcha Pty Ltd — a recording and publishing company with particular focus on the protection of Indigenous Australian cultural properties (songs, dances, stories… et cetera.). Our objective was to protect, preserve, maintain, as well as promote the *cultural integrity* of Indigenous Australian properties, as it became abundantly clear to us that the unique Indigenous Australian notion of *collective custodial ownership in perpetuity* is not addressed or catered for in the applicable legal document such as the *Copyright Act 1968.*

For example, under Aboriginal Customary Law, *songmen* and/or *songwomen* are the epitome of wisdom. They keep laws in stories, songs and dances, which are in turn passed down from generation to generation. In contrast to Anglo-Australian laws, time limits are not attached to the ownership of these cultural materials. Dare I say that these concepts are totally alien, if not conflicting with the Western ownership philosophy, at this point in time.

Aims and objectives

The aims and objectives of Daki Budtcha, in summary, include:

- to protect, maintain as well as promote Aboriginal Australian culture — songs, music, dance, drama and stories to the international audience;
- to engage in and facilitate cross-cultural exchange of ideas, knowledge and experience between the Indigenous Australians and other Indigenous races of the world;
- to encourage and support Aboriginal Australian artists and other minority performers in the exploration of overseas markets;
- to educate, enlighten and enhance the knowledge on non-Aboriginals generally about Aboriginal Australia and vice-versa;
- to revive and revitalise the Turrbal and Ningy Ningy Aboriginal languages, heritage and culture in South-East Queensland;
- to represent a point of contact for non-Aboriginals interested in making direct contact with the indigenous Australians.

Principal activities

The activities of the company include:

- music production;
- marketing and promotions;
- publishing;
- distribution;
- artists' management;
- multimedia services;
- theatre production;
- consultancy and educational services;
- film and video production.

Its particular focus is the global market.

Copyright and the indigenous Australian culture: issues of ownership and cultural integrity

The issues of ownership, copyright and cultural integrity are the very heart of indigenous survival in Australia. They are extremely contentious issues, and this is simply the reason why we deemed our pioneering role and existence in the industry as crucial.

The *Copyright Act 1968* is the main body of legal document that provides ownership and reproduction rights to creators. Within the Australian context, the role played by this Act cannot be underestimated. The period of copyright protection for a musical work is generally the author's life plus fifty years.[1] Yet, it is the very instrument that has for so long failed to recognise the unique Indigenous Australian Dreamtime principle of collective custodial ownership in perpetuity (Barambah 1997: 4).

This paper sets out, to some extent, the journey, experience, obstacles and challenges in over a decade for Daki Budtcha Records (an Indigenous-owned recording and publishing company) in its quest for the protection, ownership, promotion and maintenance of the cultural integrity of Indigenous cultural material, particularly in the music industry.

What is Aboriginal Customary Law?

The principles of Aboriginal Customary Law represent the cornerstone of the Indigenous Australian society. It was not until the High Court decision in *Mabo v The State of Queensland (No. 2)*[2] that this extremely important principle was partially recognised. It is this lack of recognition that has formed the bases of conflict and the exploitation of indigenous cultural properties[3] since European 'settlement' in Australia 211 years ago.

I will now proceed to examine the concerted effort of Daki Budtcha Records to overcome some of the deficiencies or inadequacies of the provisions within the *Copyright Act 1968* from an indigenous perspective. In approaching this task, I have consulted extensively with Maroochy Barambah, Turrbal & Ningy Ningy Songwoman and the Artistic Chief Executive of Daki Budtcha Records, particularly on the issue of Aboriginal Customary Law.[4]

Contrary to what most people might think, the concept of Aboriginal Customary Law in not uniform within Indigenous Australia. There are variations across tribes, among clans and within family groupings. These variations are totemic-based. They are very complex, and indeed a detailed discussion on this aspect is beyond the realms of this paper. Although, every effort will be made to explain this important phenomenon in appropriate context.

Why are Indigenous cultural materials exploited?

The answer to this question primarily lies in the fact that the existing legislative instrument *(Copyright Act 1968)* fails to recognise the underlying tenets of Aboriginal Customary Law. Under Western law, music is regarded as a piece of individual property — written and performed to entertain and to appeal to the listener's emotions.[5] Indigenous music, on the other hand, is seen by its Traditional Owners and Custodians as a source of life; conveying stories, songs and dances from the Dreamtime.[6]

The exploitation of cultural property/materials in the music industry has steadily increased over the years for many reasons, some of which include:

- the increased appeal and popularity of tribal chants to the ears of industry gurus;
- the search for something 'new' in the commercial world of music, which has been saturated up until now by cover versions and regurgitation.

Along with the issue of exploitation has emerged the question of what actually constitutes 'cultural property'. Should all materials emanating from Indigenous people be classified as 'cultural' or should we delineate between traditional songs which have existed from Dreamtime (typically written in language other than English) and contemporary songs which are written in relatively recent times from the experience of a songwriter, but in a historical context?

Some food for thought

Daki Budtcha would like to propose that some form of *contextual* definition be adopted. For example, a contemporary song such as 'Brown Skin Baby' by Robert Randall from the Northern Territory, under our proposed definition would be classified as a 'cultural property' purely because of its historical, social and political meaning, and the context to which it relates. 'Brown Skin Baby' is a song that directly strikes the heart of the 'Stolen Generation' debate currently raging in Australia. Put in proper perspective, it is a song that affects the lives of many Indigenous Australians and their ancestors. A similar argument may be applied to the following songs, all of which are published by Daki Budtcha Pty Ltd.

Song Title	Composer(s)
Aborigine Must Be Free	Allan Randall
Aborigine	Allan Randall / Maroochy Barambah
Yellow Sun/Dreamtime Rap	Maroochy Barambah

In view of the above, it should be noted that whilst the overwhelming majority of traditional songs (written in a particular Indigenous language other than English) can easily be classified as 'cultural property', some contemporary songs can also be defined as 'cultural property' depending largely on the nature and context of such contemporary songs. Each song will have to be analysed and assessed on its own merit. This is a very important issue yet to be considered and resolved in this whole debate.

Once materials have been classified as 'cultural property', the question of who can (and cannot) use them, for what purposes, custodial permission, ownership in perpetuity... et cetera should then be resolved.

The issue now leads us to the existing legal environment of 'cultural property'.

The Copyright Act 1968

In 1996, the Australian Institute of Aboriginal & TSI Studies in conjunction with ATSIC, instituted a Discussion Paper titled *Our Culture Our Future* in a major move aimed at finding solutions to the perennial issues of 'rip offs' in the cultural industry. Daki Budtcha Records was a major participant and contributor to this project.

As mentioned earlier, the *Copyright Act 1968* is the main body of legal document that provides ownership and reproduction rights to creators. Some of the deficiencies contained in this Act have already been outlined in the Discussion Paper (Section 4.2 - 4.2.4, pp. 37-43) prepared by Michael Frankel & Co. The important questions now are:

- Should the *Copyright Act* be amended to accommodate the deficiencies with respect to Aboriginal Customary Law? If so, what amendments should be proposed?
- Should a separate Act be implemented to recognise the uniqueness of Indigenous Customary Law? If so, how?

The Discussion Paper outlined three areas of amendments to the present *Copyright Act* (Sections 7.1.1–7.1.3: 62–64).

1. Moral Rights Amendments to allow Indigenous communities with the rights of cultural integrity and attribution;
2. Introduction of a new part to establish collecting agency for Indigenous works.
3. Extension of Performers' Rights.

Illustrative Example 1 — 'Mongungi I & II' CDs

In respect of the proposed Moral Right legislation, Daki Budtcha has already set industry standards with its recording of a traditional Aboriginal song (Gurri Nyna Nami) belonging to Songman Whadin, by ensuring that the *cultural integrity* of this cultural property was appropriately maintained in the recording of the 'Mongungi II' CD.[7] In fact, the practice already adopted by Daki Budtcha Records should be used as 'industry practice' to set the standards for others intending to reproduce traditional songs, music or stories.

Illustrative Example 2 — 'Biame' CD

In a recent case, recording of a traditional Aboriginal song was undertaken by a record company without the consent and authority of its custodians.[8] The concerned traditional song is published by Daki Budtcha Pty Ltd. The company took action.

Remedial action taken

Daki Budtcha Pty Ltd as an Indigenous-owned publisher acted on behalf of the custodians to seek remedy — both morally and economically. The result was that Daki Budtcha not only succeeded in seeking moral rights for the creator (through proper attribution), but also economic rights, in recoupment of royalties. This case was settled out of court.

This case in particular, clearly underlines the important role of an Indigenous-owned music publisher in the Australian music industry. Whilst there are deficiencies in the *Copyright Act* as it presently stands, one can argue that the expertise of an Indigenous-owned publisher can be of enormous benefits in the meantime to Indigenous people / clans / communities associated with such publisher.

The fact remains that legal instruments are not easily amended. It will no doubt take some time before existing legislation is altered to accommodate Aboriginal Customary Law or even to enact a new legislation. Given the multiplicity and complexity of Aboriginal customs and practices across Australia, the next question is: whose Customary Law is to be adopted?

In view of the above, Daki Budtcha Records has devised a methodology of 'Cultural Protocol' for the music industry in which it operates. In order to make this workable; attitudes of music industry executives have to change. Essentially, we have to educate people.

Development of cultural protocols for the music industry

Questions such as 'who owns this material?' 'who should we seek permission from?'... et cetera, are often heard in our industry. The reason for this is that by their very nature, most cultural materials (for example, songs and music) are typically not registered by their Traditional Owners or Custodians with music publishers. In an effort to overcome some of these difficulties, we have devised 'Cultural Protocol' which we believe represent a useful starting point for any person or organisation intended to use cultural material. Possible steps:

- in recording an indigenous cultural material, record companies and artists should endeavour to find out if the material is published by Daki Budtcha;
- if unpublished, endeavour to ascertain its genuine traditional owners/custodian/clans. The expertise and services of Daki Budtcha may be sought in this regard;
- whilst the second step can be very time-consuming because of historical dispossession, dislocation and removal of traditional cultural materials to archives, it is important to seek the professional advice of, say, an indigenous linguist or ethnomusicologist, in order to ascertain the rightful traditional owners. Daki Budtcha has access to the most suitable linguists/musicologists;
- once the second step is accomplished, a *written* consent and authority to use cultural material must be obtained;
- proper attribution must be made to the Songman/Songwoman (if applicable);
- mechanical (or other) royalties must be negotiated with the custodians;
- we recommend that Copyright in cultural property should remain the perpetual ownership of the Indigenous Traditional Owners or Custodians, regardless of the nature of the new musical expression, in so far as it is based on pre-existing cultural material. A good example of this is the 'Mongungi I & II' CDs by Maroochy Barambah. Although, the final composition was something the raw material (Gurri Nyna Nami) did not possess, Daki Budtcha Records attributed the ownership of the pre-existing material to the Gubbi Gubbi songman Whadin. It is a demonstration of respect that should be nurtured, developed and encouraged right across the music industry, as a standard cultural practice.

Conclusion

The role being played by Daki Budtcha Records, particularly in the music industry, in the protection, maintenance and promotion of cultural material is very significant. In the absence of legislation that recognises Aboriginal Customary Law, Daki Budtcha has embarked on a crusade to change attitudes in its industry by educating others to respect Aboriginal customs and practices. Litigation will not necessarily offer an answer, and can in fact prove to be quite expensive for the parties involved. This area of law will no doubt evolve over time as attitudes change.

Notes

1 s 32 Copyright Act 1968.
2 1992, 175 CLR 1.
3 For the definition of this terminology see Barambah 1997, p. 4.
4 Barambah, M. 1999, What are the issues facing Indigenous Australians with respect to Intellectual Property in the Digital Age? An unpublished paper presented at the Australasian Intellectual Property Conference, Coolangatta Qld. 5 - 6 March, p. 1.
5 Mills, S. 1996, Indigenous Music and the Law : An Analysis of National and International Legislation, Yearbook of traditional music, p. 57.
6 Barambah, M. 1996, as per conversation with Adé Kukoyi
7 See 'Mongungi I' (1994) and 'Mongungi II' (1995) CDs released by the Daki Budtcha Records label, for an example of proper attribution of a traditional song which honours the reputation of the creator.
8 This breach of consent and authority was in fact perpetrated by an Indigenous Australian, who claimed that her grandmother used to sing this traditional song to her as a child. She also asserted that her grandmother told her that she owned the song. This was in fact untrue. This issue underlines the consequences of ignorance. See Barambah's paper p2.

References

Barambah, M. 1997, Text of Speech at the Women & the Law Breakfast, Women Lawyers' Association of Queensland Newsletter, No. 3 December, p. 4.

Barambah, M. 1999, Official correspondence to the General Manager of the Foundation for Aboriginal & Islander Research Action (FAIRA), Unpublished, 15 April, p. 2.

FOREPLAY LIST: ROTATE ON THIS!

RICHARD MARGETSON

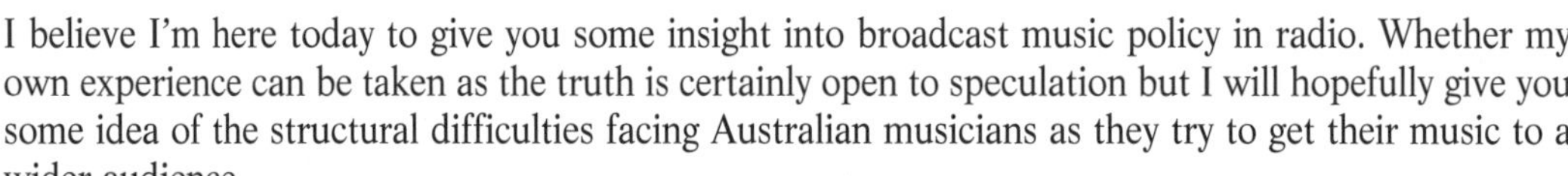

I believe I'm here today to give you some insight into broadcast music policy in radio. Whether my own experience can be taken as the truth is certainly open to speculation but I will hopefully give you some idea of the structural difficulties facing Australian musicians as they try to get their music to a wider audience.

My own initial experience of radio was through community broadcasters 5MMM (now 3D Radio after the sale of its callsign to the Austero/MMM network) and then as an employee of University Radio 5UV, both in Adelaide.

Community stations are almost always the first entry point for bands and solo artists as they embark on a career of super stardom. 3D has as its basic charter the promotion and broadcast of local artists. They have an on-air quota of the amount of Australian music played on air and they pay special attention to their own melee of Adelaide rock bands. The problems that face community broadcasters are innumerable: one is that apart from their own occasional commissioned surveys, it is difficult to ascertain their exact audience sizes. In the AC Neilsen surveys for South Australia most of our community music broadcasters are listed under the title OTHER FM and rate collectively (and these are not direct figures), around about 2.3 to 3.5 percent of the audience. Interestingly these figures lift dramatically in the demographic of 18 to 24 where they can be around (on a big survey!) six percent of the audience.

But why am I mentioning this in the context of music? Why do the survey figures matter? Well to many of us they don't that much, but if you want to 'move units' and let's face it, that's what a record company wants to do — you need to get a bigger audience. And also you probably need to catch a large younger audience: the music business is really relying on that demographic to buy its products, especially when it comes to *new* artists. Sure Elton John will still sell a million to the big disposable income spenders, the middle agers, but Silverchair are probably not relying on the 'Mums and Dads'. That's in no way to denigrate the importance of grass roots broadcasters who are often able to take the risks and be much more daring with their airplay — and also give musos their first taste of the medium: does my recording sound any good on air? How did I handle the interview? Most of our current crop of bands would no doubt tip their lids to community broadcasters as the first supporters of their work.

So let's get to the big game, the place where most contemporary music is getting played and heard: Triple J. OK, I hear the rumble of discontent already, but there is still no doubt that mainstream contemporary musical taste, and music sales figures, are almost directly attributable to whether or not they have been played on our national youth network. Sure notable exceptions can be pointed to — Savage Garden, Tina Arena — but it's not a bad rule of thumb.

So having said that *every* band wants to get J airplay deep down (!!), if you get on, the J's announcers speak to fifty-six transmitters nationwide and spread the word about what a great act you are! Silverchair are the most obvious case in point — a band who was completely unknown outside of Newcastle until they went on SBS television with a song called 'Tomorrow'. Soon afterwards this song was played on the J's nighttime 'Requests' program (notably the band still had no record contract) and due to overwhelming response, it was played again and again until it be came the biggest selling single in Australia that year.

Now we all love a fairytale, and Silverchair have already entered rock and roll mythology but it does illustrate a point: commercial radio would not have, and really does not play unsigned acts, and certainly would struggle to play an Aussie band who have no management representation or record company reps pressing for the track to be played. Triple J did and does. Currently the 'Unearthed' project is giving musicians in regional Australia the chance to be discovered, recorded, and then given airplay. This in turn has led to some of those acts getting recording contracts (Grinspoon are currently the most successful). Triple J may not have totally created that situation, but it's certainly a heavy bargaining chip for bands if they are negotiating with record companies.

But to say that the selection process is ideal would be stretching the truth a little. During my time at the J's I was involved in a number of the Unearthed listening processes. When we unearthed Perth a small group of us had to listen to EVERY entry — around 900 tapes were sent in! Similar numbers for the Adelaide one by the way. Have you ever seen 900 listings in the weekend gig guide??!! That's an indication of how important the bedroom and rehearsal room band members see Triple J airplay in their careers. To select the Unearthed winners we had to then whittle it down to four. That means sitting down in a room and listening to thirty seconds at least of every tape all day... sure you get a large amount of execrable dross, but eventually you have to decide between about twenty real contenders and that's when it gets tough. So really it comes down to: do I like this song? Eventually it's simply personal taste from the staff who've managed to get to the listenings to decide who the 'best new acts' are. So if you've lost along the way, don't take it too personally, there's an element of lottery.

Similarly with general airplay. Each week I would receive around thirty to fifty CD's, mostly from record company reps, some from small independents and some directly from bands all across the country. Triple J does have a general music meeting originally open to all staff members, but of late only to on-air staff. This is unlike most commercial stations that usually rely on a Program Director and Music Director.

If I managed to listen to 30 seconds of every CD I ever received during the week, I probably had not done a lot else! But that was always my aim. You then, once again, make your own personal choices on what you like. Then you are able to give a little air time via Triple J's playlist, which allows for DJ's to play a 'Your Choice', usually about one or two tracks each hour (a regular music shift at the J's plays about 12-14 tracks an hour).

Once you've done that you may decide to throw it into the bearpit of a Triple J meeting — people sitting with the stereo up and listening to tracks, which may have been suggested personally or a pile of tracks selected for listening by the Music Director. Sometimes a well-placed cruel insult for a song could totally kill its chances after a few seconds, (oh all those promotional budgets wasted!). Often it was best to keep a low profile and show no favouritism if a track you liked was played and you wanted it on the playlist. If someone in the room knew it was you who had brought it, that may start the gags flowing: 'not another Margo soppy track', or whatever, which similarly could dud it out of contention. I've seen perfectly good songs destroyed by great gags and never get played again. So it's once again somewhat of a lottery process, even though the collective musical knowledge of the room is pretty high. Add to that, staff who have been wined and dined and entertained and freebied by the music biz till kingdom come, which may, just a tad, influence their decisions. The promotional schmoozing budgets for major record companies are pretty phenomenal and I don't care how hard you try; it is very hard to maintain your independence.

More and more, radio stations are at the mercy of what is pushed at them, rather than what they discover themselves. Also think of how many songs are added to a playlist in a week (perhaps six to eight in a week at the J's, often one or two at a commercial level). So, if in one music meeting you hear ten guitar tunes and one dance tune for example, for the sake of balance, the dance tune has a higher chance of being added even if all ten guitar tunes are deadset killers and the dance tune is only pretty good.

So... you (the band/solo artist) manage to survive that process, you get selected as being on the playlist, then the actual rotation of the song becomes an issue. This is in the hands of a Music Director and a computer selection system which selects some tracks to come around every four hours and others to come around every five days!! Depending on its A, B or C category, a song can be thrashed for a short period (novelty songs at the J's originally went under a Z category, so the rock version of the song 'Ma Na Ma Na' would be played only for a few weeks but about every ten seconds until the audience goes mad). But if the elected new tune gets onto the playlist, the playlist can still be manipulated to 'hide' a song into rare appearances and outside of peak listening times (would you rather your song was heard on 'Drivetime' or on a 'Midnight to Dawn' shift). You would have to be a major conspiracy theorist to believe that the greatest song in history was held back by deliberate low rotation selection... but there's definitely some fodder there for minor conspiracy theorists to go on with.

Having said all that, Triple J still does play new music. You're still more likely to hear it first there and the record biz knows that. Commercial radio undoubtedly looks to the J's to find the hits first, because for all sorts of reasons, which my colleagues from commercial radio will no doubt explain, they can't take the risks. However, if you do get on the commercial list, rub your hands in glee — not only will you probably stand out as one of the few new acts amongst the 'GOLD', but you are likely (in Adelaide at least) to be reaching around fifty percent of the 18-24 market, and around thirty percent of the available 25-39's. I know — there's no accounting for public taste!

I was also going to speak more about my current push for local music on the ABC local radio station 5AN, but I see that my allocated time is up.

Hopefully this didn't discourage all the musos in the room today who maybe trying to get their music heard nationally.

ANOTHER ROOT: AUSTRALIAN HIP HOP AS A 'GLOCAL' SUBCULTURE – RE-TERRITORIALISING HIP HOP

TONY MITCHELL

> *Un nouvelle ère... plus prospère... pour moi et mes frères je me grise car je pénètre dans cette nouvelle ère où n'ont pas prise les peurs qui me tenaient naguère le style évolue de TUNIS à HONOLULU il sort du secteur qui lui était dévolu...*
>
> *(A new era... a more prosperous one... for me and my brothers... I'm intoxicated because I can break into this new era where the fears that held me back don't exist any more the style has evolved from TUNIS to HONOLULU and it's coming out from the sector where it was devolved...)* Ménélik, 'Another Root', on Nobukazu Takemura, *Child's View, Bellissima!* 1994.

In his track 'Another Root', the Afro-French rapper Ménélik speaks of a new era of confident, emergent global hip hop which has evolved from Tunis to Honolulu, and illustrates it by rapping in French on a 1994 album by the Japanese jazz musician Nobukazu Takemura which was recorded in London, Paris, Osaka and Tokyo. These 'other roots' which hip hop has developed outside the USA coincide with what Russell A. Potter, in his book *Spectacular Vernaculars,* has diagnosed as 'a vulnerable time' for hip hop in the USA, 'reminiscent of rock and roll during its late-seventies lull' (1995:147). Paul Gilroy has usefully argued that rap music is a 'popular modernist' vernacular expression (1993:45) in that it represents a search for wholeness and integrality in its sampling of a variegated black musical history rather than celebrating a Eurocentric postmodern fragmentation, displacement and relativity. Gilroy has also advanced the notion of a black Atlantic diaspora which unites a multiplicity of black popular musical forms into a cohesive sense of modernist continuity and tradition which is a vital expression of an Afrocentric vernacular, but recent manifestations in global rap music suggest it has gone well beyond the boundaries defined by 'blackness'.

Gilroy's modernist argument was adopted and distorted by Potter into an orthodox postmodernist reading of African-American hip hop in *Spectacular Vernaculars,* which is subtitled 'Hip Hop and the Politics of Postmodernism' in a travesty of Gilroy's argument. Potter suggests that the globalisation of what he regards as an essentially African-American musical idiom is a kind of deformation:

> *as (hip hop) gains audiences around the world, there is always the danger that it will be appropriated in such a way that its histories will be obscured, and its messages replaced with others... even as it remains a global music, it is firmly rooted in the local and the temporal; it is music about 'where I'm from,' and as such proposes a new kind of universality* (1995:146).

In Potter's myopic view, hip hop can only be considered universal if it remains rooted in black urban USA. Like a number of US academics, including Tricia Rose, who have celebrated African-American hip hop as an essentialist expression of African-American culture, Potter refuses to look outside the parochial, provincial and increasingly atrophied and brutalising parameters of US hip hop at ways in which it has been increasingly appropriated, indigenised and re-territorialised all over the world. Rap music and hip hop culture are now just as 'rooted in the local' in Naples, Marseilles, Sydney, Auckland, Cape Town and the Shibuya district of Tokyo, where rappers also proclaim 'where they're from', as they do in Compton or the South Bronx.

In an Australian popular musical context, one of the more inane embodiments of postmodernism's obsession with decentring relativity, displacement and fragmentation is McKenzie Wark's mantra 'we no longer have roots, only aerials' (1997:30). This expression, parroted at monotonously regular intervals, borrowed and taken out of context from the Brazilian musician Gilberto Gil, amounts to a complete misconception of the evidence provided by global hip hop, which is almost always about the celebration of roots in place, neighbourhood, home, family and nation. It is this dominant aspect of topos and geography which makes rap such a fertile area of study, especially in its manifestations outside the USA. The rhizomic (to use Deleuze's term) global diaspora of rap music has been spreading ever wider and reaching more far-flung places and obscure ethnic minorities: one of many examples of this is the Nuuk Posse from Greenland, who rap in their native language about such issues as the dominance of the Danish language in their country (Barnes 1997:65).

From Compton to Canberra: rap's multicultural diasporic flow

Hip hop's rhetorical forms of MCing, and DJing — which have their historical roots in Jamaican sound systems, as well as graffiti writing and break dancing — are all ways of celebrating a poetics of place, or talking about where one is from, and signifying one's place in a subculture that is both local and global at the same time. The hip hop nation is international as well as national. Roland Robertson (1995) uses the term 'glocal', combining the global and the local, to emphasise that each is in many ways defined by the other, and that they frequently intersect, rather than being polarised opposites. Robertson adopted this blend of local and global from its use in Japan to describe the adaptation of global farming techniques to fit local conditions, and its subsequent use as a marketing buzz word to refer to the indigenisation of global phenomena. In his work on Japanese rap music, Ian Condry has noted a Japanese rapper, ECD, who uses the metaphor 'from the Bronx... across the ocean a spark flew and lit a fire' to describe the local hip hop scene in Tokyo (e-mail to the author, 16.3.98). This indicates that although US rap was the inspiration, the local scene caught fire on the fuel that was already there. While indigeneity and ethnic identity are perhaps more complex issues to define in Australia than they are in Japan, the metaphor could also be applied here. It was echoed in a slightly different context by Brisbane DJ Damage from the rap crew Towering Inferno when he stated 'Fire is a symbol of hip hop. If you can't cut it, you get burnt.' (in Jee, 1996a).

But this does not mean that rap's roots aren't problematic. It is usually claimed that rap and hip hop originated in the south Bronx in the early 1970s when Kool Herc and others began holding street parties with turntables and breakdancers and MCs started rapping. Kool Herc was recreating the sound systems of his native Jamaica, complete with toasting — an early form of rapping. Break dancing was derived from Puerto Rican dance steps, and a lot of the early breakdance crews like Rock Steady Crew were predominantly Puerto Rican, as were some of the first graffiti artists like Futura 2000. According to early protagonists like Africa Bambaataa (in Owens, 1994:67), there were also quite a few white kids around too. This means that rap's origins are, if anything, a multicultural hybrid rather than an expression of an African-American monoculture. This has made it easier for rap to be adopted in other parts of the world, where hip hop's advocates' claims to an essentially (or essentialist) black identity are not so pressing, and where rap is often further hybridised and combined with local idioms, musical forms and dance moves. Rap's multicultural origins are frequently magnified and amplified in other parts of the world: in France, which probably has the biggest hip hop scene after the USA (the January 1998 issue of US hip hop magazine *Source* states there are 120 French hip hop crews, but that is a conservative estimate), there is a high proportion of rappers from West African, North African, Arab and Mediterranean migrant origins; in Germany there is a significant proportion of Turkish, Croatian and other 'guest worker' migrant rappers, while in Australia there are rappers from Lebanese, Pacific Islander, Chilean and Filippino backgrounds. This multicultural diasporic flow in hip hop suggests it is a form which can be adopted and adapted to express the concerns of ethnic minorities everywhere.

One exception to the myopia towards global hip hop displayed by many US academics is George Lipsitz, whose book *Dangerous Crossroads* (1994) is only partly about rap music, but is one of the few attempts in the US popular music academy to look at non-African American musical hybridities, and music and the poetics of place. Lipsitz examines the globalisation of popular music in its US and African diasporic contexts, but goes out of his way to refer to ethnically-inflected popular music in other parts of the world, including Australia and New Zealand. In the following sentence he attempts to sum up the global parameters of popular music:

> *Through the conduits of commercial culture, music made by aggrieved inner-city populations in Canberra, Kingston, or Compton becomes part of everyday life and culture for affluent consumers in the suburbs of Cleveland, Coventry or Cologne* (1994:4).

Music made by aggrieved inner city populations in Canberra? Compared with Kingston, Jamaica, and Compton, Los Angeles? But perhaps this is not as strange as it sounds. Koolism are a rap group from Canberra, consisting of former members of the group Easybass (formerly Urban Poets) whose 1995 cassette album *Space Program* is considered one of the most impressive local rap releases (Blaze 1996). One track from Koolism's self-produced, eponymous tape is called *Juss a Brown Fellow.* In it, Tongan rapper Fatty Boomstix raps about the racial discrimination and phobias suffered by Pacific Islanders in Australia before mapping out the diaspora of what he refers to as 'Australasian rap', following a rhetorical track from Australia to New Zealand through the Pacific Islands of Fiji, Samoa, Tonga, Vanuatu, the Solomon Islands and New Caledonia. Koolism's tape is peppered with Aussie references, from Shane Warne to John Howard to Crocodile Dundee to Dawn Frazer — who are all 'dissed' or criticised — and Boomstix's accent is unmistakably Antipodean, but there are ethnic undercurrents here which take it beyond a self-conscious celebration of Australianness.

Koolism's reterritorialised rap illustrates how the black ethnic identity markers of much US rap have become brown ethnic identity markers in Pacific Islander rap. This is something which is much more predominant in Aotearoa/New Zealand, where rap was much more easily absorbed into Maori and other Polynesian rhetorical traditions — like *patere* in Maori, which means a form of abusive public discourse — one Maori dictionary even translates it directly as 'rap'. Maori rappers such as the Upper Hutt Posse, Dam Native, Losttribe, Moana and the Moa Hunters, DLT, OMC and Che Fu have successfully managed to combine rap with vernacular expressions of Maori militancy which often incorporate the use of the Maori language, and some have even managed to obtain commercial success. Some of these hybrid Polynesian appropriations of rap have manifested themselves here in Australia as well. Gold Coast rap crew Warcry, for example, consist of two Australians and two New Zealanders, J Ray and Donovan, who were founder members of the New Zealand break crew The Smurfs in 1982, out of which Upper Hutt Posse emerged. Warcry are the first Queensland hip hop crew to release an album, entitled *The Art of War* (Jee 1996c). Fijian rapper Trey, one of the few women rappers on the Sydney scene, illustrates the Pacific Islander indigenisation of hip hop in a sequence from Paul Fenech's film about Sydney hip hop, *Basic Equipment* (shown on the ABC in February 1998 as part of the 'Loud' festival). Comparing graffiti to cave-painting and rap to the Fijian rhetorical form *alali*, Trey points out the diverse ethnic backgrounds of some Australian rappers, and launches an invitation to Pauline Hanson to get down with them. Her reference to Hanson is no accident — one of her tracks on her self-titled, self-produced tape *Trey (The Rhymin' Edifying Young'un)* is called *One Nation Party* and she is the first Australian rapper to have recorded a 'diss' of Hanson (closely followed by the aptly named Sydney posse Et-nik Tribe). Trey's emphasis on equivalences between hip hop and Fijian cultural formations indicate how rap music has been indigenised or 'glocalised' in the Pacific region. It is unlikely, however, that Koolism or Trey will be heard in Cleveland, Coventry or Cologne, since only fifty copies of their tapes were released. This illustrates how Australian hip hop is still a distinctly fragile, underground community phenomenon, both in terms of its oppositional stance towards mainstream Australia and the way it is ignored by the Australian popular music industry.

Sydney hip hop and the western suburbs: kickin' to the undersound

Ian Maxwell (1995) has noted that the two rap albums by Australian artists which had any noticeable impact on the local music scene in the mid 1990s both contain references to Australian hip hop's underground status in their titles: Sound Unlimited's *A Postcard from the Edge of the Under-side,* released by Columbia/Sony in 1992 — the only Australian rap album to come out on a major label — and Def Wish Cast's *Knights of the Underground Table,* released on the independent Random Records in 1993. It is also no coincidence that both groups originated in the Western Suburbs of Sydney, an area traditionally regarded as working class, underprivileged and crime-ridden, with a large proportion of immigrant inhabitants and deprived of many of the social and cultural amenities enjoyed by the inner and northern suburbs of the city. As Diane Powell has stated in *Out West,* her book about the Australian mass media's 'demonisation' of Sydney's Western Suburbs, the area is comparable to a ghetto:

> *Ghettos do not exist in discourse about Australian cities. Yet most Australian cities contain areas that are segregated along class, economic, cultural and ethnic lines. Ghetto is not an appropriate word for these low density suburban, rather than high density inner-urban, areas. However, in Australian culture, to live in some suburbs is to suffer an equivalent stigma to that borne by people living in the ghettos of Europe or America* (1994: xiv).

The Western Suburbs are generally perceived as the geographical roots of hip hop culture in Sydney, partly due to the strong concentration there of non-Anglo migrant communities such as Greeks, Italians, Lebanese and Vietnamese, whose youth were attracted by the racially oppositional features of African-American hip hop and adopted its signs and forms as markers of their own otherness. Muggings, killings and heroin dealing attributed to the Vietnamese street gang the 5Ts in Cabramatta have also fuelled the mass media with stories about ghetto-styled street wars and migrant criminal subcultures linked to hip hop, which are often highly exaggerated. In their song 'Tales from the Westside', Sound Unlimited reconstructs a history of the Sydney hip-hop scene in the Western Suburbs, locating its origins in the suburb of Burwood in 1983: 'Let's get back I'll start at Burwood park / hip hop breakin' after dark / many crews would join the fray travel from east to west upon the train / some to break some to inflict pain'. This breakdance scene, initially influenced by Malcolm McLaren's video 'Buffalo Gals', echoes similar phenomena in a number of countries throughout the world.

Sound Unlimited, who earned the scorn of Sydney hardcore hip hoppers after they teamed up with the Antunes brothers, formerly of New Kids on the Block, and pursued a blatantly commercial pop route, began as the Westside Posse. They were first featured with a Public Enemy-influenced track called *Pull the Trigger* on a compilation of Australian rap called *Down Under by Law* released on Virgin Records in 1988. This compilation, the first collection of Australian rap, (which included Mighty Big Crime, Swoop, Sharline and Fly Girl 3) shows how far it has progressed since then — nearly all the tracks here show their US influences in very obvious ways. It has been described by Blaze as 'very poor' and 'a tub of lard', although he claims *Pull the Trigger* was 'the closest to what we wanted'. Blaze also notes that the first 'true hip hop' release in Australia was in 1988 by Just Us (consisting of Maltese DJ Case and Mentor) who released an independently-pressed single entitled *Combined Talent/My Destiny,* which Blaze states was 'very indicative of the western suburbs in Sydney at that time' (1994:2).[1]

A number of other rappers have built on the mythology of the Westside as the originary source of Sydney hip hop, including Bankstown residents 046, whose name is based on their post code (and whose debut album *L.I.F.E.* was produced by prominent DJ Vame) and the White Boys, whose album *Westside* chronicles a train journey from North Sydney to the West, among other things, but who were considered 'wack' by most of the inner city Sydney hip hop scene. Similarly solo rapper D Man, also from Bankstown, released a number of commercially oriented, mainstream rap singles and an album which sank without trace. The more satirical Fathom sample the line 'There's a feeling I get when I look to the West' from Led Zeppelin's *Stairway to Heaven* to make their point on their track *Westerly Winds.* Miguel D'Souza has claimed that the film *Basic Equipment* managed to 'document what has happened to hip hop culture in the West, and re-emphasise the point that resistance still is at the core of Western suburbs hip hop', but he also argues that Sydney hip hop has become gentrified in the mid 1990s and moved away from its Western suburbs origins to an inner-city base:

> *Hip hop has made the move from being a culture and underground movement that expressed Western Suburbs' youth's resistance to the negative attitudes to them, their culture, their suburbs and their lives through the adoption of a culture and music so fundamentally opposed to good, middle class values. It has moved to being a culture adopted by hip university students, those with a background in the performance arts, the academy and, most of all, the inner city. It isn't hip hop any more* (1998:2).

The Next Level record shop in Liverpool Street, Slingshot Concepts in Surry Hills, and the 2SER radio program *The Mothership Connection* (formerly hosted by D'Souza) and the dance music street paper *3D*, where local rap releases have been regularly reviewed in the column 'Funky Wizdom' (formerly written by D'Souza), could be seen as the most prominent focal points of this inner-city base. But this does not mean that Westside hip hop has disappeared, as 'Hip Hop for Palestine', an event held by members of Sydney's Lebanese community in Granville Town Hall in May 1998, featuring a fiery performance by the Lebanese and Aboriginal rappers South West Syndicate and graffiti art by Ser Reck (formerly of Def Wish Cast) indicates. As Iveson has argued, hip hop has been an important identity marker for indigenous Australians and youth of non-Anglo ethnic backgrounds, many of whom are located in Sydney's West:

> *Young people in this position have been forced to seek out the materials to develop a culture that is relevant to their cross-cultural experiences. In hip hop, some found a culture which has the means to fight back against the experience of racism, by addressing the segregation and victimisation experienced by people of colour. Rap talks about racism, and other elements of the culture like graffiti and hip hop style provide the means to make space in segregated Australian cities for cultural production. The appeal of hip hop to ethnic and indigenous young people in Australia lies significantly in its valuing of that which isn't white in a white racist society'* (1997:42).

This reterritorialisation of hip hop from a black American vernacular expression into an often 'non white' migrant Australian context echoes similar appropriations in Europe and elsewhere. Iveson goes on to note 'far from representing the loss of Australian national identity in the face of global capitalism, Australian hip hop artists are engaged in the project of attempting to build a multicultural national identity in place of a racist monocultural model that is now gaining strength in Australian national politics' (1997:47).

Australian hip hop nationalism and US cultural imperialism

The Anglo-Australian group Def Wish Cast (who consisted of Ser Reck, Die-C, Defwish and DJ Vame, until they broke up in 1996), have also drawn on Westside mythology. They identify themselves in strongly nationalistic terms in their 1992 debut EP, entitled *A.U.S.T. Down Under Comin Upper,* which announced the arrival of Australian hip hop in no uncertain terms. The track 'A.U.S.T.', which Ian Maxwell has described as 'the unrivalled anthem of Australian hip hop', (1994:7) attempts to give the Australian hip hop scene equal weight to those of the USA and UK:

> *A.U.S.T.... an island that many never look twice at as being associated with rap — on hip hop charts they come across a new discovery U.K., U.S., what A.U.S.T.... Hold up a new flag our*

own turn for the better/The letters that stand alone not in the shadow of any other country Def Wish Cast from A.U.S.T.

Lead rapper Def Wish's rapid-fire ragga rap, which has been described as 'syllable ballistics', was influenced more extensively by Jamaican rappers from the U.K. than African-American rappers, and is almost incomprehensible at times. Maxwell (ibid.) uses Def Wish Cast's hybridity of influences to contest the American cultural imperialism thesis which has frequently been expressed in the Australian mass media, most notably in a prominent feature article in the *Sydney Morning Herald* in 1994 by Richard Guilliatt, entitled 'U.S. eh? Why Young Australia is so Smitten with American Culture'. This article examined widely expressed concerns that Australian youth were not only turning to American basketball and other sporting heroes and clothes and rejecting the previously strong local and national sporting traditions of cricket, swimming and rugby league, but also embracing MacDonalds, US cultural icons like James Dean, and television programs like *The Simpsons* and *Melrose Place.* Guilliatt suggested that Australian youth were being subjected to 'an unstoppable geyser of American pop culture' which threatened to flood a hard-won Australian cultural identity. Interviewing Western Sydney rapper Sean Taylor of the group Voodoo Flavour, he pointed to his use of 'pilfered' US hip hop jargon such as 'phat', 'chill', 'props' and 'kickin' as an indicator of 'African-American culture as the sine qua non of cool for Australian youth', identifying hip hop as 'the dominant youth style'. Statistics provided by an advertising agency survey demonstrated that ninety percent of Australian young people's favourite programs were from the USA, 85.1 percent wore American sports clothes, the favourite sport of 92 percent was basketball, and 87.31 percent rented only US videos. But Guilliatt countered his extended dramatisation of this widespread US cultural invasion and loss of local identity with the suggestion that US influences had been just as predominant in Australia in the 1960s and 1970s. He concluded with an apparent open-ended ambiguity, opposing a characterisation of the global village as Los Angeles with a portrayal of Def Wish Cast's 'broad Strine accents' and association with 'a growing clique of hip hop crews pursuing an Australian identity' as evidence of 'a wave of patriotism' in a youth culture which found strong cultural and social affinities with US cultural forms.

What emerges most strongly from Guilliatt's article is the globalisation of these US cultural icons and the universality of local panics about their contaminating influence, and a neglect of the strong local cultural indicators which are expressed even in the adoption of these imported and borrowed forms. While young Australians might easily be mistaken for Americans if regarded solely in terms of their clothes and visual appearance (and photographs accompanying the article served to prove this point), the singularity of Australian speech patterns, social practices and cultural forms of expression, along with the wide variety of ethnic origins — Chinese, Korean, Lebanese, South American, Greek and Italian — of many young Australians attracted to hip hop culture, is still unmistakable. And since the social realities of life in the urban ghettos of the USA are vastly different from the relative comfort and affluence of Australia, the fetishised American artefacts of hip hop culture tend to take on a strong imaginary quality.

The development of a national Australian hip hop scene was given some degree of 'official' recognition by the release by local independent label Mushroom's subsidiary MXL in 1995 of *Home Brewz Vol. 1*, a compilation of eleven Australian hip hop tracks by mostly unrecorded and almost exclusively male 'bedroom' hip hop practitioners from Sydney, Canberra, Melbourne and Adelaide, including Voodoo Flavour, Koolism, Mama's Funks and Groove Terminator. Robert Brailsford's liner notes expressed the prevailing sense of fragility:

apart from having a hip hop history, it is a history being built on. The main problem being Australian hip hop suffers the same fate as English or for that matter Zambian hip-hop. The prevailing attitude is that only American hip hop is real... The main challenge for Australian hip hop is to discover and consolidate what makes it unique. I don't really think anyone knows what that is, but Home Brewz should provide some clues (1995: 89–90).

The album's diversity of styles is immediately noticeable, with trip hop, ragga, acid jazz and funk influences predominating. As a grouping together of exponents of a virtually invisible underground movement, the album is a valuable indicator of some of the developments in the national hip hop scene. The release in March 1998 of *Home Brewz II*, which included a track by the female crew Womb-Mind-Speak Collective (which includes Trey), and contributions from Brethren, the Adelaide-based Fuglemen, Sleek the Elite, Fathom, Et-Nik Tribe, MetaBass'n'Breath and others, continued this expansion of the national hip hop scene. But as D'Souza commented in his liner notes to *Home Brewz II*, the scene, despite its growing diversity, remains a largely cassette-based, underground cottage industry, mostly ignored by the national music industry:

> *Australian hip hop crews have persisted with the 'tape' culture, the underground of the hip hop culture that satisfies demands with dubs made via the same double cassette-deck that also functions as their recording studio. Satisfying the immediate needs of local audiences, crews have managed a type of success sometimes known as 'props' from their own communities, the differing sub-entities of the hip hop nation in Australia. Subsequently, what has resulted is a shared spectrum of sounds, ideas and styles that differs as much as the districts that hip hop massives and crews inhabit.*

Hip hop's appeal to Australian youth of non-English speaking backgrounds as a vehicle for expressing their otherness within Australian culture has already been noted, but one important example of this is Brethren's 1996 self-titled mini-album which includes a track in Spanish, based on the Chilean saying 'pass me your spoon and I'll return it full', meaning 'I'll tell you of my experiences'. This track, which got some airplay on Triple J, contains the line 'Que passa Gough Whitlam, Ciao Pinochet', which sums up the experience of migrating from Chile to Australia. (Brethren also incorporated some Spanish rap in their 1998 single 'Slingshot', included on *Home Brewz II*). The development of Spanish language hip hop is a long story, but it was probably generated by Los Angeles based Chicano rapper Kid Frost, who began rapping in Calo, a form of Spanglish used by Latino prisoners in the USA. Frost later jammed with Italian rappers in Rome, encouraging them to start rapping in their own language and dialects, and he provided a model for Calo, a Brazilian rapper who raps in Portuguese (and who learned his skills from listening to Kid Frost's albums over and over again). MetaBass'n'Breath, a Sydney crew who include two Anglo-Americans and whose beats incorporate traditional music from Australia, Asia and South America (Iveson 1997:44), released a notable album of world music-inflected hip hop, *Seek*, in 1997, which includes two tracks in Spanish — evidence that Sydney rappers are looking at global rap influences rather than exclusively US ones. One of their tracks, 'Dialogue', as Iveson has indicated, addresses multiculturalism and the 'connections and common ground between cultures and people. They emphasise that these connections require the acceptance of diversity on more than a surface level' (1997:47).

It is worth noting in passing that Spanish and Italian are much more suitable languages than English for the dense, multiple rhymes of rap. In strictly musicological terms, rap could be traced back to *recitativo* in 17th century Italian opera. It is no coincidence that a 1998 album called *The Rapsody Overture* combines predominantly Italian operatic arias with raps by L.L.Cool J, Onyx and Redman, and the results are not as disjunctive and discordant as might be supposed. One local attempt to combine rap and high culture was 'Hip Hopera', an Australia Council funded community project run in 1996 by the theatre group Death Defying Theatre with young people in the Western Suburbs of Sydney. This managed to unearth a number of new teenage and pre-teen rap posses, including South West Syndicate, whose work was showcased on an album entitled *Danger.* The result was then toured around schools and community centres in the Western Suburbs. Although it contained input from Ser Reck of Def Wish Cast and Baba, who later went on to join MetaBass'n'Breath, this was in many ways a synthetic project based on workshopping rap music with suburban kids, and had a community theatre orientation which conflicted with some local rappers' ethical concepts of hip hop. The Funnel Web

Crew, for example, featured in *Basic Equipment,* operate as a kind of hip hop family for delinquent and dispossessed youth, and hang out literally underground in a tunnel where they do graffiti. As they put it, 'hip hop's the only thing we've got that's ours, and we don't want to see it going into schools and people charging for it'. This suggests that the educational tropes of hip hop don't always correspond with those of institutionalised education.

Another important local rap album is *Sleekism,* the 1997 debut album by Sleek the Elite, a flamboyant and witty freestyler of Lebanese extraction who raps about Australian racism, political life, capitalism, sexual encounters and solidarity with Aborigines and Lebanese culture (although it is unfortunate that Sleek makes references to 'ho's'; one positive aspect of Australian hip hop is that much of it is free of the misogyny and homophobia of US gangsta rap). The track *Child of the Cedar* includes references to his own Lebanese background and Aboriginal land rights, and adds Middle Eastern musical inflections.

In March 1998 Urban Xpressions, Australia's first local hip hop festival, ran for 10 days in Sydney celebrating 15 years of local hip hop. Organised by Trent Roden of Slingshot Concepts, manager of Brethren and MetaBass'n'Breath, Baba (Baruch Israel of MetaBass'n'Breath) and Trey, this was a highly successful event showcasing the four elements of local hip hop. It included breakdancing demonstrations in Hyde Park and elsewhere, an exhibition of graffiti art, MCing, DJing, graffiti and breakdancing workshops, open mike, freestyle and 'Reflex Poetics' events, a fashion show of hip hop/street wear and a special showing of French hip hop film *La haine* at the Dendy Cinema. There were also performances by local rap crews Brethren, Celsius, Metabass'n'Breath, Trey, Fathom, Sleek the Elite, Koolism and DJs Soup, Dr. Phibes (of The Next Level), Nick Toth, Sheep, Blaze and others in Martin Place, Taylors on Central, Goodbar, the Globe and other central Sydney locations. There were two panel discussions at University of Technology, Sydney on Australian hip hop[2] and the Australian music industry, race, ethnicity and gender in hip hop, and Australia's role in the global spread of hip hop. These panel discussions included Ser Reck of Def Wish Cast; Celsius and Kilawattz; Trent Roden; Heidi Pasqual of local dance and hip hop record labels Creative Vibes and Mother Tongues; Miguel D'Souza; Baba; Trey; graffiti artist and youth worker Sharline Bezzina (aka Spice); Sleek the Elite; Adelaide rapper, radio DJ and journalist Quro of the Fuglemen; rapper, breaker and writer Mistery from Brethren; Bevan Jee, hip hop website creator and Brisbane rep of the San Francisco hip hop label The Bomb; and Blaze, originator of the central Sydney Loungeroom record store and Parallax record label. These panel discussions also established the beginnings of a dialogue with academia. Getting media coverage on Triple J, 2SER. Skid Row, the ABC's youth program *Recovery* and in the *Sydney Morning Herald's Metro* and *3D,* the festival provided proof that Australian, or at least central Sydney hip hop was alive, well and flourishing, and perhaps emerging from the underground to claim some much-deserved exposure. As Bevan Jee (1996b) has reported, it was pre-dated by the first Annual East Coast Funk Festival held in Brisbane in July 1995, possibly the first hip hop festival of its kind, attended by 500 people and involving Brisbane hip hop crews Towering Inferno and Recipe for Disaster, as well as Warcry performing with members of Def Wish Cast, Brisbane DJ Da Master, and Sydney group Easybass.

The final event of the Urban Xpressions festival was 'Closing Ceremony' at the Globe in Newtown, MC'd adroitly by Trey, who performed some of her own numbers, and featuring the vibrant, energetic and highly imaginative skills of Fathom, Celsius, the Cyberforce Breakers and MetaBass'n'Breath. The headlining act, visiting San Francisco based African American underground crew the Mystik Journeymen, appeared much less interesting than the local crews, largely since they seemed content to reproduce (or parody) most of the cliches and orthodoxies of US rap. But the Globe was packed, with more than 200 fists pounding the air for them, perhaps illustrating Iveson's claim that 'for many hip hop fans, the measure of authenticity is whether or not the rapper is black and American' (1997: 45). It was an apt celebration of an event which has helped to put Australian hip hop more noticeably on at least the local map. Coinciding with the release of *Home Brewz II,* which features most of the rappers involved in Urban Xpressions, as well as relatively new recordings by Trey, Koolism,

MetaBass'n'Breath, Fathom, DJ Soup, Moonrock and others, it showed that after fifteen years in the shadows, local hip hop is diversifying and spreading, but remains to some degree united by its dedication and commitment to global hip hop culture. Ultimately, Australian multicultural hip hop bears witness that hip hop and rap music have become an indigenised, 'glocal' phenomenon.

Notes

1 Blaze (1996) also chronicles a number of other important (and extremely rare) early Australian hip hop releases by Melbourne-based Park Bench Royals *(One Time Live/I hate Hi-nrg,* 1989), Melbourne-based AKA Brothers *(Coming Out large/Poetry in Motion/Tall Poppy Syndrome,* 1989), and Melbourne-based Rize & Tarkee *(Let Yourself Be Yourself/Called to Add Mind,* 1990) who later become Mama's Funkstikools, and were featured on a global rap compilation, *Planet Rap,* released by US label Tommy Boy in 1993. Adelaide based Finger Lickin' Good released a 6 track EP, *Illegitimate Sons of the Bastard Funk,* featuring DJ Groove Terminator, in 1993, and a Melbourne compilation by Organised Rhyme Productions featured tracks by *Rising not Running, Doo Dayz,* and *Brudas United as One.* The Sydney group Illegal Substance released Off da back of Da Truck album in 1994, and Fonke Nomaads and the Urban Poets (later Easybass) were featured on a jazz compilation, *Undertones.* Blaze's own group Noble Savages produced an 8 track cassette album in 1994, and Capital Punishment a 6 track tape, produced by DJ Vame. Melbourne woman rapper MC Que produced a 6 track tape in 1995.

2 See Andrew Bradley's paper, 'Driven By the Sonic Language Passion', in this text.

References

Blaze. 1994, 'Australian Hip Hop/Kangaroo Style', Bomb 42, http://www.thehub.com.au/~bombaust

Brailsford, R. 1995, Liner notes to *Home Brewz Vol. 1,* MXL/MDS.

Barnes, J. 1997, Review of Nuuk Posse, *Kaataq, The Wire* no.158, April, 65.

D'Souza, M. 1998, *'Hip hop & Sydney's Western Suburbs — A Brief Pot-Stirrer',* paper given at Urban Xpressions Festival.

D'Souza, M. 1997, Liner notes to *Home Brewz Vol. II,* MXL/MDS.

Gilroy, P. 1993, 'One nation under a groove', in *Small Acts: Thoughts on the Politics of Black Cultures,* London: Serpents Tail, pp. 42, 37.

Guilliatt, R. 1994, ''U.S. eh? Why young Australia is so smitten with American culture' *Sydney Morning Herald,* 25 June, pp.1A, 4A.

Iveson, K. 1997, 'Partying, politics and getting paid — Hip hop and national identity in Australia', *Oerland* 147 (Winter).

Jee, B. 1996a, 'Towering Inferno', *Bomb* 42, http://www.thehub.com.au/~bombaust

Jee, B. 1996b, *East Coast Funk festival (Australia) Review,* ibid.

Jee, B. 1996c, 'Warcry Interview', *Eye of the Needle* #2, http://www.thehub.com.au/~bombaust

Lipsitz, G. 1994, *Dangerous Crossroads: Popular Music, Postmodernism and the Poetics of Place,* London: Verso

Maxwell, I. 1994, *Def Wish Cast 'Down Under Comin' Upper': Rapping the Westside,* Unpublished Paper, International Association for the Study of Popular Music, Lismore: Southern Cross University.

Maxwell, I. 1995, *Steppin Freestylee: improvised rap and the negotiation of community in the Sydney hip hop scene,* Unpublished paper, International Association for the Study of Popular Music, Glasgow: University of Stathclyde.

Owens, F. 1994, 'Back in the Days', in *Vibe* vol. 2 no. 10 (December- January), 67.

Potter, R. A. 1995, *Spectacular Vernaculars: Hip Hop and the Politics of Postmodernism,* SUNY.

Powell, D. 1994, *Out West:Perceptions of Sydney's Western Suburbs,* Sydney: Allen & Unwin.

Robertson, R. 1995, 'Glocalization: Time-Space and Homogeneity-Heterogeneity', in Featherstone, Lash & Robertson (eds), *Global Modernities,* London: Sage.

Rose, T. 1994, *Black Noise: Rap Music and Black Culture in Contemporary America,* Wesleyan University Press.

Wark, M. 1997,'Culture's Cannibals', *The Australian,* May 14:30.

Discography

046, L.I.F.E. Dope Runner Records, 1995.

Brethren, *Big Brother,* MXL, 1996.

Def Wish Cast, *Knights of the Underground Table,* Random Records, 1993.

Easybass, *Space Program 1996,* Self-produced Cassette, 1995.

Fuglemen, *Resuscitation,* Fuglemen, 1997.

Koolism, *Koolism,* Track Records, 1997.

Metabass 'N' Breath, *Seek,* Metabass 'N' Breath, 1997.

Moonrock, *Moonrock,* Creative Vibes, 1998.

Noble Savages, *Noble Savages,* Hell Tasty Recordings, 1995.

The Nuuk Posse, *Kaataq,* Sub Rosa SR 108, 1997.

Sleek the Elite, *Sleekism, Featuring DJ Soup,* Sleekism Records, 1997.

Nobukazu Takemura, *Child's View,* Bellissima! 1994

Sound Unlimited, *A Postcard from the Edge of the Underside,* Columbia, 1992.
Trey, *Projectile,* Self-produced Cassette, 1998.
Various Artists, *Down Under by Law,* Virgin Records, 1988.
Various Artists, *Danger,* Death Defying Theatre, 1996.
Various Artists, *Home Brews; Extra Stength Australian Hip Hop Vol. 1,* MXL, 1995.
Various Artists, *Home Brewz Vol. II,* MXL, 1998.
White Boys, *Westside,* Warlord Records, 1995.

INDIGENOUS MUSIC IN THE ACADEMY: WHOSE MUSIC, WHOSE IDENTITY?

JENNIFER K. NEWSOME

Firstly let me welcome you all here today, and say how delighted I and my colleagues from the Centre for Aboriginal Studies in Music are to be involved in this exciting and important conference.

Before I begin I would like to acknowledge on behalf of all the participants here today that we are speaking on Kaurna land, and to express our appreciation to the traditional owners, the Kaurna people, in being able to do so.

As many are no doubt aware, the mainstream tertiary sector in Australia has been very slow indeed to respond to the need for courses which are inclusive of the learning needs and aspirations of Aboriginal and Torres Strait Islander students. Across the performing arts sector as a whole, there are still only a handful of courses which aim to provide opportunities for Indigenous Australian students, and within the higher education sector there are even fewer still. During this session today we will look at some of the ways in which the academy in Australia has, to date, operated to effectively exclude the voice of Aboriginal and Torres Strait Islander musicians, and to suggest some ways in which the sector can begin to open its doors to increased participation by Aboriginal and Torres Strait Islander students.

The Indigenous 'voice' in the academy: A history of exclusion

I would like to start by looking briefly at the role of Aboriginal and Torres Strait Islander music in the Australian academy today. It would probably not come as a surprise to many to discover that this question has so far received little attention from the academic community.

To date, the engagement of the academy with Aboriginal and Torres Strait Islander musical traditions has been primarily through research. This research, conducted within the established paradigms of disciplines such as comparative musicology, ethnomusicology and anthropology, has resulted in a considerable body of documented knowledge about Indigenous Australian musical traditions, and has played a major role in the way in which these traditions have been understood and represented within the academic community.

It is notable however, that this research has been conducted almost exclusively by western trained non-Indigenous researchers, and that it has until recently tended to focus on so-called 'traditional' forms of Aboriginal and Torres Strait Islander musical expression. The reasons for this are complex and are bound up in the history of music research in Australia.

The historical focus on 'traditional' forms evolved within the context of colonial discourse in which western conceptions of 'difference' influenced attitudes towards Indigenous peoples and their traditions. In addressing this point, the eminent ethnomusicologist and educator Catherine J. Ellis commented about her early work in an article published in 1995, saying:

> *In the course of this early field work I also recorded music mixing indigenous and European forms, as part of a tradition that my own cultural prejudice then dismissed as unimportant, and which I almost missed valuable opportunities to record. They sang hymns for us with their family, father playing guitar. Then he sang some of the old shearing shed songs. We recorded these performances out of politeness, waiting always for the miracle of the 'real' performance. It was only through many visits and such singing sessions that we gradually realised that the singing we were recording was an important and widespread tradition that recreated, in Europeanised structures, the performance through song of modern Aboriginal life* (Ellis 1995:201).

Attitudes towards authenticity in contemporary Indigenous cultural expression continue to have a major affect upon the way in which Indigenous Australian cultural identity is framed. Many Aboriginal and Torres Strait Islander musicians today, who have lived their lives in areas where 'traditional' forms are no longer in common use, have been highly creative in utilising non-traditional elements to construct new forms of Indigenous musical expression. Such musicians are often faced with the question of whether their music is really 'indigenous' or not, and if it is, what is 'indigenous' about it? In this we can see the complexity of the nexus between personal identity and self expression, and public conceptions and representations of indigeneity for Indigenous musicians today.

The academy has, in general, been slow to respond to these issues and hence to the need for the development of curriculums which aim to address differences between the learning needs and aspirations of Indigenous music students and those of non-Indigenous students. In the area of music education this has resulted, until recently, in the almost virtual exclusion of Indigenous students from tertiary level education, particularly at the postgraduate level.

It is important to note that attitudes towards musical style have played, and continue to play, a key role in the design of tertiary level music curriculums in Australia, affecting decisions about the aims and content of courses, the pedagogical approaches used, and the types of prerequisites used in the selection of students. In particular, the academy has been slow to acknowledge the legitimacy of so-called popular music styles as a basis for tertiary level music education courses.

Taste and style in music are culturally determined, having their origins in early musical experiences within the family, community, and education system. Where elitist values and aesthetics persist within the academy, distinctions continue to be made between what are conceived of as great or 'high art' forms in music (such as western 'classical' music) and what are considered to be intrinsically less valuable forms, such as those derived from popular culture. Such values are 'assumed to be valid and authoritative and therefore capable of assessing other types of culture, without any questions being raised about these assumptions and their ability to pass cultural judgments' (Strinati 1995:39).

A particularly complex and contentious aspect of this can be seen in the high value placed on 'traditional' as opposed to other forms of Indigenous musical expression within the academy. The historical emphasis on 'traditional' forms within academic research has tended to reinforce the still widely held view that Indigenous expressive forms which are not based on 'traditional' elements are less authentic and therefore less valuable. For Indigenous musicians who choose to utilise popular music elements in their music, this has had detrimental educational consequences, since the persistence of such attitudes within the academy has contributed to the exclusion of Indigenous musicians from tertiary level education. I shall return to this point in more detail later in the discussion.

Low levels of involvement by Indigenous musicians in tertiary level education and hence research training in Australia have had a long term impact on the nature of music research in this country. Although it has been recognised that the Indigenous 'voice' is the primary authority upon which research about Indigenous traditions relies, there has been a remarkably slow response from mainstream academia in Australia to the need for the development of research in which Indigenous musicians are at the centre of the research process, not as 'subjects', but as the researchers themselves.

Recently, Pamela Croft, the Indigenous people's officer of the Council of Australian Postgraduate Associations, explained that Indigenous Australians were 'tired of being researched by other people', saying, 'we believe it is time to do our own research' (Pryor 1998:40).

I would suggest therefore that there is a need for targeted funding for cultural research that recognises the need for research by Indigenous musicians, who have previously been regarded primarily as research 'subjects', but who have ironically formed the basis for claims to authority in Indigenous traditions by non-Indigenous researchers. There is also clearly a need for new types of research and new approaches to research training in order to provide increased opportunities for Indigenous musicians to participate as active and equal agents in research about both Indigenous and non-Indigenous traditions, but in particular to contribute as equal 'voices' to academic discourse about Indigenous musical traditions.

As well as having the potential to greatly enrich the discourse by exploring new perspectives, developing new directions and formulating new research paradigms to meet new needs, Indigenous musicians and researchers also have the potential to overturn established understandings within academia about Indigenous music making through critique of existing research. As Edward Said has pointed out:

> *The emergence of formerly colonial subjects as interpreters of imperialism and its great cultural works has given imperialism a perceptible, not to say obtrusive identity as a subject for study and vigorous revision. But how can that particular kind of post-imperial testimony and study, usually left to the margins of critical discourse, be brought into active contact with current theoretical concerns (Said 1993: 77-78)?... The job facing the cultural intellectual is therefore not to accept the politics of identity as given, but to show how all representations are constructed, for what purpose, by whom, and with what components* (Said 1993:380).

In recent times, increasing numbers of Australian researchers have been seeking to address these issues through the use of collaborative approaches to research. However, such research continues to be primarily framed and managed by non-Indigenous researchers, and the bulk of research funding is still being awarded to non-indigenous researchers. There is therefore still much to be done in seeking to open the doors of the academy to a more central involvement by Aboriginal and Torres Strait Islander musicians in research work. A key avenue for achieving this is increased access to tertiary level education by Indigenous musicians.

Institutional barriers to the academy for Indigenous musicians

The 1997 Review of Abstudy conducted by the Aboriginal and Torres Strait Islander Commission reported that nearly all Indigenous people interviewed commented on the importance of education; recognising its significance for 'their future economic and social wellbeing'. The Review stated that Indigenous people required support to 'make (educational) choices consistent with their aspirations; including maintenance of their cultural identity' (Stanley & Hansen 1998:14). As music making is clearly a key way in which different groups in the community sustain their individual identities, music education is particularly relevant to these findings in providing an important avenue for the support and development of Indigenous musical traditions.

Tertiary level education for Indigenous musicians is critical for the purposes of advanced training in areas such as music research, music performance and composition, teacher education, arts management and administration, and community and cultural development. In view of the fact that the academy is also the traditional training ground for academics, it is vital that Indigenous musicians have increased access to tertiary education so that the number of Indigenous Australians employed as academics and researchers within the tertiary performing arts sector can increase.

In seeking to improve access to tertiary level education for Indigenous musicians, an important first step is to determine whether there are specific institutional barriers inhibiting Indigenous musicians from accessing the current system. If we take as a basic premise the view that all education serves to maintain and promote cultural traditions, then an examination of the underlying cultural and educational bases of existing courses is necessary in order to determine whose particular cultural traditions are being served by the current system, and to enable us to determine whether there are aspects of the system which act to exclude Indigenous students, and if there are, what they are.

In a case study conducted at the University of South Australia in 1995, which looked at factors affecting the performance of Aboriginal and Torres Strait Islander students at Australian universities, it was suggested that:

> *The various courses offered by Australian universities at undergraduate and postgraduate levels invariably tend to ignore any cultural differences in both content and learning styles... The indigenous student's culture is overlooked and the expectations of persistence focus on those of the dominant culture and not the persistence behaviours based on the individual student's culture... It would seem that educational institutions such as universities appear to have been unwilling, unable, or unaware of the need to meet indigenous cultural differences in respect to learning* (Bourke, Burdon & Moore 1996:2-4).

Performing arts education in Australia has developed primarily within the context of 'western' epistemological systems and Anglo-European cultural traditions. Mainstream tertiary level music education presumes enculturalisation within these systems and traditions and this is reflected in the aims and content of courses, the pedagogical processes used, prerequisites for selection to courses, and institutional cultures and systems. Aboriginal and Torres Strait Islander students are excluded from participating in these courses primarily because the majority of Indigenous Australian musicians have been enculturalised, in terms of music, primarily outside these traditions. A lack of recognition of this within the tertiary sector has resulted in a lack of appreciation of the need for courses to be inclusive of the different learning needs and aspirations of Indigenous students. This represents a key factor inhibiting increased participation by Indigenous students in tertiary level music education.

Prerequisites for entrance to courses represent an area in which there are particularly significant barriers to participation by Indigenous students. These are reasonably standardised across the tertiary music education sector and are generally based on a combination of prior musical knowledge and practical skill *within prescribed musical styles,* and presume a western-based formal educational background.

Such prerequisites include:

- an ability to read western music notation;
- a knowledge of the fundamentals of western music theory;
- a background in formal, practically based music education (instrumental and/or vocal training, and ensemble and performance studies);
- competence in the use of standard written English;
- a secondary school educational attainment of Year 12 level;
- a knowledge of the history and repertoire of western 'art' music or jazz;
- practical competence in western 'art' music or jazz styles, and
- an understanding of how to learn effectively within a mainstream higher education context.

Many educators take such prerequisites for granted, seeing them as essential for the effective learning of musical skills and knowledge at the tertiary level. But is this really so? A closer examination reveals that these types of prerequisites serve to preclude a great many proficient musicians whose musical skills and knowledge have developed outside the western educational schooling framework. Prerequisites for music courses are in fact highly culture specific, generally presuming for example that applicants have participated in mainstream western schooling to Year 12 level, and have had a background of formal western based music education and training. This training is presumed to have incorporated the learning of prerequisite knowledge in key areas such as western music literacy, music theory and history, and the development of musical skills through formal western practically based training and performance studies. These types of training normally take place during the high school years, but can often start earlier. As the majority of Indigenous musicians do not have an educational profile consistent with these prerequisites they are generally unable to satisfy such entrance requirements.

In view of the now widely acknowledged cultural diversity of performing arts activity in Australia, surely there is room within the formal education framework for an expansion of the base of performing arts education? This would provide for a more contemporary focus, which would address a wider variety of cultural priorities in terms of both educational processes and educational outcomes.

Musical style is an area in which there are quite specific culturally based prerequisites for admission to tertiary courses. The majority of mainstream courses have at their foundation, two main styles of music: western 'art' music, or jazz. Applicants are required to demonstrate their capabilities in the performance of these styles during auditions which generally form part of the selection process. Musicians not familiar with or competent in the performance of these styles, for example those whose music making experiences lie in styles such as folk music or non-western music, are not able to demonstrate the prerequisite knowledge and skills to achieve success in applying to such courses. The majority of Aboriginal and Torres Strait Islander musicians find that they are generally not equipped with sufficient background knowledge and experience in these particular styles to be able to succeed at auditions.

In order to create enhanced educational opportunities for Indigenous musicians within the tertiary sector it is necessary to have an understanding of the specific cultural and educational bases of contemporary Indigenous music making. Such an understanding is crucial to the development of music courses that are responsive to the particular learning needs and aspirations of Indigenous students.

In addressing this point I would like to draw upon the experiences of colleagues and students at the Centre for Aboriginal Studies in Music at the University of Adelaide (CASM). CASM has been at the forefront of efforts to provide access to tertiary education for Indigenous musicians, and is the first university based program in Australia to have developed tertiary level courses designed specifically to meet the learning needs and aspirations of Aboriginal and Torres Strait Islander musicians.

Work at the Centre has enabled the accumulation of an extensive knowledge base about the musical and educational backgrounds and the learning needs of Indigenous musicians, dating back to the early 1970s. This knowledge has been developed through an ongoing process of action research, utilising data derived from formal interviews, interactions between staff and students, interactions with Indigenous musicians within the community, the personal experiences of Indigenous teaching staff, and a continuous cycle of curriculum evaluation, review, and development.

Research at the Centre indicates that the majority of Aboriginal and Torres Strait Islander musicians seeking access to courses at the Centre have gained their prior knowledge of, and skills in, music from a wide and diverse range of sources. These can be represented as lying across a range of learning possibilities (Figure 1).

Column 1 represents formal music learning within a western schooling framework, while column 3 represents formal music learning within a 'traditional' Indigenous framework. For both columns 1 and 3, the chart indicates those styles of music normally represented within the formal education system, while column 2 represents examples of the wide variety of styles of music drawn on by musicians who have learned music primarily informally within an Indigenous community context.

Column 2 represents the learning base of the majority of Aboriginal and Torres Strait Islander musicians seeking access to tertiary music studies through CASM. The vast majority of applicants indicate that they are almost entirely self taught and that they have gained their musical knowledge primarily from informal sources, typically within the Indigenous community, from close relatives and friends, from community experiences such as performances, and from listening to recordings and watching television, films and videos. A very small minority report also having learned some aspects of music through formal educational processes.

Figure 1: Primary formal epistemological bases for learning music

1	*2*	*3*
Western-based music education system	Community-based learning	Traditionally-based Indigenous education system
Formalised system of instruction	Informal learning processes: Primarily self taught	Formalised system of instruction
Musical styles • Western 'art' music • Jazz • Popular styles (mainly in secondary schools only)	**Musical styles** • Contemporary Aboriginal and Torres Strait Islander music • Traditional Aboriginal or Torres Strait Islander music • Popular music: rock, reggae, blues, jazz, metal, rap, hip hop, etc • Western 'art' music. • Commercial musics • Film and video music • Folk music • World musics	**Musical styles** • Traditional Aboriginal and Torres Strait Islander music (combined with dance)

Figure 1 illustrates the key relationships between learning systems and musical style, and the relationship between these and learning processes. There are two key factors relevant to the learning needs and aspirations of Indigenous music students which can be seen from these relationships. Firstly, the majority of musicians applying to CASM do not have a musical background derived from the primary formal epistemological systems; and secondly, identification with musical style is developed primarily through informal learning processes within a community context, with diversity rather than conformity being the predominant aspect.

The level of educational achievement of applicants within the school system ranges from early primary school for students from 'traditional' backgrounds, through to tertiary level qualifications. The majority of applicants, however, report a formal educational level of attainment of somewhere between Year 9 and Year 11. Very few applicants report having completed Year 12. These findings are not peculiar to music students, but are consistent with the overall educational status of Indigenous students within mainstream schooling as a whole.

The styles of music performed by applicants at auditions for selection to CASM lie across the wide range of styles available to them within the informal learning framework represented in column 2. The predominant styles performed are styles of Indigenous music which combine Indigenous and non-Indigenous elements, such as country music, rhythm and blues, rock and reggae. Some applicants also present styles such as folk, metal and rap, and a small minority present 'traditional' Indigenous music as well as other styles. Only a very small minority of applicants choose to perform, and are able to perform, within western 'art' music or jazz styles. It is important to note that many applicants are already proficient song writers and performers prior to applying to the course, and there is commonly a high degree of originality demonstrated at auditions with many applicants performing their own compositions. This is in strong contrast with the types and styles of music performed by non-Indigenous students at auditions for mainstream courses.

In learning music primarily in the 'in between' spaces between formalised epistemological systems, Indigenous musicians have been charting a new musical course in which contemporary Indigenous identities are finding their expression through a variety of new and emerging musical forms. This is the 'third space' of which Homi Bhabha speaks, the space in which 'the process of cultural hybridity gives rise to something different, something new and unrecognisable, a new area of negotiation of meaning and representation', which 'displaces the histories that constitute it, and sets up new structures of authority, new political initiatives, which are inadequately understood through received wisdom' (Bhabha 1990:211). This is described by Kirkness and Barnhardt in the following terms: ' if considered in its totality, such knowledge can be seen to constitute a particular world view, a form of consciousness, or a reality set' (Kirkness & Barnhardt 1991:7).

An appreciation of the significance of this is, I believe, at the heart of improvements in education for Indigenous musicians. Although there is growing recognition within the research community of the significance of these new and emerging Indigenous styles of music, and their importance in the expression of contemporary Indigenous values and identities, this has yet to filter through in any degree to mainstream performing arts education. There is little appreciation, therefore, of the need to address such issues within the music curriculum.

Meeting the educational needs of Indigenous music students

Experience in working with Indigenous music students at CASM has demonstrated that the overriding principle in the design of curriculums which aim to be effective in meeting the learning needs and aspirations of Indigenous musicians is recognition of the significance of prior learning. This principle provides a firm basis upon which to build effective educational strategies and a curriculum which is culturally relevant to students.

Recognition of diversity is also a key consideration. Indigenous musicians at CASM have a wide diversity of educational, cultural, musical, familial and community backgrounds. It is necessary, therefore, for educational programs for these students to be inclusive of a diversity of educational, cultural, musical and personal needs and aspirations. This is of particular significance in the area of musical style, where it is necessary to provide learning options across a wide stylistic base.

These principles recognise the unique cultural status of contemporary Indigenous musicians, who in the process of negotiating personal and cultural identities between primary epistemological and cultural systems, are creating important new forms of musical expression. In building on the existing learning backgrounds and creative strengths of students, a deficit model of student learning is avoided, and educational considerations arising from the diverse and informal nature of students' prior learning experiences can be addressed. Recognition, both of the significance of prior learning, and of diversity, also provides a firm basis for educational strategies which aim to address important and complex issues of cultural and academic identity.

Finally, I would like to outline some curriculum design strategies based on these principles which have proven effective at CASM in addressing the learning needs and aspirations of Indigenous music students. These strategies assume an educational context supportive of Indigenous aims and values, and which is essentially intercultural and anti-racist in aiming to negotiate cultural difference and diversity through the educational process, and in seeking to address the issue of inequity in educational provision for Indigenous students through non-assimilationist approaches. They also assume the use of flexible entrance requirements that are responsive to diversity in students' prior learning backgrounds. Strategies are outlined in Figure 2.

In conclusion, I would like to emphasise the need for learning environments which are supportive and empowering of Indigenous students. At CASM we have found the creation of an Indigenous enclave within the University essential for students to be able to develop a sense of academic identity which is not circumscribed by the dominant cultural forces of the academy. We have also the found the creation of a coalition of Indigenous and non-indigenous educators from a variety of educational and cultural backgrounds highly effective in negotiating the complex territory between cultures to create a curriculum which embraces not only 'western' and 'traditional' Indigenous epistemologies but also the

Figure 2: Addressing the learning needs of Indigenous music students

- a wide curriculum base
- the use of foundational studies
- teaching of key knowledge and skills necessary to access the two primary formal epistemological systems
- the use of holistic and integrated approaches to student learning
- contextualisation of learning content and processes
- a focus on Indigenous issues and Indigenous forms of cultural expression
- a focus on analysis and contextualisation of cultural issues
- content which recognises both the significance and the diversity of Indigenous traditions and histories
- a broadly based and non-prescriptive approach to musical style
- a focus on performance and practically based learning and music making
- a focus on song and the inclusion of dance as primary Indigenous forms
- a focus on creative processes and outcomes
- emphasis on the development of higher level learning skills
- a systematic and intensive approach to the development of research skills
- a systematic and integrated approach to the teaching of formal western learning and communication skills
- a systematic and intensive approach to the teaching of music literacy
- emphasis on individualised attention to learning needs
- emphasis on the use of adult learning principles
- support for students in dealing effectively with institutional cultures and systems

learning world between these systems. Homi Bhabha describes this process as 'intervention' in 'the third space', essentially a process of 'articulating minority constituencies across disjunctive, differential social positions' (Bhabha 1990:220). The educational program developed at CASM can thus be regarded as constituting a 'site' of cultural and educational intervention, in which assimilationist approaches are replaced with an integrative philosophy which responds to the learning needs and aspirations of Indigenous students as the highest priority.

I would like to finish with a quote by Edward Said:

> *What does need to be remembered is that narratives of emancipation and enlightenment in their strongest form were also narratives of integration not separation, the stories of people who had been excluded from the main group but who were now fighting for a place in it. And if the old and habitual ideas of the main group were not flexible or generous enough to admit new groups, then these ideas need changing— a far better thing to do than reject the emerging group* (Said 1993:xxx).

References

Barwick, L., Marett, A. & Tunstill, G. (eds) 1995, *The Essence of Singing and the Substance of Song,* Australia, Oceania Publications.

Bhabha, H. 1990, 'The third space: interview with Homi Bhabha' in Rutherford, J. (ed), *Identity: community, culture, difference,* London: Lawrence and Wishart.

Bourke, C.J., Burden, J.K. & Moore, S. 1996, *Factors Affecting Performance of Aboriginal and Torres Strait Islander Students at Australian Universities: A Case Study,* Canberra: Australian Government Publishing Service: 9.

Commonwealth Government *1997 - 1998 Budget* http://www.deetya.gov.au.budget information.htm#14.

Crowdy, D. 1998, 'Creativity and Independence — Sanguma, Music Education and the Development of the PNG Contemporary style' in *Perfect Beat* 3, 4, NSW: The Pacific Society for Research Into Contemporary Music and Popular Culture.

Dunbar-Hall, P. 1993, *Teaching Popular Music,* Australia: Science Press.

Ellis, C. J. 1985, *Aboriginal Music,* Australia: University of Queensland Press.

Ellis, C. J. 1995, 'Whose Truth?' in Barwick, L., Marett, A. & Tunstill, G. (eds), *The Essence of Singing and the Substance of Song,* Australia: Oceania Publications.

Ellis, C. J. 1986, 'The Musician, the University and the Community: Conflict or Concord?' in Inaugural Lecture 1985-87, Armidale: University of New England.

Hayward, P. 1992, *From Pop to Punk to Postmodernism,* Australia: Allen and Unwin.

Kirkness, V. J. & Barnhardt, R. 1991, 'First Nations and Higher Education: The Four R's — Respect, Relevance, Reciprocity, Responsibility' in Swisher, K. (ed), *Journal of American Indian Education. Arizona: Center for Indian Education,* Arizona State University.

Pryor, C. 1998, 'Review bid to axe postgrad Abstudy', in *The Australian,* 3 June, Australia: Nationwide News.

Reid, C. & Holland, W. 'Aboriginal Rural Education Program: A Case Study in Anti-Racist Strategies' in Vasta, E. & Castles, S., *The Teeth Are Smiling,* Sydney: Allen and Unwin.

Said, E. W. 1993, *Culture and Imperialism,* G. B. Chatto & Windus Ltd.

Spurr, D. 1993, *The Rhetoric of Empire,* London: Duke University Press.

Stanley, O. & Hansen, G. 1998, *ABSTUDY: An Investment for Tomorrow's Employment,* Australia: ATSIC Review Report, Commonwealth of Australia.

Strinati, D. 1995, *An Introduction to Theories of Popular Culture,* London: Routledge.

BRIDGING THREE WORLDS

DAVID PAGE with STEPHEN PAGE and CATHERINE BEALL

Today's generation has no choice but to face and challenge the political and social issues of just being born Aboriginal. Obviously, where you are born determines your Aboriginal lifestyle and future. Whether you're from the bush, the hick country town or the city, we all have similar stories to tell and what better way to tell them than through song.

We are a race of different skins and cultural lore but we all share one thing — the existence of this compelling white world. We need a modern day corroboree of song that will help us understand who we really are as Indigenous races.

But the differences within us are over shadowed by a white cloud of ignorance. Our family or clan structure, kinship and languages need to be brought back out from under the clouds into the sun, so we can practice elements of emotion that help us determine the future for our children.

Styles of music from all over the world have strongly influenced us for many years. For the past two hundred years our people were told not to practice what we do best — sing and dance our stories — but they couldn't stop us, it's our blood and soul.

The stories of the modern day Aborigine need to be told and targeted to larger mixed groups. The first priority is to target our own communities, both city and remote, comprised of urban, country and traditional worlds and to break down the prejudices between our own peoples.

The contemporary Aboriginal music scene is raw but young. Emerging artists need to collaborate and network with each other to reinforce their existence and motivate the practice of our natural sharing abilities.

Okay, so many styles of music flow through the creative blood of all people who create and develop their music. But when you belong to a culture and a race of people who deliver a history that goes back thousands of years it is special to feel part of.

You know that being an Aboriginal songman or songwoman is a gift you cannot ignore, for the creative blood is passed down. Our relationship with the land and the respect we have for one another has been, and still is, told through song. So we know who we really are and where we come from.

Being Aboriginal music men and women trying to break into the world music arena is not easy. But when given the opportunity to develop a project that is well planned and can help more than one artist we are given hope as a race of human beings.

Many Indigenous performers have to work twice as hard as the average Australian in this field to fit into the mainstream music industry. And then, they are often catalogued and slotted into a pigeon hole when it comes time for the country to award these people for their hard work in creating an original style of music and story-telling.

Over the next few years I will be working towards the establishment of a music recording studio and label based in Sydney called Nikinali. Nikinali has been given government-sponsored premises at The Wharf alongside the Bangarra Dance Theatre, Sydney Dance Company and the Sydney Theatre Company.

I hope Nikinali will give us all an understanding of networking and collaborating by sharing the similarity of cultural expression through song form. Cultural music maintenance is rare within the urban Aboriginal music industry. Indigenous performers who are working at making it in the mainstream music industry are not often given the opportunity or the break that they deserve.

With the political and social issues we are left to face and challenge, it is essential to maintain our cultural values by sharing and passing down our talents. The first CD which Nikinali produces will feature artists from all areas of our land. This adds to the uniqueness of the project. The versatility within the contemporary black music scene needs to be branded and delivered so that all people are aware that it's very much alive. This project can only reinforce the platform for young indigenous artists by nurturing and developing their talents and the ability to carry on and pass it down.

The purpose of Nikinali is:

- To help develop the styles of emerging Aboriginal and Torres Strait Islander artists
- To help given them recognition
- To increase the Australian Indigenous music market
- To encourage role modelling for future generations
- To develop each performer's experience of song writing and recording processes.

After all our peoples have been through, we must work together to strengthen the foundation that embraces all Aboriginal stories of heartache, dispossession, reconciliation, celebration, land rights, identity, safety, simplicity, forgiveness, survival, integrity, love, children, and our future.

Is it our place as young urban Aborigines and Torres Strait Islanders to become the social workers so badly needed to heal the wounds? Are we the voice for our people to cry for better social and welfare care? Surely it is not us who are going to be the ones to record and communicate the essence of our cultures? Could it be that people our age with little or no direct experience of traditional culture are going to be the ones to carry it on?

I have been associated with the Bangarra Dance Theatre for a number of years and have always felt that when Bangarra visited the homelands or the island communities we became the 'band aid' company. We find ourselves standing in the middle between the white and the black communities. Somehow in our work, people both here in the city and way out there in remote regional communities see hope: hope for reconciliation, hope for a better future for the young people, hope for the survival of at least the essence of traditional culture.

Working over the past five years with my brothers Stephen and Russell, and the artists of Bangarra, I have been strengthened in my beliefs and purpose. As an artist I am here to communicate with and to entertain people, to connect with and to challenge people's feelings and thinking. I have always been aware of the many different audiences there are for me to explore.

When we manage to find the right ingredients for our dance theatre works we manage to reach a universal audience. What touches our own communities, also touches the mainstream audience. People may have varied and quite personal responses to the work, but essentially they feel connected in some way.

But then I am more than an artist, I am an Aboriginal artist. And this is where the biggest challenge lies. On the one hand, I want to project Indigenous peoples in a positive light, providing an all important role model for young Aboriginal and Torres Strait Islander people. On the other hand I want all Australians to understand the pain, the difficulties, the realities of being an Indigenous Australian. For this reason I think my work is rather bitter sweet. I hope it is full of contrasts — optimistic, depressing, joyful, sad, shocking and light-hearted.

Bridging the three worlds is the central aim of our work. We hope to provide a link or bridge between mainstream society, Aborigines, and Torres Strait Islanders. So few people outside of our own communities and perhaps a few government departments truly appreciate the differences among the many Indigenous people of Australia. For them very often black is black.

We have a huge task in educating people about our Indigenous heritage, about retaining the languages, the stories, the lands. There is so much talk of multicultural Australia — what about the need for people to develop a sensitivity towards the many cultures that form Indigenous Australia!

It is our experience to perform one day in the city of Sydney, the next in the homelands of Arnhemland and then to reach the international audience through CDs and radio airplay. To mean something to such a diversity of people is a big responsibility. We must be more than an artefact, a tourist attraction, a smoke screen covering the truth of our people's existence. We need to give people a sense of how human nature and experience is fundamentally the same for all people the world over. We need to cross barriers of language, technology, time and place. Dance and music are the best possible conveyors of these experiences and these messages.

Over many years my brothers and I have developed a strong, close relationship with Bundak Marika, Djakapurra and Janet Munyarryun and their family in Hirrkala, Arnhemland. We are from the Munaldjali Clan, Yugambeh Tribe in South East Queensland. Our experience is urban, theirs is traditional. Having this closeness is not always easy, but for us it is a great honour and it is enduring. Together we have shared our stories, our dreaming, our dance and song.

We have learned to be more external about our work, less prepared to work with the unconscious experience, more inclined to argue over concepts between ourselves. Essentially our experiences are about identity, about belonging and connecting somewhere. This gives us a feeling of unity, and within that each person's story gives variety and shape to the overall work.

In my collaboration with my brother, choreographer and director, Stephen Page, together with Djkapurra Munyarryun we draw on our sense of the spirituality of the land and set it within a context that can be seen and heard, and hopefully understood, by all peoples. Stephen's program note for 'Ochres' reads as follows:

Spirituality is an integral part of our lives. For Indigenous Australia, spirituality centres around the land. The nurturing and life giving capacity of even our hardest terrains has been the mainstay of Indigenous religious beliefs. Incorporating the earth into spiritual ceremonies is done by many tribes using various ochres. Having the different colours such as white, yellow, red and black, ochre is applied in designs according to your totem so that your totem spirituality is awakened during the paint up. There are no time constraints, no boundaries, there's an apparent timelessness around the ritual.

Maybe through these essential forms, as we dance and sing, the essence of our traditional cultures can be expressed. Then when we have the resources and desire to develop the mix of traditional with contemporary forms, maybe we can be some kind of universal voice.

I have always learnt from my brothers and sisters, my mother and father, uncles and aunties — may we all dance and sing in unity. This creative process has strengthened my ability to do what I do best: believe in myself, my people and the land.

My language is gone, my tribal song and dance from long ago were not passed down to me, but I am still part of the dreaming. We the urban Aboriginal Indigenous people of the world, can only spiritually express the cultural identity that burns inside us. Through music, dance and visual art we have taken what belongs to us and shown the world what has always been.

SMELLS LIKE EXTREME SPIRIT: PUNK MUSIC, SKATE CULTURE AND THE PACKAGING OF EXTREME SPORTS

CATHERINE PALMER

Introduction

Certain leisure activities that have grown exponentially in popularity since the mid 1970s have seen their adherents emerge as a significant social class.[1] Sports such as rock climbing, mountaineering, skate boarding, B.A.S.E and bunjee jumping, street luge and snow boarding, to name but a few, now occupy key places amongst the leisure pursuits of the young (or the young at heart). In addition to their relative newness or novelty value, the defining characteristic of these extreme sports is that they provide their practitioners with a substantial chance of injury or even death. Undertaken at great height or at great speed, these are high-risk sports that are not for the faint hearted.

It is this 'taste for the extreme' (Midol 1993:23), that I take as my point of departure today. Specifically, I am concerned with exploring the ways in which this notion of risk taking, living on the edge or 'catching the buzz' as it is known amongst extreme athletes, provides a mechanism through which they constitute and present themselves as a heroic class apart. Extreme athletes are the characters who, in urban mythology, live hard and die young, and it is this theme of living on the edge that is avidly incorporated into the narratives and practices of extreme sports people.

Although this motif of heroic risk taking can be elaborated in a number of ways, this paper explores but one, namely, the music industry. While this may seem a curious site for expressions of 'extremity', I argue that music, particularly punk music, plays a critical role in disseminating this symbolic capital amongst extreme athletes. Elements of a hard core punk scene are readily appropriated by these young men and women when constituting and presenting their own group identity.

To illustrate this argument ethnographically, I will first briefly describe the character and composition of an extreme sports community in Adelaide, before moving to a consideration of the ways in which one particular 'youth culture celebration' provides an occasion at which this dovetailing of extreme sport and extreme music can be played out. The event that I have chosen to examine is 'Indy Fest 500', a music festival which took place in Adelaide in April 1998. As I make clear in the following pages, Indy Fest, as it is more commonly known, offers a key locale at which the heroic life of the extreme athlete can be enacted, and at which the very self of the extreme athlete can be presented. In addition, as I will elaborate shortly, it is the centrality of punk music to the staging of Indy Fest that allows these extreme athletes to reflect, express and resonate aspects of their distinctive social and sporting lives.

Fearless figures: skaters, climbers and mountain bikers

While the umbrella of extreme sports clearly encompasses a range of sporting subcultures — skaters, mountain climbers, mountain bikers, amongst others — there are nonetheless certain features common to them all.[2] The practitioners of these 'frontier challenge activities' are young, usually male, and the reliance on expensive equipment (boards, bikes, climbing gear and so on) suggests they are also affluent. Importantly for this paper, these high-risk activities are all spoken of by their adherents as being sports that can injure or even kill. As one local skater, Ben, notes:

> *...most skaters I know have at least one broken bone to their name. Whether it's a 'swell bow', a broken toe, a knee blow out, or a head bongo, if you can't take the pain, then you won't stick with it for long. Part of the learning process of skating is falling on your arse.*[3]

Similarly, Dave, a rock climber, maintains that 'everybody who climbs gets hurt. If you don't get hurt, you're not trying'.

In other words, the discourse that surrounds these sports plays with the notion that they offer much, much more than other sports. Extreme sports take their adherents faster, higher and further than all others, and certainly, such themes articulate with popular sentiment. Simon, a highly accomplished mountain biker, describes his sport as being:

> *...all about going out there and pushing yourself. It isn't some feeble fashion show or dumb popularity contest. It's all about having a fucking blast. It's about putting the smack down on the laws of physics, and it's about cheating death.*

As befits the discourse of extremity, boundaries are pushed and personal limits are transcended. To quote Melissa, one of the few female skaters I have encountered:

> *...when you're faced with a 15 foot half pipe*[4]*, someone's got to do it. All it takes is overcoming that fear, taking the extra push and going for it.*[5]

As detailed in such narratives, extreme athletes constantly push themselves to their limits, further compounding the dangers to which they are exposed.

Indeed, the behaviours and conversations of skaters, climbers and mountain bikers continually reinforce their perceptions that they are driven men and women who know no limits. The sports that they play are not for the faint hearted, and their ability to rage harder than most is a key part of their internal social discourse. The song by the Beastie Boys, 'You've Got to Fight For Your Right (to Party)', has an almost anthemic quality amongst mountain bikers, while the three fingered 'ecstasy salute' is a common means of biding one another farewell. Equally, the reputation of skaters for high speed living is a matter of some pride for Melissa, as is evidenced in her following comment:

> *Who's always up the latest, having fun, or as others see it, causing problems? Skaters!! Who can drink the most beer? Skaters of course!! Who can mosh the hardest? It's skaters!!*

While I will expand on this theme shortly, it is important to note here that drug taking and incredibly high levels of alcohol consumption are de rigueur modes of behaviour within this culture of extremity. An apposite comment by Ben reflects this extreme mentality: 'on Friday nights, I just sleep where I fall'.

Extreme music

Irrespective of whether one skates, climbs or mountain bikes, there is a certain commonality in their appreciation of particular styles of music. Punk is a genre of choice for extreme athletes, and it is this link between sport and music that I wish to explore now. As I argue in the following pages, the dangerous, 'in your face' and 'on the edge' characteristics of extreme sport are reflected in the character of punk music.

In positing a link between extreme sport and extreme music, I am not suggesting that skaters and climbers *are* punks — the class base and attendant ideological project of each activity is clearly different. Whereas punk has long been taken to represent the consciousness of working class youth, extreme sports are amongst the cultural pursuits of the relatively well to do. What I am suggesting, however, is that the aggressive nature of punk, with its associated dangers of moshing and its long history of tragic heroes who lived hard and died young, resonates with the construction of self as it is presented by extreme athletes. As Simon Jones (1988) has noted, young people use music to situate themselves historically, culturally and politically, and it is through punk music that extreme athletes do precisely this.

That the genre of punk music is embraced by skaters and climbers is perhaps not surprising. The emergence of 'arguably the most dystopian and nihilistic postwar counterculture' (Humphreys 1997:150) in the mid 1970s coincides with the rise in popularity of extreme sports. While it is not my intention to document the historical development of punk, it is important to note that two distinct musical traditions converge in the style of punk that is listened to by extreme athletes here in Australia. The anarchic, aggressive British tradition of The Sex Pistols, manifested in the music of contemporary bands such as Black Grape, The Prodigy, The Happy Mondays and White Zombie, merges with the American tradition of The Velvet Underground, Iggy Pop, Blondie, The Ramones and The Patti Smith Group, which comes to life in the 'fun' style of punk that is played by groups such as Rancid, Green Day, Burn the Priest and Offspring, as well as in the alternative 'Seattle' music scene which has produced bands such as Pearl Jam, Sound Garden and, of course, Nirvana.

Played at relentlessly high volume, contemporary punk can be characterised by its absence of ballad or melody, and by its use of very fast, often intricate, rhythms and percussive lines. Punk is, to quote Roland Barthes, 'muscular music' (1977:149). With its 'raw' lyrics that are constructed around simple syllables, punk eschews the 'cooked' style of dance, techno or other forms of popular music' (Frith 1978:159) that are defined by their high levels of studio production. Ugly and harsh, the musical equivalent of giving the finger, the style of punk that is embraced by local skaters and climbers is both aggressive and chaotic. For these young men and women, punk must be either 'hardcore', 'noise core' or 'crusty', and the bands that are listened to must be ones that 'you can go sick over', to use the local parlance, or that 'have big style'.

Punk intersects with the lives of extreme athletes in a variety of ways. Skate and climbing magazines, rather than more mainstream outlets such as *Rolling Stone* or *Smash Hits,* advertise punk CDs, as well as reviewing the concerts of international artists. Gigs for local bands such as The Blood Sucking Freaks are advertised in climbing gyms, along with 'bass player wanted' and other such announcements, which are pinned to their walls, as well as to those of suburban bike and skate shops. Mountain bikers listen to punk so as to get psyched for training, while bands such as Offspring, Down By Law, Green Day and Blink 182 blast from the car stereo when travelling to out-of-town climbing destinations such as the Flinders Rangers or the Grampians.

Equally, the fashion style of climbers and skaters borrows heavily from 'thrash fashion'; a style described by one punter as 'clothing you can mosh in'. Loose fitting pants (often Rip Curl, Quicksilver or the US import labels of FUCT, Porn Star, Globe and Zoo York), Vans (which are a particular brand of suede sandshoes that are popular amongst skaters), and long sleeved T-Shirts printed with the names of punk bands or the slogans of the No Fear clothing company, characterise the dress and appearance of these extreme athletes. In the presentation of this particular look of extremity, a stylistic bricolage of sorts takes place in which two distinct subcultural styles are merged so as to form and enact a new cultural logic.

However, it is in the ways in which certain characters are elevated to positions of heroic pre-eminence amongst extreme athletes where the intersection of punk and sport is made most apparent. Every subcultural group creates its own heroes; and for climbers and skaters, their musical heroes are those who publicly dramatise this notion of 'life on the edge'. In particular, bands and singers who battle addictions with drugs and alcohol are seen as embodying risk and extremity in their purest forms. Being 'drug fucked' as Melissa puts it, is the mark of a truly heroic life.

Certainly, punk has a long tradition of overdose deaths, most famously that of Sid Vicious, and the discourse of alternative rock routinely expounds the notion that true stardom is, and must be, a fatal attainment. The heroin fuelled suicide of Kurt Cobain, the alcohol binges of The Replacements, the public 'detoxes' of Shaun Ryder of the Happy Mondays and Perry Farrell of Porno for Pyros and Jane's Addiction (the name says it all) position these artists as heroic figures in contemporary times. In each instance, the addiction of the artist is seen as a risky pay off for their genius. To quote one fan, whose words I lifted from one of the many Nirvana home pages on the world wide web, 'Kurt Cobain put a gun to his head... but the echo of that shot still has not died' (http:// www.kaiwan.com/rockrap/archive/arch124a.html).

I argue that this construction of artist as gambler opens up a new imaginative space between the listener and the singer, with many extreme sports playing fans supporting punk artists who openly admit to an involvement in the drug scene. As Melissa recounts, 'I went and bought the Black Grape CD, *It's Great When You're Straight... Yeah!* because the guy [the lead singer] said he had taken lots of drugs'. As such accounts make clear, the public articulation of their involvement in drug taking ensures that the punk entertainer remains, for the extreme athlete anyway, a heroic class apart from other performing artists.

Perhaps predictably, drug taking is an extremely popular pursuit amongst climbers and skaters, with everything from beer and dope, to ecstasy, speed and heroin, being routinely and widely consumed by these young people. More than this, drug taking is seen as a badge of honour amongst climbers and skaters. The harder one plays, the greater the degree of subcultural acceptance.

The analytic point to emerge from such anecdotes is that contrary to the popular view that sees drug taking as a means of escape, for extreme athletes, drugs are about heightening their emotional responses rather than dulling them. Drugs are about living for the moment, rather than escaping from it. The movie *Trainspotting,* with its graphic depiction of drugs as offering an intense, exciting rush, is a popular favourite amongst extreme athletes, and such media representations of drugs as fun resonate with local opinion. As Simon (the mountain biker) notes with regard to the taking of ecstasy:

> *I think people are looking for ways to transcend the boredom of just getting by, and if you've ever dropped an E [ecstasy tablet] then you know there is more to life than just shopping.*

Such narratives construct for the extreme athlete a heroic life that knows no limits. It is here that I draw on the work of Mike Featherstone to further elaborate this notion of a heroic life. As Featherstone identifies:

> *If everyday life is usually associated with the mundane, taken for granted, common sense routines which sustain and maintain the fabric of our daily lives, then the heroic life points to the opposite qualities... It points to an ordered life fashioned by fate or will, in which the everyday is viewed as something to be tamed, resisted or denied, something to be subjugated in the pursuit of a higher purpose* (1992:160).

Performing extremity: Indy Fest 500

So far, I have detailed a series of mini performances, through which a heroic life can be enacted, through which an extreme spirit can be presented. As I have already made clear, the physical risks of skating and climbing, as well as the dangers of drug taking, articulate the close relationship between action and experience for extreme athletes.

The remainder of this paper focuses on the *major* performance of Indy Fest, illustrating some of the ways in which the grand narratives of risk taking and living on the edge can be elaborated through these sorts of 'youth culture celebrations'. Despite the festive atmosphere of such occasions, fairly profound renderings of the very core of social identity are nonetheless expressed and embellished at these events. Notions of individualism, the heightening of emotional responses, the transcendence of personal limits and perceptions of death and danger are all articulated by those in attendance. Once again, it is the centrality of punk music to the staging of Indy Fest that allows climbers, skaters and mountain bikers to reflect upon and express aspects of their heroic life.

Indy Fest is by no means a unique or an isolated event. A veritable global calendar of alternative music festivals exists at which skaters and climbers amongst others, can, to use the local expression, 'really go off'. Usually running over several days, these grand performances include Lolapalooza in the United States, Glastonbury in the United Kingdom, and closer to home, Livid, the Off Shore Festival in Torquay, Victoria, as well as the local events of Somersault, The Big Day Out and, of course, Indy Fest 500. This last festival provides a fairly recent ethnographic example of the intersection between extreme sport and extreme music. As I argue in the following pages, a key part of the success of Indy Fest is its capacity to reconstruct the genre of punk music so as to marry extreme sport with extreme music.

Taking its name from the Indy Car 500, the slot car race held annually in the American city of Indianapolis, Indy Fest 500 is seen as providing all-round thrill seeker entertainment. Staged annually each April, Indy Fest is held in the grounds of Adelaide University, immediately providing a clue as to the demographic make up of those in attendance. Billed as 'South Australia's biggest alternative music festival', Indy Fest is a twelve hour extravaganza that merges skate culture with punk culture.

Offering an overload of excitement and entertainment, Indy Fest serves to dramatise the intensity of an extreme lifestyle in a variety of ways. The subjective experiences of risk taking and living on the edge are constructed, not simply through the engagement of skaters and climbers with specific musical texts, but also through a broader range of goods and resources. Mosh pits, gyroscopes, skate ramps, BMX jumps, fashion parades and beer tents are provided at Indy Fest, all of which offer seminal sites at and through which one can articulate his or her extreme spirit. In other words, a unified system of signs and symbols is present at Indy Fest, out of which a range of materials can be assembled to reflect and enact the spirit of extremity.

To illustrate the merging of skate and punk culture, one has to look no further than the list of acts that performed at 1998's Indy Fest. The band line up included The Living End, TISM (This is Serious Mum), Sick of it All and Something for Kate, who are all influential players in the Australian punk/indie rock scene. In addition, several professional skaters were recruited from the American cities of San Diego and Richmond, Virginia, to help entertain the crowds with their 'head flips', 'ollies', 'drop ins' and a range of other skating manoeuvres.[6]

Once again, two distinct subcultural styles were combined so as to enact a new cultural logic. As one member of the audience, Josh, describes it:

> *I went to Stage 4 where 99 Reasons (a local Adelaide band) had just begun it's set. They were incredible. The punk songs were as good as anything I'd heard, and the ska got everybody skanking. The skaters went sick, so it wasn't like watching a normal band. It was more hard core than that.*

For this particular punter, extreme music festivals, like extreme sports themselves, promise to take him faster, higher and further than all others. More than this, events such as Indy Fest bring to life the subcultural syncretism of extreme sport and extreme music. Ben, the party hard skater who sleeps where he falls, describes his experience of this year's Indy Fest:

> *Skating on a ramp, next to a live band is pretty exhilarating. There's a connection between the harsh music and the thrill of the skate. It's all about high energy levels. Skating is high energy, the music is high energy. Hard and fast, the whole lot of it. It's a buzz you just have to catch.*

Whether in the beer tent or on the skate ramp, Indy Fest provides several opportunities at which being 'in your face' and 'on the edge' can resonate with the on ground responses of those in attendance.

Moshers and madmen

While the skate ramp and the beer tent certainly offer sites at which to enact some sort of extreme spirit, few locations raise it to symbolic pre-eminence in the way the mosh pit does. At every alternative music festival, a large part of the audience adds a unique atmosphere by engaging in a practice known as moshing, and Indy Fest is no different. A highly corporeal, dangerous, activity, moshing is a generic term used to describe the practice that involves rough, physical contact between concert goers. Slamming, pogoiing or skanking in time to the music sees bodies deliberately and repeatedly collide with one another — as one 'mosher' puts it, 'you get pounded'. In other forms of moshing, members of the audience are passed across the top of the crowd, often over distances of several metres, in a practice known as crowd surfing, while in another variation, concert goers leap from the stage into the (hopefully) waiting arms of the crowd below, in a sport known as stage diving.

Not surprisingly, the mosh pit (the area in front of the stage) is a seriously dangerous place. Broken bones, blood noses and lost teeth are frequent occurrences: at a Metallica concert, a young man was taken away in a neck brace, while at a Smashing Pumpkins concert in the United States, a woman was trampled to death. However, far from suggesting an increased need for care or caution, such instances have been appropriated by local moshers as some sort of macabre learning curve in which they simply learn from the mistakes of others. As Dave recognises:

> *Nobody wants that kind of hardcore carnage. I mean, no-one should die at a concert, but if you've got a good set of people in the pit — by this I mean big people, medium people, and little people, including girls, then the mosh pit will be well behaved, and it won't become a 'fight 'till you die' concert.*

As befits the construction and presentation of self by skaters, climbers and others, mosh pits are transformed into places where they can emerge as daring figures who routinely enact the spirit of extremity when stage diving, slamming, skanking or crowd surfing. For moshers, the very real prospect of injury, or even death, strikes the tension between risk taking and tragedy that is part and parcel of living on the edge. Rules and unruliness exist simultaneously in a precarious balance. To quote Dave again:

> *There's always going to be accidents, but as long as certain places are set aside for moshing, and you can find a place that isn't in the middle of bum fuck, then nobody needs to get hurt. It is a set of consenting people who want to mosh, not just 'if you are in the way you get hit'.*

In other words, moshing embodies the heroic life of the extreme athlete. It is a perilous expression of identity, experience and lifestyle. It epitomises the enactment of those heroic accomplishments which hinge on the heightening of emotional responses. One mosher describes the experience as 'a freedom, an inhibition, like I've never felt before', Dave describes it as 'better than sex', while another describes it as 'going beyond drugs and alcohol'.

As the example of moshing demonstrates, aspects of an extreme lifestyle are repeatedly amplified through events such as Indy Fest. Offering a range of sites at which an extreme spirit can be presented, enacted, embodied and legitimated, the importance of events such as Indy Fest is that they serve to *spectacularise* extremity. Whether on the skate ramp or in the mosh pit, when extremity is dramatised through particular performances, its cultural resonance becomes most pronounced. As Palmer & Jankowiak have noted, 'it is through performances, whether individual or collective, that humans project images of themselves and the world to their audiences' (1996:226). It is through performance, in other words, that 'the self' can be most strongly and unmistakably presented. As my (necessarily abbreviated) account of Indy Fest has illustrated, it is the centrality of punk music to the staging of this event that allows skaters in particular to both reflect upon and perform aspects of their distinctive social life.

Conclusion

To conclude, what I have tried to do in this paper is to show the processes by which some of the narratives and practices of skaters, climbers and mountain bikers come to find a certain resonance with the genre of punk music. My discussion of an extreme lifestyle, with its emphasis on 'catching the buzz', illustrates some of the ways in which this extreme spirit can be repackaged and represented for public display in the grand performance of Indy Fest.

That the genre of punk music strikes a chord with the ways in which extreme athletes present themselves makes for a serious and contradictory challenge, both to punk's historical roots and to its political leanings. My intention however, has not so much been to explore the ways in which sport and music are used to resist hegemonic structures and institutions, as it has been to outline the ways in which certain ways of thinking and talking about dangerous behaviour have become crucial narrative themes in the packaging of an extreme sports identity.[7] Despite the festive rhetoric of 'a youth culture celebration', Indy Fest is nonetheless a slick commercial production that commodifies and trades upon the spirit of extremity.

Certainly, dominant norms and values can be and frequently are challenged through sport and music, but my project has not been to invoke this particular spirit of resistance, but to describe an extreme spirit. Part of my reluctance to pursue this thread of resistance stems from my own cynicism about the self-construction of a heroic life as is presented by skaters and climbers in Adelaide. These are rich, university educated, kids who skate, climb, listen to punk, mosh and drop Ecstasy, which perhaps begs the question as to just how dangerous, just how risky, just how confronting any of this actually is. But, whether or not these are seriously risky activities is not the point. That skaters, climbers and mountain bikers think they are is what matters for this paper, and with this in mind, I would like to conclude with a quote from Erving Goffman:

> *when an individual plays a part, he implicitly requests his observers to take seriously the impression that is fostered before them. They are asked to believe that the character they see actually possesses the attributes he appears to possess, that the tasks he performs will have the consequences that that are implicitly claimed for it, and that, in general, matters are what they appear to be* (1959:9).

Notes

1 Extreme sports are known elsewhere as 'whiz sports'. First appearing in France in the early 1970s, whiz sports grew out of a conflict between the skiers and the coaches of the French Ski Federation. The clash revolved around two divergent notions of training. Some skiers spoke out against the work oriented nature of training and proposed more playful practices. As Midol and Broyer suggest, they 'promoted a concept of fun that should be experienced in the here and now' (1995:206).

2 In pointing to the risky nature of these activities, I do not wish to suggest that there is a universality to the experience of risk. The subjective experience of each extreme sport ensures that the meaning and interpretation of risk remains unique to each. For some, the dependence upon equipment produces the 'fear factor' that its practitioners seek, for other sports, that they are undertaken at great heights increases the chance of injury or death, while for B.A.S.E jumpers, getting busted by the cops is one of the risks that accompanies this particular sport. Thus, as Hilliard points out 'each leisure activity has its own dimension of risk taking behaviour, and the form of risk taking differs markedly from one activity to the other'(1989:311).

3 The highly specialised nature of skating argot is clearly of note.

4 A half pipe is a ramp that literally looks like a pipe cut in half. What Melissa is referring to is the nerve racking trick of skating from the top edge of the ramp.

5 The female skater is a notable exception. Females who are associated with skating are commonly placed in the marginal role of girlfriend or supporter and are often referred to as 'Skate Betties'.

6 San Diego and Richmond, Virginia are widely regarded as the 'homes' of punk and skate.

7 This marks a break with typical ways of analysing sport and music as subcultural resistance. See Hebdidge (1979), Thornton (1996), Cushman (1995) and Nerhrig (1997) with regard to music, and Birrell & Richter (1987), Donnelly (1988), Gray (1992) or Humphreys (1997) with regard to sport.

References

Barthes, R. 1977, *Image, Music, Text,* London: Fontana.

Beal, B. 1995, 'Disqualifying the official: an exploration of social resistance through the subculture of skate boarding' *Sociology of Sport Journal* 12: 252-267.

Birrell, S. & Richter, D. 1987, 'Is a diamond forever? Feminist transformations of sport', *Womens Studies International Forum,* 10: 395-409.

Cushman, T. 1995, *Notes from the Underground: Rock Music Counter Culture in Russia* (Suny Series in Sociology of Culture) New York: State University of New York Press.

Denski, S. & Stolle, D. 1992, 'Metal Men and Glamour Boys: Gender performance in heavy metal' in Craig, S (ed.) *Men, Masculinity and the Media,* Newbury Park: Sage.

Donnelly, P. 1988, 'Sport as a site of 'popular resistance' in R. Gruneau (ed.) *Popular Culture and Political Practices* , Toronto, Garamond Press.

Featherstone, M. 1992, 'The heroic life and the everyday life', *Theory, Culture & Society* 9:159-182.

Frith, S. 1978, *Sound Effects: Youth, Leisure and the Politics of Rock,* London: Constable.

Goffman, E. 1959, *The Presentation of Self in Everyday Life,* Middlesex: Penguin.

Gray, J. 1992, *Mountain biking as counter culture,* Paper presented at the North American Society for the Sociology of Sport Conference, Toledo, OH.

Hebdige, D. 1979, *Subculture: the Meaning of Style,* London: Routledge.

Hilliard, D. 1989, 'Finishers, competitors and pros: a description and speculative interpretation of the triathlon race' *Play & Culture* 1(4):300-314.

Humphreys, D. 1997, 'Shredheads go mainstream? snow boarding and alternative youth', *International review for the Sociology of Sport* 32/2:147- 60.

Jones, S. 1988, *Black Culture, White Youth,* London: Macmillan.

Midol, N. 1993, 'Cultural dissents and technical innovations in the whiz sports' *International Review for the Sociology of Sport* 28:23-33.

Midol, N. & Broyer, G. 1995, 'Towards an anthropological analysis of new sport cultures: the case of whiz sports in France' *Sociology of Sport Journal* 12:204-212.

Nehrig, N. 1997, *Popular Music: Gender and Postmodernism: Anger is an Energy,* New York: Sage Press.

Palmer, G. & Jankowiak, W. 1996, 'Performance and imagination: towards an anthropology of the spectacular and the mundane', *Cultural Anthropology* 11 (2):225-258.

Thornton, S. 1996, *Club Cultures: Music, Media & Subcultural Capital,* Wesleyan University Press.

POPULAR MUSIC: SCENES, IDENTITIES AND CULTURAL CAPITAL

MOTTI REGEV

❖

I mean maybe I make too much of this. Let me not state this as the way it was but as the way I took it to be at the time. I felt that it was almost like a resistance movement. I felt that the autonomy that kids felt was incredibly important, that they really felt that they were an army almost in disguise... that it was a whole alternative lifestyle, that it was a secret society. The look itself was an unanimous look, it was a look which individuals could recognize in each other, but their employers couldn't see, their parents couldn't see, and importantly enough, couldn't object to either. And yet, just by slight changes in the way that you carried your overcoat, you know, if you carried it on the left hand, it meant that you were up to the minute; or if you had an umbrella and held it half way up one week; or if you had a hat, a bowler, and didn't wear it, or if you had a bowler and wore it... I mean, all these little details, even to the point where sometimes which button you did up on your three-button jacket showed whether you were really up to the mark or not.[1]

The things to which I want to draw your attention in this short excerpt are, first, the phenomenon Peter Townshend is talking *about,* namely, mod subculture and by metaphor 1960s counter culture in general; second, the text of music/movement/image captured in The Who's performance; and third, the representation in the 'present tense' of the excerpt of Pete Townshend as a mature, relaxed, prestigious elder of rock culture. The relationship between the first two things on the one hand, and the third one on the other hand, is at the focus of this paper.

This extract from an interview with Pete Townshend, songwriter and guitar player from The Who, and unofficial spokesman for the 1960s rock music scene in general and for the 'mod' subculture in particular, typically reflects the inseparable connection between music, body movement, visual appearance and identity that characterizes popular music in the second half of this century. The 'mod' visual appearance, the way the members of The Who move on stage while singing and playing, and the music itself — sound and lyrics — are jointly but one typical moment in a history of 'scenes' or 'subcultures' in the second half of this century. From the 'teddy boys' to 'hip-hop', 'rave' and 'club-culture', the history of popular music in the second half of the twentieth century reads like a series of cultural identities. Each one of them has been characterized by a musical style, and a specific visual image as well. Thus we have, at times, this inseparable connection between sonic textures, as expressed in vocal delivery, 'colour' of musical instruments and rhythm, typical haircuts, clothing articles, body gestures and ways of dancing, as expressed in the actual conduct of musicians and fans, or in their representation on film, television and photography. In addition, as can be learnt from the Townshend interview, much of these identities have been perceived by their members and leaders as expressions of resistance against adult culture.

But the representation of Townshend in this documentary exemplifies an additional element of the history of popular music in recent decades, namely the legitimization of some of the contents, meanings and practices of rock culture, and the canonization of some of its works and musicians. From 1950s rock and roll up to the very recent hip hop, grunge and dance scenes, popular music's contents and meanings have been increasingly legitimized as major expressions of contemporary culture.

In what follows, I want to offer a broad sociological re-examination of our understanding of the relationship between such identities and their processes of legitimization. My general proposition is that these identities, as 'scenes' or 'subcultures', are in fact the avant-garde, real life cultural workshop in which aesthetics and meanings are formulated, in order to later be selectively adopted by mainstream culture and transformed into legitimate cultural capital. They are, in other words, the constantly changing frontier of a contemporary, continuous struggle over the redefinition of legitimate cultural capital.

This paper is divided, roughly, into three parts. The first part is an assessment of the centrality of subcultures or scenes in the popular music of recent decades; the second reviews the major theoretical perspective within which subcultures have been studied, namely, as expressions of resistance and rebellion; the third part offers an alternative theoretical perspective, which looks at subcultures and scenes as stages, or moments, in a wider cultural struggle over the classification and redefinition of legitimate cultural capital.

Adapting a concept that was originally associated with the sociology of deviance, popular music studies tended to use the term 'subculture' for the socio-cultural entities in which music and visual image are closely connected. The concept implied a self-conscious socio-cultural formation, located in places and contextualized in space and time. In other words, it implied a sense of real life community. The work of the global culture industry, however, spread the contents and meanings associated with each subculture to millions of youth around the world. For a large proportion of them, living in small cities or in countries on the periphery of Anglo-American culture, membership and participation in subcultures was never full and complete, but rather partial and sporadic. Mediated through radio and television programs, magazines, films or advertisements, such remote membership in subcultures could often mean blurring the difference between them, and membership in more than one way. It was an act of consumption, a life style component, rather than the real thing of full membership and participation.

Realizing this, the concept of subculture has been replaced in some quarters of popular music studies by the concept of scene, a term that was taken from the vocabulary of fans and musicians. Here, the sense of identity which is embodied in music and appearance has been transformed to imply something which is less confined in terms of place and less defined in terms of social organization. Rather, a scene is a socially looser cultural framework, in which the existence of a community is, to a large extent, mediated through mass media consumption, making it more of an imagined, or even virtual community, spread in space, yet very real in its existence for its participants and members. In retrospect, one might claim that all past subcultures were, in fact, scenes.

Be it as a subculture or as a scene, the triangle of music, visual images and identity remains a cornerstone of popular music studies, an essential unit of analysis. It dominates the historical and sociological image we have of popular music history, and in particular pop/rock history. I am saying this in order to emphasize that the following brief historical description of our perception of the role of scenes is based on such images and is not necessarily a verified empirical truth. Conventional knowledge within this context of popular music studies identifies two turning points or dividing lines in the history of popular music in the second half of the 20th century. One is the advent of rock'n'roll in the mid 1950s, the other is the splintering of the pop/rock tradition into a plethora of scenes and niches in the early to mid 1980s. The first dividing line symbolically represents the very emergence of music and appearance as twin cultural tools for constructing identity. Conventional knowledge tells us that before rock'n'roll, popular music was regarded mostly as pure entertainment, and if its production and consumption did contain elements of identity construction, they were not connected to specific forms of visual appearance.

The first twenty-five years of rock culture, from 1955 to 1980, which I think we can refer to by now as the *formative* period of the rock era, are typically characterized by a series of consecutive subcultures or scenes. Each one of them, until the punk subculture of the late 1970s to early 1980s, is usually regarded as a response to the decline, or sell-out of the former one. Our image of rock history of that period contains a strong element of linearity, of development, which culminates in the subculture, or scene, of punk — probably the ultimate, or ideal-type subculture.

The period following the decline of punk, that is the last fifteen to twenty years, is characterized, in contrast, by the coexistence of subcultures or scenes. Our perception of the socio-cultural map of popular music in this period emphasizes plurality of scenes and even their subdivision into 'niches'. The socio-cultural map of popular music, within pop/rock tradition, currently includes several major scenes, like hip hop, electro-dance, metal, alternative and the set of local scenes contained under the Western ethnocentric name of 'world music', or 'world beat'. Each one of these scenes is often subdivided into certain niches of style and appearance. The point I want to stress is their coexistence in time and space: each one of them contains, separately, a type of linear change of innovation and then legitimization that resembles the one which dominated the whole field in its formative period.

What do we make, theoretically, of this description, of this image we have of the history and socio-cultural mapping of the field of popular music? I think that one major concept that has long been at the core of our understanding of scenes and subcultures is, indeed, resistance. Following the ideology of fans and musicians, subcultures and scenes have been theorized as expressing, implicitly or manifestly, resistance and rebellion against dominant culture. Generally inspired by a Marxist tradition of the Gramscian type, popular music studies tended to interpret the combined meanings of appearance and sound within various scenes as expressions of critique, of refusal to be assimilated into or be part of dominant mainstream culture. Scenes have been understood as the locus of struggle of young people against meaninglessness, consumerism, competitiveness, nationalism, racism and so on.

One major consequence of this theoretical perspective has been a certain skepticism, a scholarly critique of the transformation of subcultural contents and meanings into components of mainstream culture. Concepts like 'co-optation' or 'incorporation' have been in use for referring to the 'loss of authenticity' or commercialization of what were initially authentic meanings of resistance or subversiveness.

Thus, the succession of subcultures in the formative period of rock is sometimes portrayed as a sort of cyclic process of resistance, co-optation and as a response, a new, revitalized subculture of resistance. The coexisting plurality of scenes in the past twenty years is sometimes perceived as a sort of competition regarding the true core of resistance. Namely, where does true rebellious authenticity reside these days: is it in the 'alternative' scene? in the hip hop scene? in the techno scene? or maybe in the various indigenous world-beat scenes?

I think a continuing academic focus on the theme of resistance and authenticity tends to ignore or at best distort a major historical and cultural fact about popular music. Namely, that much of the meanings and contents of past subcultures have been institutionalized as components of legitimate culture. Some musical works of earlier subcultures have even been canonized as 'masterpieces' of contemporary civilization. Chuck Berry, Bob Dylan, Talking Heads, New Order, Public Enemy and Nirvana are just a handful of names among many whose works have been consecrated through various discursive practices as 'masterpieces' of rock as a musical art form. In other words, the other side of the co-optation and commercialization of scenes and subcultures is legitimization. 'Loss of authenticity' is in fact institutionalization.

Taking this knowledge, this historical and cultural fact into consideration, I want to argue that individual scenes in the field of popular music, and the pop/rock culture as a whole, are and have been essentially moments in a wider contemporary, partially successful struggle over the redefinition of legitimate cultural capital. This argument is inspired and influenced by Weberian sociology in general and by the sociology of Pierre Bourdieu in particular, and I want to say just a few words of clarification.

For a major tradition in sociology, whose founders are Max Weber and Thorstein Veblen, the core of conflict and struggle in society resides in concepts like status, prestige, legitimacy and recognition. Largely within this tradition, Bourdieu's notion of cultural capital, or more precisely legitimate cultural capital, is a relatively recent and influential conceptual addition. One possible definition of cultural capital is: institutionalized and widely shared cultural signals used for the demonstration of social respectability and even social superiority. The two most relevant types of cultural capital here are: firstly, *embodied* cultural capital, that is, preferences, attitudes, and body language; secondly, *objectified* cultural capital, such as art works, books, and domestic artifacts of various sorts. Throughout modernity, legitimate cultural capital has been associated with high culture and the humanities. Ownership, mastering and knowledge of preferences, attitudes and body language, of art works, books and other objects associated with high culture, have been the major components of legitimate cultural capital with which members of prestigious classes demonstrated and practiced their social superiority.

I think that what we have been experiencing since the 1960s, as a deep cultural change, is to a large extent a classificatory struggle over the institutionalized contents of legitimate cultural capital. In this struggle, speakers for and producers of contemporary cultural forms — that is, cultural forms associated with broadcasting and with the culture industry, for which the derogatory term 'mass culture' was in use — have been claiming legitimacy and demanding recognition. In other words, they were working for the inclusion of these cultural forms within legitimate cultural capital. Film, television and popular music are the three major cultural forms around which these struggles have been waged.

In a wider sociological perspective, this classificatory struggle is homologous with the emergence of new class fractions in contemporary urban and industrialized societies. It has been noted by many sociologists of the past twenty years, that changes in the spread of higher and professional education, and the emergence of new high-tech, business-administrative and cultural industry related professions, has produced social categories variously known as the new class, the new middle class, the professional class and other names. These classes, or class fractions, have gradually generated structured interests in distinction, in formulating and defining a cultural identity different from those older or traditional prestigious class fractions. In fostering an identity of their own, they have perceived themselves to be socially superior, yet different from earlier privileged classes. Being media literate, the status interest of these class fractions produced a homology with the struggle for the legitimacy of film and popular music, in which the latter became the major ingredient in the new cultural capital of these class fractions.

Within the context of this struggle, and in regard to popular music, scenes and subcultures have been serving as the cases and examples where popular music is demonstrated to have 'serious' meanings of identity construction and aesthetic value. Scenes have provided the materials, the evidence, around which the claim for legitimacy and recognition for popular music as a serious cultural form has been formulated.

However, the success of this struggle, that is, the success to gain recognition and legitimacy for popular music, has the consequence of dismantling the sense of micro-identity of scenes and subcultures. Legitimacy means disappropriation of contents, meanings and musical works from their subcultural context, and making them publicly and generally available as components of much larger taste cultures or taste categories.

It is exactly at this point, the issue of legitimacy and recognition, that the 'cultural capital' perspective drastically differs from the 'resistance' perspective in the theorizing of popular music. As long as we talk about 'struggle', the differences between the two are minimal. Both perspectives perceive the practices, contents and meanings of scenes and subcultures as the embodiment of a contest over meaning and of new forms of identity. There is a crucial difference between the two perspectives of 'success', that is, the success of a given social or cultural movement to realize its goals. The perspective of resistance tends to equate the legitimization of the meanings and contents of a given scene, its full or partial institutionalization as part of mainstream culture, with 'failure'. The academic vocabulary speaks in this regard, as I said, about co-optation or incorporation, as a sort of transcription of the fans notion of 'selling out'.

Thus, from the resistance perspective, the formative period of rock is sometimes characterized as a consecutive process of incorporations of subcultures, of moments of resistance, into dominant culture. So much so, that after the perceived co-optation of punk in the early 1980s, there has been much debate about the 'death' of rock.

From the cultural capital perspective, the legitimization and recognition of practices, contents and meanings originally associated with scenes and subcultures is, by way of contrast, a realization of a cultural transformation, the success to make legitimate culture into something different from what it used to be. Scenes and subcultures serve as arenas of exploration and formulation of contents, meanings and practices which later become the tools with which contemporary forms of distinction are practiced. Scenes are the socio-cultural test grounds in which specific species of objectified and embodied cultural capital are generated.

I think that one of the major contributions made by Bourdieu to the sociology of art and culture is that he made us realize that much of what has been going on during modernity in the fields of art, under concepts like innovation, avant-garde or canonization, can be better explained and understood by adapting concepts such as heresy, orthodoxy and consecration, originally associated with the sociology of religion.

Applying this perspective to the history of popular music, we realize that the logic of heresy inscribed in rock culture is, in fact, a strategy for gaining eventual legitimacy and recognition. Examining scenes in this way, we realize that, sociologically, the demand for legitimization is unavoidable. The seeds of institutionalization are there, at the core of any scene or subculture.

I want to demonstrate this by saying a few words about my current study of the trance music scene (psychedelic trance or Goa trance) in Israel. I hope most of you are familiar with this specific subculture of electronic-psychedelic dance music; outdoor, weekend-long raves, with the colorful back-to-nature and futuristic visual style of posters and graphics.

The seeds of a demand for legitimacy which I just mentioned, are to be found in the growing dissatisfaction of musicians with their role as providers of dance tracks. This produces a growing split between the subcultural regime of value, in which the functional role of the music for dancing and raves is emphasized, and the artistic regime of value, in which musicians and other industry professionals push the music towards variance, sophistication and recognition as a general form of expression.

I believe this split exemplifies the nature of the processes at work in all contemporary scenes and subcultures.

Notes

1 Interview with Peter Townshend from the film *Cool Cats — 25 years of Rock and Roll Style,* directed by Terrence Dixon, Delilah Films, 1983.

CROSS-CULTURAL PERSPECTIVES ON GUMLEAF PERFORMANCE BEHAVIOUR

ROBIN RYAN

Anyone can toy with a gumleaf, but its mastery as a musical instrument is the property of specialists who rarely play a tune 'straight'. The unique form of musicianship exclusive to the art of gumleaf features devices such as wobbles, waa-waa, slides and shivers. Their manifestation is the result of collective creative development, but is subject to varied cultural inflections. Whereas non-Aboriginal Australia projects gumleaf music as a national icon, most Aborigines view it as a 'traditional' cultural activity. Two discrete agendas of cultural symbolism are therefore attached to gumleaf music.

Based on the observations of Aboriginal and non-Aboriginal gumleaf players viewed over five consecutive years, this paper seeks to demystify the improvisational grammar of the gumleaf and to show how — with its strong emphasis on western notions of musical property — the canon of competition compromises the eco-cultural, social, physical and musical qualities which so markedly characterise the Aboriginal gumleaf music tradition. In particular, the Aborigines' energetic, holistic performances still bear the influence of their half-century long gumleaf band tradition and their ecological interaction with the natural environment. This paper concludes with a cross cultural scheme for conceptualising the variable performance behavior of Aboriginal and non-Aboriginal gumleaf musicians respectively.

As the year 2000 approaches, the intensification of nationalist discourse places particular importance on the Australian people's possession of musical and other icons. Although the practice of leaf playing extends beyond the island continent, gumleaf playing is an identifiably Australian activity, with the sound as well as the sight, smell and taste of gumleaves begging the construction of an Australian identity. This paper focuses on a gumleaf music-culture connection which embraces environmental, physical and musical qualities which lie outside of the mainstream popular music circuit.

The Aboriginal and non-Aboriginal[1] leaf music traditions have impinged one on the other yet each basically commands its own unique flavour in Australian music. By drawing on aspects of the uniqueness of oppositional aesthetic systems, I will present a preliminary cross-cultural scheme for conceptualising the idiosyncratic musical behaviour of each cultural group. Rudimentary features of gumleaf performance, such as grip, stance and gesture, will be divided from features of musicianship such as tone and timbre, loudness and ornamentation in my analysis of eleven Aboriginal and non-Aboriginal leafists respectively. To fit in with the theme of this conference I will afford particular attention to the work of leading Aboriginal gumleaf exponents Herbert Patten and Roseina Boston, and I thank each for authorisation.

I did not set out to represent competition as a contradictory cultural site, but as this study progressed it inevitably took on the nature of a personal account. I became sensitised to ways in which

Fig. 1: Roseina Boston

Fig. 2: Herbert Patten

the invading culture has suppressed indigenous expressions of leaf music in order to advance their own socio-political and nationalistic agendas. Furthermore, I contend that the considerably rich Aboriginal contribution to leaf playing has been compromised by a canon of competition which upholds artificial rubrics as to how Australian gumleaf music should sound. A result of this is that the musical standardisation demanded of participants in gumleaf contests exposes the few remaining Aboriginal contestants to a subtle grey-out or loss of distinctiveness, which all but disenfranchises them from their cultural, spiritual and environmental attachment to gumleaves as sound producers.

The combined feedback of indigenous musicians and research participants[2] revealed a consistently possessive attitude to the gumleaf instrument as Aboriginal cultural property, with most asserting that their ancestors possessed a long and skilled association with leaf soundmakers,[3] and all deeply committed to the notion that gumleaf music is 'traditional'. Most remembered hearing leaves played in the local circulation of a mission or fringe settlement. Naturally enough, this evocative ingredient of everyday life led to their conceptualisation of gumleaf music as a tangible aspect of their background and heritage. Their use of the term 'traditional' in relation to the activity serves to redress the notion that it might be 'untraditional', even though none could say how the gumleaf instrument was bound to tribal teachings or mythology.

Twentieth-century proliferation of the practice of gumleaf playing, including both the band and competitive solo traditions, has veered to the southeastern crescent of the mainland (see Map 1). Gumleaf bands emerged as a popular movement in the 1910s — if not sooner — as Europeanised musical idioms began to prevail upon Aboriginal popular taste. As a result of the processes of culture contact, Aborigines were compelled to substitute Western musical repertoires for traditional songs and dances. As they incorporated these into their oral music-making, tunes were easily adapted to suit the pitch ranges and idiomatic qualities of leaf instruments. Classical trills, jazz 'blue' notes and waa-waas were definitely of introduced origin, but it is not yet possible to say whether the techniques of sliding between notes, pulsating leaf vibrato, wobbling, and playing the leaf 'no hands', emerged indigenously or by introduction.

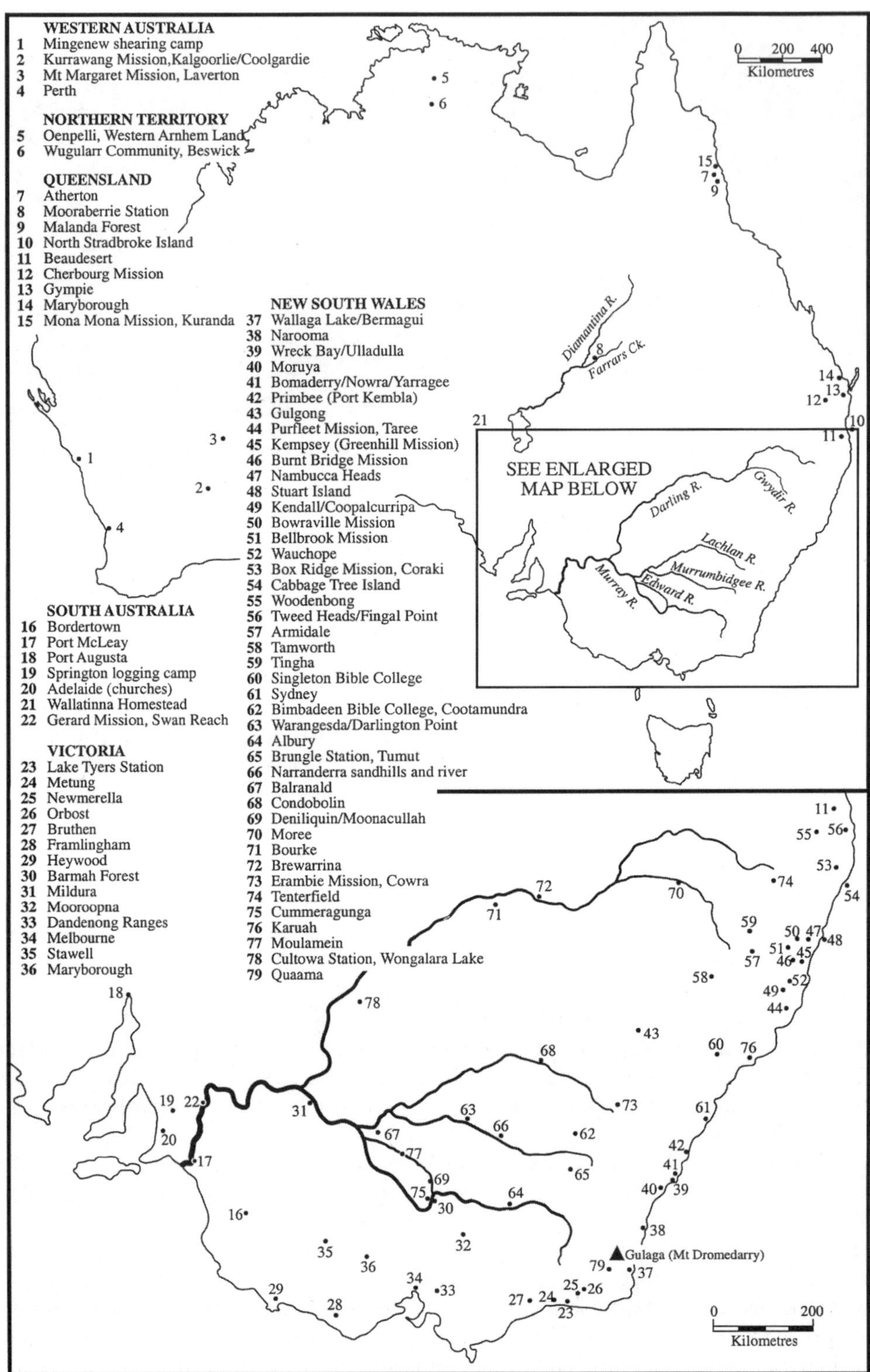

Map 1: Documented locations for Aboriginal gumleaf playing (sources complied 1892-1998)

Gumleaf ensembles mushroomed well into the mid-twentieth-century, often constituting quartets, trios and duos rather than formal bands. On the southern coast of NSW, the Wallaga Lake Gumleaf Band linked a localised form of indigenous musical practice with its Westernised counterparts over a period of approximately sixty years, beginning in the 1910s. A relatively autonomous group, they flourished in the 1920s and 1930s, when their popularity extended far beyond their own community.

The Wallaga Lake Aboriginal Station was not formally attached to a church mission, therefore remnant traits of Aboriginal performance behaviour were exhibited in conjunction with the step-dancing, singing, accordion and fiddle music which supplemented gumleaf items. Jimmy Little Senior often dressed in tribal paint and threw spears on stage, an indigenous form of clowning which had been spurred on by the fashionability of vaudeville and blackface minstrel shows during the previous decades. To the rhythmic beat of a kangaroo-skin drum, gumleaves were played loudly in parts to simulate the shots and shells of the battlefield in the more tear-jerking acts. Although they occupied the bottom rung in society's ladder, the bandsmens' music was alive and wandering, carefree, yet polished — so much so that they were co-opted to march at the opening of the Sydney Harbour Bridge in 1932. Likewise the Lake Tyers Gumleaf Band of Gippsland, Victoria was highly vulnerable to the cultural and financial exploitation of tourism and was regimented to stir up a martial spirit for World War II.

The John Meredith Collection at the National Library of Australia contains oral historical evidence that several elderly and recently deceased gumleaf players were taught by Aborigines during the early twentieth-century, enthusiastically 'adopting' a perceived Aboriginal leaf instrument. Some earlier instances of gumleaf playing emerged amongst settlers, with the Salvation Army having played a crucial role in encouraging the practice of gumleaf playing from the 1890s. Most notably, Captain Tom 'Mudgee' Robertson[4] nurtured gumleaf pupils around 1900.

The leaf gained popularity as a form of 'novelty noise' in the 1920s, thus furnishing an economical source of amusement during the 1930s Depression. As a means of remuneration the practice persists among at least three individuals up until the present day.

Contexts for the non-Aboriginal leaf music tradition included stage shows, amateur hours, fairs, harmonica and dance bands, and homely bush bands. Some cross-cultural sharing of gumleaf music probably occurred in shearing sheds, even though Aboriginal and non-Aboriginal men did not share the same world-view and cultural heritage.

The attempts of Aboriginal leafists to articulate their inner cultural space includes the transformation of (perceived) pre-existing cultural traits into emblems of identity. Leaf birdcalls form part of their evolutionary interpretation of leaf music, as well as reinforcing one possible solution for its roots. Herbert Patten and Roseina Boston hail from widely separated locations yet independently expend intense energy in their loud, holistic performances. With their cooperation I identified some predominant native flora and fauna and we recorded the birdcalls which they produce on specific leaves in a deliberate 're-enchantment' of the environment (see Table 1).

Herbert's own research indicates that the mopoke owl and black swan or *guniyaruk* calls were culturally significant for his ancestors, the Brabuwooloong branch of the Kurnai of Gippsland. The 'on-water' and 'in-flight' calls of the *guniyaruk* form a powerful part of the way in which Herbert understands his life within the Australian environment.[5] Herbert tries to reproduce these sounds in his various performances and talks for the Aborigines' Advancement League, Melbourne.

Gumbaynggir Elder Roseina Boston is a great-niece of Possum Davis, who conducted the 1920s line-up of the Burnt Bridge Gumleaf Band. Roseina connects her gumleaf sounds with the beautiful natural environment at Nambucca Heads, NSW where she reports that special totems such as storm birds, rain birds and screeching black cockatoos were 'bestowed' on her people by ancestral spirits to strengthen self identity. 'This is how we played the leaf,' Roseina claims, 'imitating birds, just as we imitated animals and birds with our dancing'.

More than anything else, Roseina enjoys playing her gumleaf to the birds, in fact, they often gather around her as she plays and she believes that they talk back to her. She produces the cacophonous laughs of her personal totem, the kookaburra, on a brittle gum leaf, using a technique called 'shivers'.

SPECIES OF BIRD	CALL DESCRIPTION	MUSICIAN	SUITABLE LEAF
1. Owl (mopoke) of Gippsland	atmospheric call inspired fear of dark	HP	Terpentine
2. Gippsland Black Swan (Guniyaruk)	on-water: subdued 'ooo' in-flight: loud, gutteral squawk night-time: growl in the throat	HP	Gippsland Mahogony
3. Eastern Whipbird	male: whipcrack female: whistle and trill	HP	Box
4. Lyrebird on Gulaga (Mt Dromedary, NSW)	imitates Koori Lone Whistle	HP	Box
5. White Sea Hawk	a 'whipping' sound	HP	Yellow Box
6. White Cockatoo	low-pitched 'Cocky' talk	HP	Yellow Box
7. Robin Redbreast	whistle followed by 2 or	HP	Yellow Box 3 lower or higher notes
8. Turtledove	subdued warble with an abrupt ending	HP	Yellow Box
9. Rainbow Lorikeet	similar to a wolf whistle	HP	Yellow Box
10. Bush Magpie	beautiful, balanced	HP	Yellow Box 'stereo' turnaround
11. Black Cockatoo (a rain-bringer)	high-pitched squeak kee-ya, kee-ya ('someone's coming!')	HP	Yellow Box
12. Kookaburra	laughter, chuckles and croaks	RB	Brittle Gum
13. Leatherhead (Soldier Bird)	'look out!' (a warning)	RB	Brittle Gum
14. Willy-Wagtail	twittering prattle	RB	Brittle Gum
15. Eagle (NSW)	shrill, silvery cry	RB	Spotted Gum
16. Curlew (Death Bird)	ghostly descending wail	HP	Yellow Box

LEGEND: HP = Herbert Patten
RB = Roseina Boston

Table 1: Birdcalls produced by Aborigines on leaf instruments

Roseina once noticed some boys preparing to shoot parrots and pleaded with them not to do so. When they did not heed her she instinctively plucked a leaf from the nearest spotted gum, simulated the eagle's tremulous screech, and scattered the parrots.

Many illustrations could be made of the reinforcement of Aboriginal cultural identity through gumleaf playing. In short, my observations show that when Herbert and Roseina entered the Australian Gumleaf Playing Championship a compromise was made with regard to their particular beliefs, capacities and strengths as their own awareness of what they are trying to convey as Aboriginal persons comes into conflict with a 'deforming space'; 'deforming' since all competitors were required to operate under the same eurocentric criteria.

The annual Golden Gumleaf Award had been operating at the Golden Wattle Festival in Maryborough, Victoria since 1977 and constituted the major gumleaf competition of its type.[6] Following the initial promotion of the event,[7] twenty-two inquiries were received from Victoria, New South Wales, South Australia and Queensland. One inquiry, written on 10 July 1977, read as follows:

> *I heard that white-man WALLY FRENCH play a gum leaf other (sic) night on TV Chan. 2 Sydney - Me, blackfellow Australian gum leaf player - I think I leave him for dead. Please send me application form for competition. Cedric Barnes (Harrison 1997: 2).*

The provision of a venue 'open to players of any background' attracted the participation of five Indigenous adults and one child between 1977 and 1997,[8] but the Golden Gumleaf Award had always been organised, sponsored and adjudicated by non-Aboriginal officials and had only ever produced non-Aboriginal champions.[9] Since the majority of contestants are non-Aboriginal, I applied extra data from my fieldtrips to construct Tables 2 and 3 (Aborigines viewed at the contest are marked with an asterisk).

INDIGENES	GRIP	STANCE	GESTURE
ATKINSON, J *	2/h, t/l	s/m	natural body language
BALLANGARRY, J.I.	2/h	s/m	corroboree steps
BOSTON, R *	2/h, t/l	s/s, t/f	tells stories with leaf
BULL, W. (Bill)	1/h, 2/f/t, b/l	n/a	n/a; arrested for busking
DUNGAY, J. * (Goorie)	2/h, b/l	s/w	cheerful busking antics
GROGAN, C.	2/f, b/l, c/f, n/h	s/m; h/b	played leaf to cattle
MARR, B. (Goonabahn)	1/h (2/f)	s/m	animated quartet player
PATTEN, H. *	2/h (cf/sf); t/l	s/w; d	pronounced corroboree steps
THOMAS. T. (Guboo)	1/h or 2/h	m/d	jitterbugging
THORPE, W.	2/h (c/f); t/l	s/w	extroverted only if sound is good

NON-INDIGENES	GRIP	STANCE	GESTURE
BERRIS, M.	1/h or 2/h (c/f)	s/s	plays on a potted tree
BOSTON, H.	2/h, t/l, n/h	s/s	plays 'no hands'
CARTER, D.	2/h (c/f); t/l	n/a	copied mouth organ gestures
ELWOOD, P.	2/h (c/f), b/l	s/m, t/f, l/f	embraces leaf, climbs tree
EVA, W.	2/h, b/l	s/s	sedate; mimes flute fingerwork
GRAETZ, K.	2/h (c/f)	s/s	no particular gimmicks
LOCKWOOD, W.	1/h or 2/h (cf)	s/s	jumps from tune to tune
McLAUGHLIN, W.	1/h, 2/f, b/l	s/s	no particular gimmicks
REUTENS, V.	2/h (s/f)/n/h	s/m, t/f, b/l	Klezmer-like antics artistic fingerwork
ROBERTS, F	b/l (cf), n/h	s/m, s-s, l/f, t/f	microphone effect with hands
WILMOTT, J.	2/h (c/f)	bends knees, t/f	hands over nose, thumb up

LEGEND: HAND GRIP: 2/h = 2 hands; 1/h = 1 hand; 1-2h = 1-2 hands; n/h = no hands; 2/f = 2 fingers; 2/f/t = 2 fingers & thumb; c/f = cupped fingers; s/f = spread fingers **MOUTH GRIP:** b/l = bottom lip; t/l = top lip **STANCE: s/s = standing steady; s/m = alternates between steady & mobile stance; s-s: moves from side to side; l/f =** leans forward; s/w = standing/walking; s/t = sitting; d = dancing; t/f = taps foot; h/b = on horseback

Table 2: Variations in gumleaf performance behaviour (i) rudimentary features

It can be seen from Table 2 that gumleaf grip, stance and gesture are rudimentary features that, by and large, remain discrete to individuals rather than specific musical traditions. Interestingly enough, the three oldest players represented (namely Guboo Ted Thomas, Bert Marr and Walter McLaughlin) all grip the leaf with one hand only, although some Lake Tyers bandsmen had used two hands. Playing leaf 'no hands' was a common performance trait at Wallaga Lake as well as amongst Aboriginal stockmen. Today the tendency of most players is to hold the leaf with two hands. According to my sampling, Aboriginal musicians rest the leaf on either the upper or lower lip, whereas non-Aboriginal musicians more commonly rest the leaf against the lower lip. In some cases gumleaf grip may be determined by whether one's musical background lies with a vocal or instrumental tradition. Philip Elwood, a non-Aboriginal busker, purports to place his lips against the leaf in the same manner as he does the trumpet, whilst Salvation Army officer Mike Berris has a background in French horn which influences his embouchure and concept of tone.

INDIGENES	TECHNIQUES	LOUDNESS	TONE/TIMBRE
ATKINSON, J. *	slides	average to full	clear and bright
BALLANGARRY, J.I.	slides	average	shrill
BULL, W. (Bill)	slides	full	shrill and sweet
BOSTON, R. *	slides, shivers, vibrato	full	shrill and piercing
DUNGAY, J. (Goorie)*	bird tape backing	average to full	trumpet-like, clear and bright
GOLDEN-BROWN, A.*	slides	average to full	clear and bright
MARR, B. (Goonabahn)	slides	average to full	different timbres used in Taree gumleaf quartet
HERBERT, H. *	blue notes/vibrato slides/harmonics	full, resonant, vibrant	saxophone-like, 'muddy', 'dirty' or 'rough' jazz
THOMAS. T. (Guboo)	slides/vibrato	full	sharp/piercing
THORPE, W.	slides/vibrato	depends on character of tune	sharp/piercing

NON-INDIGENES	TECHNIQUES	LOUDNESS	TONE/TIMBRE
BERRIS, M.	classical trills	thin (soft)	whistle-like, clear
BOSTON, H.	slides	average to full	trumpet-like, clear
CARTER, D.	wobbles/slides/ vibrato	average	sweet/silvery/liquid, clear
ELWOOD, P.	slides/wobbles busker/climbs tree	thin/medium	thin, sweet/clear/smooth and clean
EVA, W.	wobbles/waa-waas, trills	average	silvery/flute-like, liquid
GRAETZ, K.	slides	thin/medium	whistle-like/thin
LOCKWOOD, W.	'minstrel' whistling/bird trills	full	shrill/birdlike
McLAUGHLIN, W.	'straight' tunes	average	trumpet-like, bright
REUTENS, V.	wobbles/waa-waas	thin/medium	smooth, clear and clean
ROBERTS, F.	tongue trills	average/full	saxophone-like, bright
WILMOTT, J	classical trills	average	ocarina-like/clear/liquid

Table 3: Variations in gumleaf performance behaviour (ii) musicianship

Even though at least a dozen male competitors learnt to play the gumleaf from Indigenous people, each went on to develop his own characteristic manner of playing. Inaugural champion Les Hawthorne became attached to the same cured leaf on which he perfected the trilling method for almost forty years. He kept the leaf pressed between the pages of his Bible, so that it retained the resilience of a playing card.[10] The late Fred Roberts, who learnt from Aboriginal leaf player Shady James, formed a family bush band at Tatura, Victoria. His daughter Wendy Eva is presently the only woman to have held the Australian gumleaf music title.[11] Fred and Wendy each adopted their own distinct style of playing, with Fred having perfected the art of playing the leaf 'no hands' whilst accompanying himself on accordion, and Wendy playing a dried leaf to her own 'mimed flute' fingerwork.

Varying degrees of human expressivity characterise the musical behaviour of gumleaf players. In their own communities Aboriginal leaf players performed standing, walking, dancing, seated – even up a tree or reclining on the ground. Their physical expression is usually relaxed, although the body language of the gumleaf bandsmen featured in the 1934 film *The Squatter's Daughter* was restricted to big-toe tapping whilst subject to white control. Herbert Patten often breaks into a spontaneous dance sequence whilst playing the gumleaf, displaying antics which he saw used at community dances and parties from the 1950s on. However, he can only move freely because he has his leaf technique 'down pat'.

Aboriginal performance behaviour is also moulded by the culture-specific symbols of language and dress, the previous amount of interaction with hosts, and the perceived cultural distance between traditions. Country and western dress, for example, is a by-product of the Aboriginal performers' minority position within non-Aboriginal society. Roseina Boston goes to great lengths to dress the part of the Aboriginal country and western artist (Figure 1), and also exploits the gumleaf as a means for enhancing her storytelling prowess.

During contests the gestures of non-Aboriginal players are comparatively restrained, with the exception of six-fold champion Virgil Reutens, the 'Larry Adler of the gumleaf'. When performing the 'gumleaf blues' Virgil sways his body backwards as he taps one foot. His strength as a performer lies in facility and reliability — indeed he is hardly ever seen to change leaf. (By far the most common reason for missed beats is the tearing or splitting of a leaf, in which case players swap to its underside or snatch a new leaf).

Most adjudicators of the Golden Gumleaf Award were media personalities who regard 'showmanship' and originality in presentation as a virtue,[12] although in recent years conservatorium trained musicians have been invited to judge. By 1994 players were being judged solely on musicianship, namely pitch, timing, whether they produced enough air to support phrasing, and on their uniqueness in portraying an item. In 1995 a new adjudicator stressed pitch, timing, individual creativity and musical definition; in 1996, clearness of tone[13] (which he defined as a 'violin-like quality'), musicality and improvisational ability; and in 1997, pitch, timing, dynamic contrast, overall musicality, ability to meld phrases together, and a 'violin-like quality'. With no textbooks on gumleaf playing to use as a precedent, the notion that a gumleaf should sound like a violin belies our common human tendency to resort to comparative descriptions. However, my collection of anecdotal evidence also indicates that the gumleaf has been mistaken for clarinet, trumpet, flute, ocarina, human whistling and the female voice.

In my view, a leaf should be free to sound like the species of leaf that it is rather than a weak imitation of a conventional instrument. Competitors from different areas have a range of pre-conceptualised gumleaf sounds in mind. Whereas one might prefer the sound of a tin whistle, another conceptualises the sound of a saxophone. A player's preference is partly conditioned by the timbre[14] of the particular leaf to which he or she has adjusted.[15] Timbre brings a certain personality or 'colour' to bear on the interpretation of a musical theme. Philip Elwood describes the timbre of the yellow box leaf as 'mellow' and that of the red ironbark as 'trumpety'. He chooses a yellow box 'Stradileaf' for romantic pieces; a red ironbark leaf for bright, sparkling major key tunes.[16]

Furthermore, the timbre of a single leaf may be altered by a change in a player's technique. In his interpretations of jazz, for instance, Herbert Patten deliberately produces the 'muddy', 'thick' timbre appropriate to a 'blue' note by humming into a leaf rather then merely blowing it. His 'wah-wahs' are produced by placing the leaf on the lower lip, so that one hand is free. He slides into long notes by manipulating his lips, cups his hands in front of his mouth to achieve a muted effect, or spreads them like a cone to aid dispersal of the sound (Figure 2). The imagined words of a song can modify gumleaf performance considerably through change of accent. In approaching the leaf as a seasoned singer, Herbert carefully enunciates the syllables of words in his mind as he plays.

As a child of about seven, Herbert noticed great-uncle Lindsay Thomas producing deep, resonant notes on a gumleaf. Herbert still emulates this style of playing, indeed his leaf can be heard at a distance of five hundred metres through thick mountain scrub.[17] Loudness depends on blowing pressure, and to a lesser extent the thickness and width of a leaf. The high-pitched gumleaf has been known to steal the tune from a tenor saxophone when the latter reaches the top of its range, its intensity can even drown a vocal part. The tendency of Aboriginal competitors to play the leaf louder than their non-Aboriginal counterparts reflects on their adaptation of an alfresco tradition which in some places once incorporated the echoing of leaf sounds across rivers or mountains. When teaching the gumleaf to younger Aborigines, Herbert and Roseina encourage loudness as a virtue, dismissing soft sounds as 'tinny' or 'anaemic'. Differences in gumleaf embouchure may also contribute to loudness, as Aborigines tend to play the leaf on the inside of the mouth. Unlike the other players interviewed, they cope well with *eucalyptus* nausea.

If we take the stance put forward by Curt Sachs (1943: 46) that 'an organist improvises in another style than a flutist (sic) or a violinist; every instrument creates its own style', then it follows that the gumleaf improvisational tradition should remain a most individualistic one. However, as the outcome of collective creative development, gumleaf improvisation relies on a stock of musical clichés which are not always the individual inventions which virtuosos claim them to be. Balanced on an artistic knife-edge with respect to musical proportion, competitors need to strike a delicate balance between improvising whilst at the same time applying 'good taste' and restraint in avoiding excessive use of sliding, vibrato and surface embellishments. The late Dudley Carter was a master of the 'wobble', which he produced by altering the position of his lips whilst vibrating his fingers back and forth. His smooth, vibrant tone was characterised by warmth and emotion and his clear-cut ornaments executed with innate musical sense.[18]

Over the five year period between 1993-1997, I observed and recorded the rendering of the compulsory tune. In 1993, five non-Aboriginal competitors played 'God Bless Australia' in fairly strict time with average loudness. Mike Berris played leaves attached to a potted eucalypt sucker named 'George Bush' to enhance his environmentally responsible presentation. This, and the standard jokes attached to performances on fig leaves in clubs, highlight leaf music as a form of Aussie humour. Herbert exhibited his own set of cultural values as to what constitutes 'good' gumleaf music. He used a louder tone than the other players, made striking use of gesture, and added extra rests between notes and phrases.

The selection of tunes such as 'Pub With no Beer' inadvertently appropriate the gumleaf instrument to perpetuate a maudlin Aussie identity, an outworn type of nationalism which is not necessarily appropriate as the turn of the century draws near. Nevertheless in 1996 ten entrants played 'Pub With no Beer' with a great deal of variation in tempo, style and timbre. Roseina Boston, amongst others, adhered to a country backbeat à la Slim Dusty, whilst Virgil Reutens added tinges of jazz to his rendition. As differing genres of leaf music have been performed side by side they have often exerted an influence of one on the other, although some patrons complain about the degree to which 'gumleaf jazz' has shaped other genres to its own image.

With respect to free choice repertoire, multi-instrumentalists Jeff Wilmott and Mike Berris are familiar with band marches, light classical melodies and old-time dance music, but most others opt for well-known songs.[19] Only one so-called 'traditional' Aboriginal melody has ever been performed at the competition,[20] the most obvious difference in samples of repertoire from each cultural group being the high percentage of hymns and war songs selected by Aborigines.

In its projected cultural symbolism, the gumleaf is undoubtedly an icon from which people have squeezed a quintessentially 'Australian' essence, although in my view the epithet 'Australian' is often applied in a restrictive way which serves only to trivialise the beauty of leaf playing. Through such agents as gumleaf contests and television commercials, gumleaf playing has increasingly become a site of hegemonic domination. The sentimental, 'give me a home amongst the gumtrees' style of nationalism projects gumleaf playing primarily as a white Australian bush performance tradition, whilst the Aboriginal solo tradition still bears the influence of the gumleaf band tradition as few Indigenous players would choose not to engage with their past heritage.[21]

The mutual and differential attitudes of contestants towards the competitive rubric reflect on the broad consequences of acculturation in the interface of psychology and culture. It is equally important to examine an Aboriginal leafist's 'reflected self' as well as the eco-cultural context from which local gumleaf playing traditions spring. Herbert and Roseina's avifaunal leaf music communicates something of the culture that they believe brought this medium into being. Both uphold the gumleaf to be a powerful and meaningful symbol of their identity, even though as individuals they are enmeshed in the complex social web associated with representation and the connections between music, identity, politics and power relations.

Shrinkage of Aboriginal musical culture resulting from the interference of European civilisation is obvious when we consider that almost all gumleaf repertoire used by Aboriginal players derives from the Western musical landscape. However, the types of sounds produced by competitors may differ vastly when they are juxtaposed to compete through an annual compulsory tune. Allowing for individual divergences, those aspects of performance behaviour which most readily distinguish the two schools of gumleaf playing are summarised in Table 4. The Aboriginal aesthetic involves extroverted body language, a penchant for loud dynamics, some tonal ambiguity and a leaning towards slow tempos and long pauses between phrases. All these features are culturally determined and generally idiosyncratic in their divergence from the practice of non-Aboriginal players.

FEATURE	INDIGENES	NON-INDIGENES
GRIP	leaf on top or bottom lip	leaf on bottom lip
STANCE	standing, sitting, walking, reclining, dancing on horseback, in treetops	standing
GESTURE	Men: extrovert women: sedate	less pronounced (excepting Virgil Reutens)
TONE AND TIMBRE	shrill, brass-like	whistle-like (mainly)
LOUDNESS	full, resonant	average
TEMPO	*ad lib,* some time-lag between phrases	fairly strict doubling the speed
SPECIAL TECHNIQUES	slides, shivers 'blue' notes, wobbles	wobbles, waa-waas

Table 4: Cross-cultural model for variation in gumleaf performance behaviour

(Sampling: 11 Aboriginal players; 11 non-Aboriginal players)

At best I have made a small statistical statement, but it indicates how some aspects of the Aboriginal gumleaf performance tradition still reflect the social and environmental principles of Aboriginal culture, not just those which had been adopted and adapted from European models.

My musical vision for maintaining a continuum of the tradition into the new millenium involves the establishment of a Gumleaf Music Festival which would provide instruction for beginners, folkloristic leaf presentations, and the opportunity for creative items to emerge with the gumleaf medium specifically in mind. Apart from 'Concerto for One Gumleaf' which Neil Seymour created and performed at the 1983 contest, I do not know of any other tunes which have been composed on or for the leaf. This is an area which could prove advantageous in showing how a tune might carry something of the character of the instrument itself.

Notes

1 In this paper I introduce individuals according to whether they are 'Aboriginal' or 'non-Aboriginal' since Aborigines are not necessarily 'black' and some non-Aboriginal leaf players are of Asian or mixed racial descent.

2 Most of my research participants live in NSW and Victoria; such a study has not yet been exhausted in other states.

3 The hunting leaf and child's leaf music toy, for example, may constitute tangible links between past and present. Aborigines living a tribal or semi-tribal lifestyle possessed a centuries-deep bond with the native flora, including multi-layered levels of understanding in relation to habitat, wildlife and totemism. Non-Aboriginal leafists, by contrast, often play introduced leaves. A more detailed discussion on this topic is forthcoming in my thesis *'A Spiritual Sound, A Lonely Sound': Leaf Music of Southeastern Aboriginal Australians, 1890s-1990s,* Monash University.

4 Born in Mudgee, NSW (birthdate unknown); 'promoted to glory' in 1927.

5 On one occasion in 1994 Herbert also mimicked the Eastern whipbird at a particular location on Gulaga (Mt Dromedary), NSW. He then crouched behind a tree and played the Koori Lone Whistle, a freemason-like signal through which Kooris disclose their identity to one another. A nearby lyrebird imitated the whistle immediately.

6 Others are the smaller-scale local 'Golden Leaf Award' held at the annual Bangtail Muster in Armadale, WA since 1991, and a South Australian state competition initiated in Karoonda on 5 September 1997 by former champion Cliff Dobbins.

7 Veterans were encouraged via local advertisements to come out of hiding to teach youngsters the skill. All who volunteered were non-Aboriginal men, most of whom hailed from Central Victoria.

8 Namely Ambrose Golden-Brown, Gordon Edwards, Herbert Patten, Roseina Boston, James Dungay and five-times Junior Champion Jarrod Atkinson.

9 Champions selected from 1977-1997 were Les Hawthorne, Dudley Carter, Wendy Eva, Cliff Dobbins, Fred Roberts, Keith Graetz, Virgil Reutens, Philip Elwood and Jeffrey Wilmott, with five having won the prize on more than one occasion.

10 Comment made by former adjudicator Terry McDermott, 5 October 1997.

11 National champion in1982 and 1985, Wendy is also the only person to date to have played a gumleaf solo in the Melbourne Concert Hall. This she did by invitation for the National Salvation Army Week Concert in 1973.

12 In 1984 the adjudicator took into account each contestant's ear for music, control of the leaf, choice of personal number, and the rendering of the compulsory tune, whilst in 1985 judgement was based on audience reaction, showmanship, the actual playing of the leaf, and choice of number. By 1989 criteria focussed on presentation, musical ability, tunefulness, and personal appearance (Harrison 1997: 12-13, 17).

13 Champions often speak of their 'gumleaf tone', the intensity of which they modulate to express fuller sentiment in their renditions of songs. My understanding is that they use the word 'tone' with reference to the timbre, pitch and strength of a gumleaf note in the same way that we ascribe 'tone' to the human voice. Variables include the species of leaf selected and the cultural background of players, who incorporate those qualities of tone which they like into their own tone via natural discrimination.

14 That property which distinguishes it from another leaf sound of the same pitch or loudness.

15 The variety of sounds which can be produced on countless species of leaves may even approximate the variety of sounds made by the human voice. In 1982 the adjudicator observed that every contestant in the finals played on a different type of 'gumleaf'.

16 Explanations of timbre are inadequate, with leafists and adjudicators sometimes resorting to dichotomous descriptions drawn from their visual, aural, tactile and taste bud senses, for example, rough or smooth, sweet or sour, liquid or dry, thick or thin, clear or muddy, dirty or clean, sharp or flat.

17 Lindsay Thomas was a member of the Lake Tyers Gumleaf Band, Victoria. The measurement described here was assessed with the help of Aline Scott-Maxwell on 15 February 1997.

18 Examples may be heard on tape TRC 2539/076 (National Library of Australia).

19 Philip Elwood's current repertoire of about fifty songs includes several Beatles numbers, Australian folk songs, and songs of the British Isles.

20 Herbert Patten rendered an untitled Yorta Yorta love song before playing the 1996 compulsory tune.

21 Roseina's great-uncle Possum Davis conducted the Burnt Bridge Gumleaf band, NSW.

References

Harrison, M. 1997, *Australian Gumleaf Playing Championship History 1977-1997,* Maryborough, Victoria: self published.

Sachs, C. 1943, *The Rise of Music in the Ancient World, East and West,* New York: W.W. Norton.

TRADITIONAL WORLD MUSIC AS POPULAR MUSIC: ISSUES OF RESPECT, AUTHENTICITY AND THE SPECTRE OF CULTURAL IMPERIALISM ILLUSTRATED BY THE CASE OF TAIKO — TRADITIONAL JAPANESE DRUMMING

PAULENE THOMAS

❖

Traditional culture is the current buzz! This is evidenced by Irish pubs, reiki groups, yurt style buildings, yoga classes, Polynesian healing clinics, Native American dance classes, WOMAD festivals, African drumming groups, belly dance troupes and all kinds of traditional music becoming popular music. This is a wonderful way of increasing international knowledge and understanding but it also has a far from wonderful side. The case of matsuri taiko (traditional Japanese festival drumming) illustrates this.

Matsuri taiko is essentially folk music. It is more than 1000 years old and its origins are explained in the Shinto myth of Amaterasu the Sun Goddess which forms part of the creation stories of Japan. Historically, taiko occupied a central role in village life — it told the time, warned of danger, scared animals away from the crops, encouraged soldiers going into battle and entertained the gods whose presence was the reason for and centre piece of all festivals. Due to Japan's geography and the difficulties of travel, communities remained isolated for long periods and many different styles of taiko evolved. Themes of taiko pieces were taken from life such as farming, fishing and forestry, dancing to please the gods or the ancestors and demon drumming to frighten away enemies. Taiko was at the centre of traditional Japanese life although not as an entertainment. This was reflected in such proverbs as 'if you play taiko badly demons become angry' and 'if you play taiko at mid-night ghosts appear'.

Despite its long history, taiko's time as a performing art has been brief, only beginning in the aftermath of World War Two when Japanese concerned about the rapidly increasing westernization of their society, looked for ways to attract young people back to their traditions. One answer was community based taiko groups providing culturally based social activity and entertainment. Taiko gradually grew in popularity until the first fully professional group (now Kodo) was formed in 1971. By 1975 they were touring internationally and other professional groups were forming. City administrators were getting involved — setting up taiko festivals and purchasing equipment for local groups. This trend reaching its zenith in the early 1990s when the small city of Ota spent over A$1000000 on one great Odaiko — a giant taiko. Thus taiko's future as a performing art was assured. Meanwhile, in the 1960s, the first overseas taiko groups were formed in North America by Japanese/American communities wanting to preserve links with their ancestry, eventually growing to over 50 groups in 25 years. The 1980s saw interest spread to Europe and groups formed in Germany, France and the UK. Australian groups formed in the 1990s and there are already four groups here presenting authentic taiko: AtaruTaru Taiko and Taiko School (SA); BacchiAtari (Qld); Murasaki Taiko and JAPEP Wadaiko (Vic) and TaikOz/Synergy (NSW). These groups all started from close contacts with Japan and world taiko[1], as well as a knowledge and love of its traditions.

Their performances and regular visits from Japanese groups signal taiko's arrival as popular musical entertainment in Australia. So far so good — respect for the art form and its traditions, close international contacts, friendship, fun, exciting entertainment and growing popularity, *but* taiko's popularity has brought it to the notice of a much less desirable element with a very different agenda. Taiko's fast growing popularity is very easy to understand. It has a strong visual element that makes it look just as dramatic and spectacular as it sounds. It exudes community spirit, teamwork, strength and vigour, it is accessible to ordinary people of all ages and it is the heart of a fascinating culture.

Sadly some musicians are oblivious to all this. They are attracted purely by taiko's burgeoning popularity. They are not interested in taiko's unique musical traditions, its role in its culture or its intrinsic qualities. Their intent is to scramble onto a popular bandwagon and exploit it however they can, especially since they perceive taiko as very easy to pick up and audiences as uncritical. True, many traditional pieces (developed by and for ordinary villagers rather than specialist musicians) do have quite simple rhythms. But each one also has its own meaning, special forms, stances and movements. And often kiais (shouts) or parts of songs go with particular pieces. For example, Taikobayashi, a 400 year old piece, has a very simple songline which anyone hearing it a few times could easily pick up, but there are also movements, changes of position, kiais and a variety of possible arrangements as well as other traditional percussion instruments.

Thus to present even the simplest traditional piece takes a bit of study and cultural understanding. To pick up the basics from some brief exposure, reproduce them as you see fit and claim to be presenting authentic taiko is not only dishonest, it is extremely arrogant and offensive. No culture is so lacking in depth that aspects of it may be understood from the most cursory glance. It is hard to credit, that in 1998, there are still people who believe they can give the musical traditions of others the once over, select what appeals to them and present the results as authentic world music! This lack of concern for the feelings and rights of the traditional owners would do any imperialist proud. Yet this is being done and not just by ignorant and unscrupulous individuals. There are music schools claiming to teach traditional music despite having staff who have not studied or performed such music. The result of this is musicians and music teachers with no sense of how offensive and dishonest it is to claim to present traditional world music on the basis of sketchy, casual instruction. This ties into an idea of traditional music forms being so childishly simple, that they can be taught by people with no background in them at all.

It is widely recognised that when a culture is debased, respect for its people is equally diminished. This has been seen all over the world in the recent histories of indigenous peoples. Traditional music has specific meanings and functions and is closely bound up with the identity of its people, whether these people are an indigenous population struggling to revive and protect their culture or the people of an industrial super power. Taiko is still important to Japanese identity as shown by its prominence in the opening and closing ceremonies of 1998's Nagano Olympics and its use as a gesture of friendship between Prime Minister Hashimoto and Russian President Yeltsin during the latter's April visit to Japan.

There are thousands of taiko groups in Japan ranging from kindergarten to professional level, and with tens of thousands of Japanese coming to Australia each year for a variety of purposes no-one should expect to present phony imitations of taiko and not be caught out. Musicians who attempt to compose taiko pieces after very limited experiences are like a classical musician who, after a few hearings of jazz, attempts to compose an authentic piece. But when the genre is part of another culture the results can be offensive as well as substandard.

To give an example: last August when AtaruTaru Taiko was performing in Japan, I was approached after a concert in Adelaide's sister city, Himeji, by two young women who said that, on a recent student exchange to Adelaide they had seen so-called taiko presented at a rugby game that was so strangely executed that they felt it must have been a joke or a send up of Japan. I informed both the club and Adelaide City Council's Sister City Committee and stressed the point that if aspects of other cultures are to be presented at big public events they must be checked for authenticity. Imagine the reaction if a group of local 'entertainers' presented a dubious version of the haka to a crowd with a substantial New Zealand content! Would-be imitators must be made aware that a bad imitation of a piece of cultural material is a parody and most people do not appreciate seeing their culture parodied by outsiders.

Apart from issues of honesty and respect there are also legal considerations in presenting traditional music. The fact that a type of music is very old does not give automatic exemption from issues of copyright and intellectual property. Many taiko groups that work in traditional style write and perform a lot of original material. Anyone who sees a performance and assumes that because the style is traditional they can copy the work and present it as they please could be making a huge mistake. Even when the piece is genuinely traditional, it is still not necessarily free from copyright. Most traditional taiko pieces can be arranged in a variety of ways and still retain their authenticity. Though not in just any way, so while the copied arrangement could be very old and in the public domain, it could just as easily be five years old and someone else's property. How does a person who knows virtually nothing about taiko tell the difference? Indeed how do they tell which elements are part of basic song and which are peculiar to that arrangement?

Taiko groups presenting traditional pieces customarily explain the area of origin, meaning and arrangement of each piece. Those who cannot do so give good reason to suspect their authenticity if not honesty. Another trap for the ignorant imitator is that certain configurations of drums have recently been developed by particular groups and individuals. Prior to World War Two, only a limited number of set ups were used. Copy the wrong set-up or claim a piece with a modern set-up is traditional, and risk exposing yourself as a fraud.

Contemporary technology makes it possible to pick up bits of information about traditional cultures previously accessible only by diligent study. Big taiko events and professional groups now have Web Sites on the Internet and so it is quite easy for all sorts of snippets of information to be picked up and used by unscrupulous individuals to create an impression of knowledge where none exists. What cannot be picked up is respect for the culture, understanding of and ability in its musical traditions and forms, and a grasp of what is in the public domain and what is not. Nevertheless, pieces continue to be lifted off the Internet and CDs in ways that demean both the art form and the rightful owners of the material because musicians assume the audience won't know the difference. However, as more people experience authentic taiko their exposure as frauds comes inexorably closer.

Many musicians in Japan and the US are now combining taiko with a variety of other instruments to produce different styles of music. And some very exciting and innovative compositions are resulting. There are also taiko groups working on very contemporary pieces using synthesisers and drum machines, as well as traditional taiko, to create new sounds. All forms of music continue to evolve with musicians pushing the boundaries through collaboration, use of new technology and unusual combinations of instruments. But this is very different from groups claiming to present traditional taiko, substituting inappropriate instruments because they don't possess the correct one and don't know enough about taiko to know how the lack of a certain instrument in a particular piece can be covered without sacrificing authenticity. A group that claims to be presenting a traditional piece, then uses taiko in a post WW2 set up with a set of bongos, is making its ignorance and lack of respect for the integrity of the piece, and the art form, very clear. We can only hope that Adelaide will not see such a spectacle again.

Another give away of the taiko phony is non-Japanese names for allegedly traditional pieces — especially when there turns out to be no direct translation into Japanese of the supposedly traditional piece's English title.

Elements of taiko are also moving into popular music through various styles of New Age music and through some of the rhythms of taiko being played on western instruments. The music thus produced is widely enjoyed and perfectly legitimate to present as long as the pieces themselves are in the public domain and it is not represented as traditional world music.

In view of all this can traditional world music be incorporated into music school curricula? Certainly, on two conditions. Firstly traditional world music cannot be taught properly in isolation from its culture so this information must be incorporated — and part of this entails the possession of authentic instruments — and secondly the school must have a teacher of sufficient proven knowledge on the subject. A person whose experience of Chinese history was limited to attending a few lectures would never be permitted to teach it at tertiary level, so what kind of staggering arrogance makes someone who has had minimal exposure to a form of traditional music consider themselves competent to teach it? And what sort of institution offers this dubious level of expertise to its students? Indeed what sort of institution places its students in a situation where they learn to present plagiarized pieces and substandard imitations and pay for the privilege? The bottom line is honesty and respect. Traditional world music carries the soul of its people and lifts the hearts of its audiences. It must not be reduced to a phony watered down shadow of itself by the exploitation of the unscrupulous. To its audiences I say, get involved, ask questions — to know it more is to appreciate it more. To would be performers, simply — love it or leave it alone.

Notes

1 This term refers to the taiko which has developed in the US, Canada, Germany, France and the UK as well as here in Australia, either through the efforts of the local Japanese community, whose families have brought the knowledge of taiko from Japan, or through non Japanese who have studied and performed taiko in Japan and retain contact with Japanese groups. I use it to refer to groups all over the world who are presenting authentic taiko, rooted in Japanese tradition.

GAZING AT THE SPICE GIRLS: AUDIENCE, POWER AND VISUAL REPRESENTATION

MANDY TREAGUS

❖

In considering the current Spice Girls phenomena, how are we to regard their huge girl fan base and the ways in which these fans gaze? Do we see this audience as passive consumers duped by the marketing machinery of late capitalism, or as active participators in the promotion of new models of female subjectivity? How are we to account for the ways in which young girl fans view the Spice Girls if current theories of the gaze seem inadequate?

While it is difficult to describe the identification process, Diana Fuss suggests that 'in perhaps its simplest formation, identification is the detour through the other that defines a self' (1995:2). In sociological studies of fans, especially young females, it has been found that a large part of the appeal of fandom has come from relating to other girls who are also fans. For instance, Sheryl Garratt has said that the greatest motivation for her and her group of friends in following the Bay City Rollers in the 1970s was a 'desire for comradeship' (1984:144). Such comradeship has often been expressed in the bedroom culture described by Angela McRobbie and Jenny Garber: that sometimes safe interior space formed, in opposition to male street culture, as a permissible place in which female adolescence can be negotiated (1976:220). This is born out by a study of young girl fans done by the University of York, which concluded that 'girls thought that girl power was about having fun with your friends' (Spice Girls…':1). Such comradeship is achieved through rituals of identification, such as those produced through interaction with the musical products of the star/s.

In the case of the Spice Girls, such identifications are produced in very specific ways. The girl fan's viewing position is complicated by the fact that the most common representations of the Spice Girls appear on television, 'a medium which has been seen as 'feminine' and one in which the division between image and audience is much more blurred (Joyrich 1996:40). As a medium which is also 'intimately tied to consumerism', television is most often viewed as 'low culture', and its audience theorised as passive (ibid.). The music video clip can be seen as an extreme example of television's dominant qualities. Functioning as both product and promotion, it is commonly fragmented, inconclusive and polysemic. As viewers of music video clips, Spice Girls' fans are placed stereotypically as passive objects, the ultimate consumers. Though the group *has* been heavily marketed, this in itself is not enough to account for the extraordinary success it has had. What then are the elements from which the audience has made such resonant meanings for themselves?

It is possible to see the Spice Girls as conventionally sexualised female figures, fulfilling admirably Laura Mulvey's notion of *'to-be-looked-at-ness'* (1975:19). The TV special, 'The Spice Girls Live At Istanbul' features their song 'Naked', during which all five women sit astride chairs which are placed so as to give the impression that all of them are, in fact, naked.[1] This program was followed immediately by 'Playboy's Really Naked Truth: Part One', reflecting the apparent view of the programmers that the two shows would have a similar audience.[2] Certainly the differences of representation between the song 'Naked' in particular and the Playboy show were a matter of degree, rather than style of representation. (The Playboy show contained more full frontal female nudity than I have ever seen on free-to-air television in Australia). So can one argue for ambiguity in the representation of the Spice Girls? And, importantly for the purposes of this paper, how are we to theorise the position of their vast fan base, a large number of whom are preadolescent girls?

The first Spice Girls hit, which was not only number one in the UK but entered the US charts at number one (as no other British debut single has done before), was 'Wannabe', and it presents a very particular version of the pop song romance, especially as presented by female performers. For a start, the style is assertive. Not only are the first few lines spoken, almost shouted, but they put the desires of the female first. Words are repeated, especially 'I wanna', so that both the tone of voice and the lyric build up an image of female self-assertion. There is an ascending circle of chords which adds to the level of excitement and the number of voices also creates a sense of power in the chorus. The other aspect that is asserted both lyrically, musically and visually is the value of female friendship over the heterosexual bond. While these sentiments might be commonplace in the work of radical female artists such as Ani DiFranco or Liz Phair (though less simplistically put), they are not common in the mainstream pop world, where romance follows much more traditional patterns. It's what 'he' wants that is generally the concern of both male and female artists, because all she wants is him. Likewise female bonds are an unspoken element which never threatens the centrality of heterosexual romance in mainstream romantic songs.

More recent UK female groups like All Saints and Eternal negotiate the potentially threatening image of four aligned women with a number of strategies. Some of those evident in the All Saints' hit song 'Never Ever' include the placement of the singer in a vulnerable and self-doubting position lyrically, in which she considers herself completely to blame for the break-up (and because a full minute of the song features spoken lyrics, they are more prominent in this song than is often the case); filming singers individually, rather than in a group; filming singers in positions which connote submission (such as eyes downcast, head-canting, hair across eyes) and above all, showing all the women to be in a state of lack because of the absence of the male. As they sing the performers walk through a house in which everyday items explode and machine gun fire peppers the walls behind them. These threats to their physical safety encode them as vulnerable, reinforcing this representation of the romantic female as weak, needy and lacking. They also appear to be objectified in terms of the display of their bodies, with much of the visual continuity provided by the constant display of cleavage. In its negotiation of the romance plot, 'Wannabe' is in stark contrast to this. The fact that both songs have been so successful shows that both carry a discourse which has found resonance in their audiences. 'Wannabe' is energetic, self-assertive, brash and expresses a confident independence which is not reliant on the male for its continuance. How much is the audience response a welcoming of the representation of this style of female subjectivity which up until the Spice Girls had only been seen and heard in independent recordings, and thereby largely been inaccessible to the young female? The fact that the response has been so overwhelming could be taken to indicate that the representation of such a subjectivity is long overdue for this audience.

In the hit single, 'Stop', the young female audience is very particularly addressed and cultivated. This is primarily achieved through the visual, though lyrically the song calls for a slowing down of the courtship process, another potential appeal to the younger girl as the female bonds are not threatened. The video is set in a working class British street, and rather than being the zone of young men, it is shown to be a place where girls play at hopscotch, skipping, cat's cradle and pat-a-cake. Not only are the young girls' activities represented, but the group are shown joining in, with the interactions of the Spice Girls mirroring that of the girls. This is a rare affirmation of girl culture in the music industry, still renowned for its 'blokeyness'. Visually it is female to female contact and activity which is predominant. At the same time the setting as a whole is an assertion of the local, commodified to serve the global promotion of the Spice Girls as product. The locals are depicted as working class simpletons who attend the local fair or drink in the pub, and who too can be coopted into enjoying the group's performance in the local hall.

Males rarely feature in Spice Girls' clips, and when they do they are never portrayed as something that would destroy the solidarity of the all-female bond of the group. This counter balances the impact of the romantic preoccupations of a number of the songs' lyrics. An extreme example of this is the clip for 'Say You'll Be There', which features the group as a band of female techno-warriors, who use martial arts and high-tech Ninja influenced weapons to capture a hapless male who happens to appear in his pick-up truck. Though the clip is presented as a narrative, with movie credits at the start introducing the Spice Girls as fantastic characters, this never develops beyond demonstrations of their skills. The shots of male bondage are unexplained, and function as symbols of male disempowerment, just as the rest of the clip serves to assert the power and fighting abilities of the women. In contrast to All Saints, these performers move confidently, demonstrate their own physical power, and don't display modes of bodily submission such as head canting. It's brash, it's assertive, and should the viewer have any doubts about its gender politics, the confused apparent pursuer is carried off on the roof of a car as a trophy. The song's ostensibly heterosexual and romantic lyrics are undermined by the show of combined female power and by the visual absence of any potential romantic male leads.

Such representations of female supremacy would be dull indeed if they were done without a sense of irony, but this is not the case. As in many representations of the Spice Girls, the irony comes from the knowing intertextuality of the piece. One of the better jokes in the movie is the casting of Meatloaf as the bus driver, and giving him the lines 'I'd do anything for the girls, but I can't do that'. In this clip's desert location and aggressive female personas, it draws on the imagery of the Tank Girl, thereby evoking a less mainstream feminist iconography (Driscoll 1998). It also refers to another icon of popular culture, in its allusion to a scene from Tarantino's *Pulp Fiction,* in which the character Mia Wallace (Uma Thurman), tells the character Vincent Vega (John Travolta) about a TV pilot she has made called 'Fox Force Five'. The clip of 'Say You'll Be There' seems to be an illustration of the five feisty women described by Thurman, characters who never made it into the realm of popular culture other than in a filmic conversation. This scenario must have a particular appeal for the Spice Girls, or for one of their consultants, as there is a direct steal from the dialogue of *Pulp Fiction* in *Spice World: The Movie,* again on the same theme, this time transmuted to 'Spice Force Five'. In this recuperation and celebration of popular culture, the Spice Girls play with the notion of the female warrior, taking on the heroic role that has been reserved in such culture for the male hero.

This sense of play in the exploration of subjectivities presents a greater range of possibilities for ego-ideals than is often the case in the area of popular culture and women and girls. The fact that there are five Spice Girls (at least in the first two albums and movie), each projecting a very specific persona, adds to these possibilities, a fact that groups have exploited for decades. In spite of this, are traditional ways of looking really disrupted by representations of the Spice Girls? Are they breaking ground or are the Spice Girls just reinscribing dominant modes of representation such as the *to-be-looked-at-ness* of women? In the negative, it is hard to deny that they project themselves as sexualised figures, who dress, at times, for maximum erotic impact. This was especially so of ex-Ginger Spice, Geri Halliwell, the former Turkish game show hostess, but is also true at times of all of them. Despite the apparently powerful personas displayed in the clip of 'Say You'll Be There', the performers at times enact stripper-like moves, caressing themselves and leaning forward to expose maximum cleavage. Apparently pandering to the male gaze has undoubtedly facilitated the group's exposure in the male-dominated entertainment industry, though it has not won them any credibility with the media as a whole. However, the question of whether the sexualised woman is necessarily a subordinated woman remains, and it provided the impetus for much of the academic debate around Madonna as a figure in the 1980s.[3]

One of the aspects of the representation of the Spice Girls which has the greatest impact on the gaze of the viewer is the function of the return gaze. The employment of direct address in many of the Spice Girls' clips means that some of the viewing power and sense of subjectivity remains with them.

Sally Stockbridge has claimed that the direct address of music performers always disrupts the functioning of the male gaze, because 'both male and female stars can 'look back' at the audience' (1990:103). The dominance of the male gaze is also undermined by the 'construction of rock stars as stars to be gazed upon, irrespective of sex, by fans both male and female' (1990:105). In contrast to groups like All Saints, the Spice Girls gaze out confidently at their audience, in a look which can be seen to signal both playfulness and power. However, while direct address may add to the power and authority of, for example, a news reader, does it always add to the power of a performer? Direct address has different functions depending on its context. If that context is a porn movie, for example, direct address can induce a fetishistic gaze which empowers the gazer rather than the performer. It could be argued that 'Say You'll Be There' functions successfully as porn, with its futuristic scenario and the direct and erotic address of its performers. It also functions convincingly as a model for the female heroic, however, suggesting that there is no one preferred reading of this clip, but rather that at least two viewing subjects are produced by it. There are, in Graeme Turner's words, 'different readings of the same text' (1993:125). I believe this kind of ambiguity has contributed to the success of the Spice Girls, who have had to be seen to satisfy conventional ways of looking, while at the same time creating new points of identification for the adolescent female viewer.

Unlike Madonna, however, the Spice Girls do not make specifically erotic or sexually transgressive clips. Early in her career, as Brian Longhurst has stated, Madonna was 'seen as an inauthentic product of the culture industry who was involved in the exploitation of others for the gain of that industry' (1995:123), a description which is remarkably close to the way in which the Spice Girls are seen most commonly today. Madonna's sexual identities, which were initially viewed as exploitative, were later celebrated as forms of postmodern play in which differing subjectivities could be explored. Why is it that we are not prepared to see the Spice Girls in this way and that any media mention of the group is not complete without a joke at the expense of their supposed inauthenticity? Have we lost our sense of postmodern fun, or is it their girl audience that makes us feel they are 'less than' in the popular music field? Madonna, though she explores different kinds of sexualities in her music clips, never entirely dispenses visually with the male lead as the Spice Girls have done so regularly, thereby providing a point of ego-identification for the male. Are the negative reactions to the Spice Girls a reinscription of the old rock/pop binary which valorises the musical passions of young men and denigrates the musical enthusiasms of young girls? And if they are seen as inauthentic, are we, in fact reinscribing the modernist notion of the artist as a gifted individual who, individually, produces 'art'? Are we attempting to reinstate divisions between 'art' and 'commerce' which would set apart some products of the music industry as high culture?

Certainly in the world of popular music, such divisions are quite current, even if they have been broken down largely in older fields. Motti Regev has argued convincingly that the way popular music attains the status of art is through two main attributes which are generally spoken of in terms of 'the jargon of subversiveness and authenticity' (1994:87). The difference between the way in which Madonna's sexuality functions in her music, her clips and in her publicity, is that this provides the site of her rebellion and subversion. Though early in her career her sexuality was seen to be a sign of her inauthenticity, its subsequent encoding as subversive in fact gave her credibility in the popular music world. The issue of authenticity is a complex one, but the history of popular music being what it is, very few women have been able to cross the boundary from mere pop to authentic rock performer. If they have done so, it has generally been via the display of attributes usually seen as 'male'. In Madonna's case, though she is not universally seen as high art in the popular music scene, she has managed to convince the music audience in general of her creative control, and is seen as a 'self-contained unit of creativity' (Regev, 1994:92). She is thus perceived as both subversive and authentic. The Spice Girls have so far failed to achieve this. Though they are given first song-writing credit on all of their songs, it is assumed by both music public and rock press that they are mere puppets in the production of musical product, thereby lacking authenticity in terms of the way popular music has come to be valued by both its practitioners and its critics. However, the young female audience is not necessarily concerned with such criteria. The almost entire exclusion of female performers from the popular music canon may be one of the reasons for this. The Spice Girls have achieved success with their audience by appealing to other criteria, which has not won them fans in the rock press, but has won them the devotion of millions of girls around the world.

If the Spice Girls do not use their sexualities as a site for subversion, do they merely reinscribe traditional ways of viewing? Most of the objectification occurs through the display of their bodies through dress, and this need not be seen as simply sexual, or as traditionally satisfying the male gaze. Each Spice Girls dresses in a distinctive way, with everything from the Marilyn Monroesque cum Playmate outfits of Ginger, to the Umbro tracksuits worn by Sporty. In between is Posh in short designer dresses, Scary in leopard skin pants and bikini tops and Baby in powder blue, pigtails and with a Chupachup accessory. Collectively, the effect draws attention but does not necessarily imply subordination. As Kaja Silverman has suggested, Western fashion 'challenges the assumption that exhibitionism always implies woman's subjugation to a controlling male gaze' (1986:139). Fashion can be seen, as it has been in connection with Madonna, as a means of exploring subjectivity and asserting the self. If, as Silverman asserts, 'clothing is a necessary condition of subjectivity — that in articulating the body, it simultaneously articulates the psyche' (1986:147), then the brash and collectively exhibitionist clothing of the Spice Girls can be seen as the expression of confident and innovative subjectivities. Their clothing marks them as female, even feminine (though not always, especially in the case of Sporty). In asserting themselves as females worthy of success, the Spice Girls have to negotiate terrain faced by female figures in other forms of popular culture. If they give up the markers of femininity, will they still be seen as women succeeding, or will they become substitute males? In asserting a brash and confident femininity, the Spice Girls leave no doubt about their subjectivity as women. Their clothing indicates that they are definitely not substitute males, though as women they do explore traditionally male roles. A big part of the way in which the young female fan views the group's clothing styles is as a form of play. This is made clear when visiting the semi-official Spice Girls Internet fan site. Maintained by 15 year old Simon Dixey, it features pictures of would-be Spices from around the world, competing to look the most like the originals (Dixey 1998). These pictures of fans, some of whom are preschoolers, show just how much fashion can be a sophisticated form of dressing up. That the fans understand this aspect is shown by their responses, and suggests that their gaze may not be so concerned with the sexualisation of bodies as with the sense of play in the dress. 'Play' is an important part of the Spice Girls' appeal. In their response to viewing the Spice Girls, many girl fans 'play out' their gaze, which is both an expression of their identification and of the fact that their gaze often has a very practical and bodily expression. My own observations, anecdotal evidence from others, and the University of York study, suggest that when young female fans, especially pre-teens, watch the Spice Girls, they do so in order to learn both lyrics and dance moves. Their activities together centre on 'dancing, role-playing and singing' ('Spice Girls…':1). The gaze of these fans has a bodily expression in which they 'do' the Spice Girls themselves, and viewing pleasure is played out in the bodily pleasures of dancing, singing and dress.

The displacement of heterosexual, and indeed, *sexual* relationships can be seen to be part of placing this music into the sphere of the young girl, who is either pre-sexual or more comfortable, if adolescent, in holding the whole sexual process at bay for a little longer. This is confirmed by the University of York study, which concluded that 'the more adult aspects of the Spice Girls go over the heads of younger fans, who do not include notions of adult sexuality in the term 'girl power' ' ('Spice Girls…':1). While the girl fan can be seen to be in preparation for heterosexuality, her current erotics appear more concentrated on the bodies of both herself and her female contemporaries, as demonstrated by the preponderance of female images in adolescent girls' magazines. How young girls might be said to view the Spice Girls is similar to the way in which they might read *Dolly* or *Girlfriend*;[4] such publications can be seen to be contributing to the internalisation of the male gaze by training girls to conform to a particular narrow model of femininity. However, while a case like this can be made regarding some of the ideological work achieved by both band and magazines, I believe that more is going on in both instances. While Mulvey's thesis can serve to explain how representation in film constructs a male viewing subject, can this account for the predominance of images of females in both women's and girl's magazines? A glance at *Cleo, Cosmopolitan, Vogue* or a dozen other similar publications reveals a preponderance of apparently erotic images of women and for women. According to Diana Fuss, women's fashion photography 'provides a socially sanctioned structure in which women are encouraged to consume, in voyeuristic if not vampiristic fashion, the images of other women, frequently represented in classically exhibitionist and sexually provocative poses' (1992:713-714). Such a tendency is also obvious in girls' magazines. Fuss suggests that though the text accompanying such images directs its audience toward identification rather than voyeurism, the images nevertheless invite a desiring gaze. She then goes on to postulate a third way of looking, 'a position that demands both separation and identification, both a having and a becoming — indeed, a having through a becoming' (1992:730).

> *Vampiric identification operates in the fashion system in the way that the photographic apparatus positions the spectator to identify with the woman precisely so as not to desire her. But in order to eradicate or evacuate the homoerotic desire, the visual field must first produce it, thereby permitting, in socially regulated form, the articulation of lesbian desire within the identificatory field* (Fuss 1992: 730).

In magazines aimed at teenage girls, similar images abound, but often include images of girls together, leading Catherine Driscoll to assert that such photography not only 'eroticise(s) looking at women' but also 'relations between women' (1995:192). This is evident in the advertising in the October 1998 *Dolly,* which features many images of girls embracing and text in which they reflect on their relationships. Regular features such as 'Friends Forever', which celebrate female to female relationships, continue this trend (*Dolly:*124). Like Fuss, Driscoll concludes that 'rather than being repressed, the homoerotics of these images and this Girl are an 'open secret'' (1995:195), but one which is contained by an understanding that heterosexuality will be the destiny of the viewers, whatever pleasures they may be taking in the now. However, girls are not the only images to be eroticised; erotics flow into the commodities themselves, so that images of girls become another of these. In this way, the Spice Girls could be seen as just another commodity aimed at a young female audience. Like many of these commodities, images of them are eroticised, and the homoerotics could be argued to be somewhat incidental to this process. However, given the 'open secret' regarding the erotics of girls' magazines, and the fact that the young female fans are well versed in reading such images, a homoerotic gaze would seem to be part of what it means to gaze at the Spice Girls.

There *are* issues of ambivalence surrounding not only the group's bodily representation but also the issue of the group's relationship with feminisms of various sorts. In their evocations of Tank Girl, use of various slogans like 'Girl Power' and 'What part of no don't you understand?' in their lyrics, interviews and net sites, the band appears to draw on strands of contemporary feminism. (A highlight of their 1998 US tour was a rendition of 'Sisters Are Doin' It For Themselves' performed by Sporty and Scary). The celebration of girl culture, the relationship between daughters and their mothers, and the promotion of female friendships is done at the expense of the heterosexual relationship and the romance plot, both of which are gestured at but not given the same emphasis, especially visually. Even the movie plot, such as it is, turns on the issue of female friendship and is capped by the birth of a girl, which, in terms of the movie, is an all-female event. In the movie's denouement, the band overcomes the forces of evil, in this instance concentrated in a partnership between an Australian media mogul and a member of the paparazzi, both male. While it is possible to see these as just empty gestures, or even a commodification of feminism itself, the preponderance of 'girl culture' elements suggests that this is a large part of what the Spice Girls are about. As ego-ideals, they offer a new form of identity which is less implicated in the dominant operations of power as they pertain to gender, class and age. They promote girl power, not women power, and they flaunt working-class accents with confidence. Theirs is not a radical subjectivity, but is does mark a shift. Popular culture is not usually the place to find radical subjectivities for girls; they can be found in the independent recording artists, the riot grrl bands and their net sites. Nevertheless, as 'a zone of contestation', popular culture can be seen to be the site of a shift in the representations of female subjectivity as exemplified by the Spice Girls. These subjectivities represent new possibilities in viewer identification for girl audiences. If, as Fuss has said, 'identifications are mobile, elastic and volatile' (1992:8), we can expect new ego-ideals to appear, and audiences to change. However, we can read the Spice Girls as a shift in the battle for hegemony in the representation of females and female subjectivity in popular music, however small a shift it might seem.

Notes

1 *Spice Girls in Istanbul* was the biggest selling music video in Australia in April 1998. Spice Girls Vol 1 was number three (Australian Wednesday 10 June, p 10).

2 Both shows were screened on Channel 10 on the 18 November 1997.

3 See for example *Desperately Seeking Madonna,* ed. Adam Sexton, *The Madonna Connection: Representational Politics, Subcultural Identities, and Cultural Theory,* ed Cathy Schwichtenberg, and John Fiske's *Reading the Popular.*

4 Robert Goldman, Rosalind Coward and Annette Corrigan all raise some of the issues and apparent contradictions around the viewing positions occupied by the consumers of women's magazines. Internalising the male gaze is one of the simpler of these positions.

References

Corrigan, A. 1992, 'Fashion, Beauty, Feminism' in *Meanjin* 51, 1:107-122.

Coward, R. 1984, *Female Desire: Women's Sexuality Today,* London: Paladin.

Dixey, S. 1998, 'Just Like Spice Competition Results' *Spice Life 4!*, http://c3.vmg.co.uk/spicegirls/spicelife/, 21 September.

Doane, M. 1982, 'Film and the Masquerade: Theorising the Female Spectator' in *Screen* 23, 3-4:74-87.

Dolly October 1998, Pitts, S. (ed.), Sydney: ACP Publishing.

Driscoll, C. 1995, 'Who Needs a Boyfriend? The Homoerotic Virgin in Adolescent Women's Magazines', in *Speaking Positions: Aboriginality, Gender and Ethnicity in Australian Cultural Studies,* van Toorn, P. & English, D. (eds), Melbourne: Dept. of Humanities, Victorian University of Technology:188-198.

Driscoll, C. 1998, 'Riot Grrls: Girl Culture, Revenge and Global Capitalism', unpublished paper delivered 27 March, Adelaide.

Fiske, J. 1989, *Reading the Popular,* Boston: Unwin Hyman.

Fuss, D. 1992, 'Fashion and the Homospectorial Look' in *Critical Inquiry* 18, 4:713-737.

Fuss, D. 1995, *Identification Papers,* New York: Routledge.

Garratt, S. 1984, 'All of Us Love All of You' in Steward, S. & Garratt, S. (eds), *Signed, Sealed Delivered: True Stories of Women in Pop,* London: Pluto:138-151.

Girl Power! Live in Istanbul 1997, video recording, Barnard, D. (director),Virgin.

Goldman, R. 1992, *Reading Ads Socially,* London: Routledge.

Joyrich, L. 1996, *Re-viewing Reception: Television, Gender, and Postmodern Culture,* Bloomington: Indiana University Press.

Longhurst, B. 1995, *Popular Music and Society,* Cambridge: Polity Press.

McRobbie, A. & Garber, J. 1976, 'Girls and Subcultures' in Hall, S. & Jefferson, T. (eds), *Resistance Through Rituals: Youth Subcultures in Post-War Britain,* London: Hutchinson:209-222.

Mulvey, L. 1975, 'Visual Pleasure and Narrative Cinema' in *Screen* 16, 3:6-18.

Regev, M. 1994, 'Producing Artistic Value: The Case of Rock Music' in *Sociological Quarterly* 15, 1:85-102.

Schwichtenberg, C. (ed.) 1993, *The Madonna Connection: Representational Politics, Subcultural Identities, and Cultural Theory,* Boulder: Westview Press.

Sexton, A. 1993, *Desperately Seeking Madonna,* New York: Delta.

Silverman, K. 1986, 'Fragments of a Fashionable Discourse' in Modleski, T. (ed.), *Studies in Entertainment: Critical Approaches to Mass Culture,* Bloomington: Indiana University Press:139-152.

'Spice Girls do not corrupt young girls, research finds' 1998, *The University of York Press and Public Relations Office,* 28 August, http://www.york.ac.uk/admin/presspr/spice.htm.

Spiceworld: The Movie 1997, motion picture, Spiers, B. (director), Polygram.

Stockbridge, S. 1990, 'Rock Video: Pleasure and Resistance' in Brown, M. E. (ed.), *Television and Women's Culture: The Politics of the Popular,* London: Sage:102-113.

Turner, G. 1993, *Film as Social Practice,* 2nd ed, London: Routledge

TOWARDS INDIGENOUS DISCOURSES IN MUSICOLOGY: REFLECTIONS FROM A NEGOTIATED SPACE AT THE MARGINS OF THE ACADEMY

ASHLEY TURNER

This paper is about the development of an Indigenous musicological discourse at the Centre for Aboriginal Studies in Music (CASM). I am intensely aware of, and would draw your attention to the somewhat complex position that this paper occupies in relation to issues of Indigenous representation. Such complexity is perhaps unavoidable when the narrative emerges from a negotiated space. If the ideas and arguments are at times obscured by jargon, as is the hallmark of much academic discourse, the fault is mine. Alternative readings are always possible, and indeed, anticipated.

Before I proceed I wish to acknowledge the fact that this conference took place on Kaurna land. I would like to thank the Kaurna elders and people for their generosity and forbearance.

From the outset I should make it clear that the Indigenous musicological discourse of which I speak is still in its infancy. Nevertheless the development is significant because, as far as I am aware, CASM is the only place in Australia where a concerted effort is being made to facilitate such a development. This effort is being made through collaborative work between Indigenous and non-Indigenous members of staff at CASM, and students.

The academic context of this emergence is a program of music studies designed to address the learning requirements of Indigenous students from a wide range of cultural and educational backgrounds. As has already been indicated in discussions convened by Jennifer Newsome (in this volume, 1999) and Anthony Pak Poy, CASM's program differs from conventional music education programs in that it adopts an inclusive, non-prescriptive approach to the styles of music which students may wish to study. This is in keeping with the principle of self-determination and the stated objective of CASM to affirm Indigenous music making *in all its diversity.* It is this rich musical diversity, combined with a strong sense and culture of community, exchange, dialogue, and critique, which gives impetus to the evolving areas of discourse at CASM.

One of the more contentious areas for discourse is ethnomusicology. Although CASM has been the site for numerous ethnomusicological interventions, a systematic program for the teaching of the discipline did not emerge until 1992. Accordingly, discourse at CASM is partially informed by institutional and personal memories of ethnomusicology as sources of power and authority emanating from outside CASM, and a suspicion that CASM formed a 'site of surveillance' and 'field of action' for ethnomusicology. The enclave nature of CASM, the sense of intense community, and its ambiguous location within but on the margins of the academy, only served to intensify the image of indigeneity conceived 'panoptically'. Given the centrality of power and difference paradigms in Indigenous education, it is useful to pursue Foucault's model of the panopticon a bit further.

Referring to the disciplining of music and musicology, Katherine Bergeron writes:

> *It is not really the watchman in the prison's central tower (nor by analogy, the conductor of the band or orchestra) that maintains order among the enclosed, but rather what such figures, seen or unseen stand for: a 'higher' authority, a 'standard' of excellence, all ideals embodied in what we call the canon. It matters little whether we conceive of this canon as a scale, a body of law, or a pantheon of great authors and their works: the effect in every case is the same. The cannon, always in view, promotes decorum, ensures proper conduct. The individual within a field learns by internalising such standards, how not to transgress* (1992:4).

In applying Foucault's model I am pointing to some of the Western-based educational functions, biases, assumptions and imperatives within which Indigenous music education has negotiated a space. The panopticon serves to remind us of the fragility of that position. CASM can be read as having been from time to time, a site of action and surveillance in which Indigenous students have formed a subject group. Those actions by outsiders have included attempts to educate, study and shape individuals on the 'inside'. From time to time the object of some of those actions, which have been partially informed by a deficit modelling of indigeneity, has been to impose an order of conduct and identity which made sense to the outsiders but which may have made little sense to those on the inside.

Clearly, this picture is vastly different to the Freireian ideal upon which CASM was founded, and I should be quick to point out that I am not suggesting that Paulo Freire's model of side by side participation and mutuality failed at CASM. Quite the reverse, the fact that CASM has continued for nearly a quarter of a century to receive the full-hearted support of Indigenous communities, suggests that Freire's ideology has prevailed. However, experience also shows that this fragile ideal needs active defence against resurgent colonial imperatives. For some people outside CASM, the image of an Indigenous enclave in the academy as a 'wilderness' that needs bringing under control is quite possibly a comfortable and enticing one.

The decision to commence a program of teaching ethnomusicology at CASM marked a turning point in Indigenous music education. When I first took up the ethnomusicology lectureship at CASM, at the beginning of 1996, students already had been introduced to several facets of the discipline. This included transcription and analysis of musical works, the experience of learning and participating in music making that lay outside one's own cultural background, surveys and area based studies of musical styles and their cultural contexts from selected locations throughout the world, and some anthropological and social theory. Note that this is more or less the standard sequence for ethnomusicological training in Western academies.

However when I first started teaching at CASM, students expressed several concerns about ethnomusicology:

1. The scientific purposes of ethnomusicology were unclear and questionable. Why try to obtain abstract understandings of music, when you could actually experience it at its most profound and essential level by simply doing it? For all practical purposes, the important truths about music were possibly self-evident, whilst the search for over-arching explanations for the relations between humans and music seemed to be a rather futile and pointless exercise, especially when one was looking for practical solutions to 'real' problems as a maker and owner of music.
2. Students recognised that ethnomusicology was linked to colonialism and that it probably had some colonial agency. As there can be no 'neutral ground' in regard to colonialism, then ethnomusicology is either part of the problem or part of the solution.
3. Many of the inner workings, canons and assumptions of the discipline were all but hidden, and probably needed renegotiating in light of Indigenous social and cultural priorities, namely: the need for practical solutions to problems facing Indigenous communities and individuals, the need for self-determination and equity, the need to have unabridged rights to represent one's own culture instead of being represented, the need to secure a negotiating position in relation to dominant powers and paradigms, the need to obtain cultural and social empowerment and justice, the need

to obtain respect for Indigenous cultures in all their diversity, and so on.

4. The imperative to decode musical works not only apparently failed to address Indigenous priorities but probably worked against Indigenous interests, because it appeared to place a higher value on cultural products than on cultural processes.
5. In regard to the musical works which ethnomusicology attempts to decode, students recognised that, on the whole, certain types of music have been more highly valued than others, that 'traditional' forms and distant places are often seen as having greater legitimacy and authority in the ethnomusicological gaze than are, for example, contemporary, close to home, Indigenous popular musical forms. The implication that traditional music was the most legitimate expression of Indigenous musical identity was offensive and wrong. Indigenous identity inheres wherever it will; in contemporary and emerging traditions, in traditional forms, in so-called 'hybrid forms', in music at the margins, in appropriated forms, and in the massively successful popular music that appears in the everyday commercial media.
6. Studying the music of distant and alien music cultures whilst one's own culture was, in some cases, in desperate need of recognition and action, appeared to be immoral and discriminatory.
7. Studying the intimate details and workings of a distant musical culture in the name of scientific interest appeared intrusive and unethical. Those intimate details were clearly someone else's business.
8. Studying the intimate details of Australian Indigenous music cultures was unacceptable when the lecturer was not Indigenous.
9. Representations of Indigenous cultures and identities were of little real worth when non-Indigenous people made the representations. This is simply confirmed by the fact that Western academic understandings and representations of Indigenous traditions are largely informed by research conducted almost exclusively by non-Indigenous researchers (also see, Newsome in this volume). Again, images of the panopticon!

This potent critique of ethnomusicology is clearly framed by a distinctly anti-colonial perspective. Such a perspective involves:

> *a practical commitment to the political consequences of representation — a rupture and a positive awareness of the way colonial representation has shaped, and misshaped, reality for coloniser and colonised alike* (Hilton, 1993: 6)*, and a need '... to move the boundaries and undo the restrictions which make it so difficult for [Indigenous people] to speak'* (Langton 1993:7).

Embedded in the critique are many suggestions for advancing these ends:

1. Above all else there is an urgent need for supporting research by Indigenous people. As Marcia Langton points out, 'one of the important interventions is the act of self-representation itself and the power of aesthetic and intellectual statements' (ibid:10). CASM students, entering into ethnomusicology for the first time, are now encouraged to begin constructing research projects straight away. By taking this approach, students learn to explore and critique the ethnomusicological toolkit from the first day out, whilst also gaining hands on experience in managing and developing skills and methods which they can then apply to their own needs as they see fit.
2. Ethnomusicology could address practical needs related to the immediate priorities of people who conventionally have appeared as subjects of study. Of course ethnomusicologists have often been activists and advocates for the people with whom they have worked, however that engagement has usually been emergent and ephemeral, and not the primary reason for doing the work. On the other hand, research proposals produced by CASM students respond to immediate and personally significant priorities, such as documenting the rapidly disappearing songs of one's own community; exploring one's own cultural background and heritage; revealing the largely ignored 'in-between' musical spaces and worlds in which much Indigenous music making happens; examining the nature of obstacles which have limited Indigenous participation; and so on.

Through this process many students have come to realise that they themselves are custodians of valuable cultural knowledge that they can reproduce and build on for the benefit of their communities.

Ethnomusicological research is thus situated at CASM as a strategy for empowerment of Indigenous people and as a means for Indigenously controlled production and representation of knowledge.

3. It follows that the gaze of ethnomusicology, conventionally turned upon and construing the 'Otherness' of research subjects, might be turned around, to search for understandings about the position of oneself and one's own music in relation to broader contexts. Some postmodernist writers have attempted this type of thing. However, the result all too often, has been epistemological confusion, due mainly, I suggest, to the fact that many of the ethnographic tools deployed still prescribe 'Otherness' at some level.
4. Issues of professional responsibilities and research ethics warrant close attention. Given pressing needs to address a history of systematic disempowerment and culture loss is there a need to overhaul the ethical codes under which ethnomusicologists work? Suggestions have emerged from class discussions that point to the need for an active rather than passive concern for wellbeing. What about the explicit incorporation of Indigenous ethical codes as is the case in the Four World's International Institute for Indigenous Sciences in Canada, which offers research degrees underpinned by Indigenous ethical codes.
5. The concerns raised by CASM students would also seem to suggest a need to re-examine the motivations behind acts of cultural interpretation, classification, and the bases of authority from which such interpretations are made. If that authority is not based at some level in a degree of ownership or otherwise legitimised stake in the represented culture, it would seem reasonable to be suspicious of the motives behind acts of interpretation and representation.
6. Translations and interpretations of cultures, when warranted, could proceed from a negotiated ethnographic space which was truly mutual. In other words, a space and approach which facilitated the production of documents and understandings that were of equal value to all parties. This would require mutual agreement about the fundamental epistemological underpinning of research methods, purposes and products, as well as institutional recognition of the academic legitimacy of non-Western knowledge systems.
7. The teaching of ethnomusicology should emphasize 'the interrogation of texts as products of our cultures' (ibid:7). By deconstructing ethnomusicological texts students could salvage personally important cultural knowledge across a range of fields, whilst also practicing empowering methods of reading. As Marcia Langton has explained:

> *the central problem is the need to develop a body of knowledge on representation of Aboriginal people — and a critical perspective to do with aesthetics and politics, drawing from Aboriginal world views, from Western traditions and from history* (ibid:28).

Conclusion

The ideas presented in this paper reflect a situation that is continuously changing. At best the solutions and readings offered are provisional. Lasting solutions will necessarily be flexible and negotiable. What is clear however, is that, as students gain a handle on the disciplines, they have insisted on their re-evaluation. One pattern that appears to be clear, however, is that if ethnomusicology is to serve Indigenous interests it will be activist, advocacy-based and oriented towards solving concrete problems.

Such a development should be welcomed by the academic community, for as Philip Bohlman suggests:

> *Ethnomusicology internalized a process of canon formulation that reflexively embraced canons not as a means of fixing the field, but as a means of constantly endowing itself with the potential to change in response to its own self-reflective discourse* (1992: 119).

Anyway, students at CASM would not let me get away with anything else!

References

Bergeron, K. 1992, 'Prologue: Disciplining Music', in Bergeron, K. & Bohlman, P.V. (eds.) 1992, *Disciplining Music: musicology and its canons,* Chicago: The University of Chicago Press:1-9

Bohlman, P. 1992, 'Ethnomusicology's Challenge to the Canon: the Canon's Challenge to Ethnomusicology', in Bergeron, K. & Bohlman, P.V. (eds.) 1992, *Disciplining Music: musicology and its canons,* Chicago: The University of Chicago Press:116-136.

Hilton, A. 1993, 'Foreword' in Langton, *'Well, I heard it on the radio and I saw it on the television': an essay for the Australian Film Commission on the politics and aesthetics of filmmaking by and about Aboriginal people and things,* Sydney: Australian Film Commission:5-6.

Langton, M. 1993, *'Well, I heard it on the radio and I saw it on the television': an essay for the Australian Film Commission on the politics and aesthetics of filmmaking by and about Aboriginal people and things,* Sydney: Australian Film Commission.

Pak Poy, A. 1998, 'A Question of Style — Curriculum Design at the Centre for Aboriginal Studies in Music', unpublished paper delivered at *Musical Visions,* 6th National Australian/New Zealand IASPM Conference, Adelaide: June 25-28, 1998.

AUSTRALIAN POPULAR MUSIC AND EVERYDAY LIFE

GRAEME TURNER

Implicit in what follows is my perception that, over the last decade and a half, the function of popular music within the everyday lives of its producers and consumers has changed significantly. Culturally, it is no longer as tightly identified with the myths of resistance and authenticity once thought to be so essential to youth subcultures. Industrially, popular music has been transformed by the convergence of media forms and systems of delivery. Formally, the relationship between sound and image has been amplified and complicated by music video, as has the distinction between product and promotion. As far as the audience is concerned, the modes and points of consumption have proliferated and new partnerships with other popular activities (computer games, for example) have developed. While it clearly remains influential, I think we have to ask if popular music is as discrete and powerful a cultural form as it once was, or might be again. For Australian popular music, there are specific influences at work which may produce profound changes in its contribution to the everyday lives of Australians in the future. Shifts in the character and scale of government support, in industry infrastructure and regulatory environments, as well as shifts in the structure of the international music industry, have collaborated in producing what I would argue is a more difficult environment for the producers and audiences of Australian music in the late 1990s than that which prevailed in, say, the mid 1980s.

In this paper, I wish to explore two issues — the convergence between popular music and other cultural forms, and changes in the industrial and regulatory context for Australian popular music — in order to map some shifts and variations in the function of Australian popular music within our popular culture.

The last time I addressed this kind of topic was for Philip Hayward's collection, 'From Pop to Punk to Postmodernism', published in 1992 but conceived in 1990. My focus then was on the industrial/cultural contexts within which Australian popular music was produced, performed and consumed. Rather than focussing on the music itself, I addressed some of the roles locally produced music played in the lives of Australians who consumed it: my starting point was the contention that Australian popular music 'works vigorously, resonantly, and memorably on Australians through the culture of their everyday lives — that is, at the points where they are most 'naturally', at their most 'unquestionably', Australian' (ibid:14). This, in the context of two decades of strong commercial development and a positive climate of government support for Australian popular music. Significantly, a great deal of what I wrote for 'From Pop to Punk to Postmodernism' was about the venues, the contexts of consumption, as distinctive features of Australian popular music's imbrication into everyday life. I would approach the topic differently now. The contexts of consumption for Australian popular music are not what they were, the nature and extent of government support has changed, and the cultural function of popular music itself — throughout the western world — may well have changed permanently. It is now a decade since Simon Frith announced that the rock era was 'over', with its provocative corollary that, far from being rooted in working class resistance, rock was always a definitively suburban fantasy (1988).

These comments were given their point by Frith's discussion of the reconciliation of the two preeminent post war popular (and suburban) cultural forms — rock music and television.[1] This leads me into the first line of argument I want to follow: discussing changes in the role that popular music plays in our lives.

Convergence has become the buzzword for analyses of the media in the 1990s. Built upon the changing technological futures anticipated for communication industries in general (with broadcasting, telephony, and information retrieval in particular), the notion of convergence proposes that what now look like different, even competing, technologies may wind up, as a result of globalising corporate structures, merging into one system of access and delivery: television networks will reach you via your home computer, for instance. Generally, I am suspicious or at least circumspect about the technological determinism that influences triumphalist predictions of large-scale technological change. Nevertheless, it is fruitful to think about what has happened to the cultural placement and function of popular music as a consequence of what must be regarded as a signficant trend towards convergence.

Let us start by looking at the merging of popular music into other media forms and with other media or entertainment industries. The reconciliation between popular music and televison which Simon Frith discusses, neatly enacted through the development of music video, has resulted in television becoming a more important point of access to popular music and a site of music consumption in its own right. During the 1980s, there were suggestions that music video had actually outstripped radio as a point of access (Burnett 1996: 82), but the most recent ABA report demonstrates that this is not currently the case: researchers found that music on radio was still valued more highly than music on television by the largest consumer group — teenagers and young adults (Cupitt et al 1996). While music video is commonly thought to have dramatically expanded television's role in promoting popular music, such arguments probably underestimate the historical significance of teen programs such as *Bandstand* or *Six O'Clock Rock* (in Australia), *Top of the Pops* (in the UK) and *American Bandstand* (in the US). Furthermore, as Grossberg insists, television has always been closely involved in the relationship between fans and popular music:

> *Fans have learned how to dance from television: they have learned how to dress and act; they have learned new organisations for desire and emotion, and sometimes they have found new objects and narratives for those desires and emotions. In fact, the generation of rock fans has always been doubly coded; they are also the television generation* (1993:189).

While music video has produced a new textual form which can be consumed in its own right or in partnership with the music text, it is hard to talk about it as a wholly autonomous form because of its relationship to a music text which can be seen as primary. Music video is less equivocally an autonomous cultural form when it is regarded primarily as a mode of promotion. Here, there is little doubt of its importance. Even in the Australian industry — where music video as a form arrived late, and where music video channels were not established until more than a decade after MTV had peaked in the US — we can find instances where the use of music video has been a more important factor in chart success than radio air play: a case in point, examined by Meret Valtwies, is the single taken from *Strictly Ballroom*, John Paul Young's 'Love is in the Air':

> *Although 'Love' enjoyed considerable chart success, ending up as one of the five bestselling Australian singles of the year, it did not get massive airplay in Australia. Albert Productions A&R director Barbara Andrews has identified the single's major promotional boost as coming from the video's frequent broadcast on TV, the use of the clip as a preview trailer for the film on Hoyts home video releases, and the general media hype around the film itself* (1993:46).

As this example suggests, music videos can promote more than music. In Australia in recent years, they have been consistently used as a nursery for growing certain kinds of hybrid celebrity/TV star/pop star. Particularly in the case of the teenage stars of popular TV soaps like *Neighbours* or *Home and Away*, a level of celebrity developed in one medium has been expanded and 'diversified' as the young stars attempt to broaden their popular appeal by producing pop singles supported with high concept videos. Such enterprises usually have the benefit of newsworthiness on their side, and thus have a good chance of being given a screening on entertainment weeklies and chat shows as well as in the music video programs. In such cases, it is the image — in all its senses — rather than the music which is the primary object of consumption (few of these performers would claim to be musically adventurous). They provide us with instances of music video operating as a site where popular music's close dependence on the image has been institutionalised, systematised and routinely exploited.

Of course, the consumption of rock and popular music has always involved a detailed and well informed interest in the image of the performers, the styles of dress and behaviour, and the visible codes of attitude. It is quite possible to see music video as, in a sense, reclaiming the traditional[2] importance of the visual in music performances through its integration of performance, spectacle and the promotion of music. Negus (1992) takes this view on video. However, more customarily, music video is regarded as displacing the music with the image. For Keith Negus, despite his recognition of the continuity between music video and traditional musical performances, 'the relationship between popular music and the star image as presented through films and television has been given greater emphasis by the growth of video' (27). There is a debate about the power relation between the music and the image in music video. Burnett, for instance, argues that MTV has increased the importance of the visual at the expense of the music, that it favours 'pretty people' over musicians, that it has turned concert tours into visual rather than music spectaculars, and that it has enabled singers like Whitney Houston and Mariah Carey to build their audience without working their way around the live performance circuit (1996:97). Grossberg sees the culture of the image, both in music video and in the cinema's increasingly direct address to a youth audience, as carrying substantial ideological consequences:

> *I want to suggest that the popularity of music video has to be located in a larger context in which visual media and images are competing with, if not displacing, music and aural images as the site of salvation and transcendence in rock culture. Further this changing topography of the media in people's lives points to an even more significant possibility; the increasing erosion of the form of the relationship between fan and music that has characterised rock culture, what I will call the ideology of authenticity* (op cit.:198).

There is some nostalgia in this diagnosis, but it is surely right to suggest that, in cinema and video, popular music faces powerful competitors for its once central role in young people's everyday lives.

More positively though, and less often noted, is music video's potential as a place where new contributions to popular music performance can occur. Rachael Gorham and Arielle Nakache's article (1993:24) on Australian music video choreography makes the point that music video offers new opportunities to artists with dance and performance skills who can now become stars through TV despite their lack of 'any primary vocal-musical accomplishment'. In this way, one senses music video may carry potentials like those of the classical film musical — a mode of performance and entertainment that has all but died out.

Which brings me to the relation between music and film. Although Grossberg suggests film is displacing music from its preeminent position with the youth audience, one would have to say that if this is occurring it may well be due to Hollywood's relatively recent discovery of the importance of popular music as more than a secondary system of narrative information (its usefulness in establishing mood and setting, the affective dimensions of a scene), and its effectiveness as a marketing device. Film has the advantage of being a more discrete and autonomous form than music video but it is making increasing use of music video and popular music soundtracks as a means of cross-promotion. Music videos for hit films such as *Titanic* are not content with simply selling the hit song from the movie; incorporating action and narrative footage from the movie into the video clip, they sell the movie too. Soundtracks are now routinely incorporated into the promotion of movies — advertised as 'featuring the music of' — aimed at a youth audience. Hollywood has become more musically sophisticated over the last decade in that it is more knowledgeable about both mainstream and more niche market popular music. This is reflected in the convergence between the production processes which result in the recording of a move soundtrack and a music CD. Specialist soundtrack producers are now a part of the Hollywood film industry, hired to increase the promotability of the product rather than to enhance the narrative with the selection of music. Their success is apparent in the fact that soundtracks now account for a significant, and increasing, component of the music industry's sales. The trend is not confined to Hollywood. A number of the most commercially successful Australian productions of recent years have relied heavily on excerpted singles and the soundtrack for promotion: among these I would include *Muriel's Wedding, The Adventures of Priscilla, Queen of the Desert, Strictly Ballroom* and less successfully, *Idiot Box.*

Given this kind of convergence, popular music as a form does stand to lose some of its autonomy as the popularity of particular musics or artists is manipulated by film industry promotion — as has been the case, say, with ABBA's music in Australian film over the last few years. Concern can be exaggerated, of course, as the two cultural forms still work very differently. Unlike film, which remains a specific event chosen for consumption on a particular day and with particular company, music remains firmly articulated to the teenager's and young adult's routine practices of everyday life as well as to moments of dedicated pleasure. What worries Grossberg, though, is the loss of what he sees as the 'ideology of authenticity', and the audience's surrender to the more clearly manipulative fantasies produced through film. According to Grossberg, contemporary youth films such as those produced by John Hughes in the1980s (*Pretty in Pink, The Breakfast Club, Ferris Bueller's Day Off* and so on) have replaced rock's 'transcendence' with a disabling cynicism:

> *If rock seems to empower its audiences by juxtaposing the transcending possibilities of everyday life against the social conditions of contemporary existence (so that everyday life is the site of the transcendence of history), these films rather cynically locate the very need for transcendence within the tortured boundaries of everyday life. If rock heroes exist ambiguously as people we relate to and people we aspire to, the star characters of these films refuse the responsibility of defining their audience's aspirations* (op cit.:198).

It's the politics of these films, then, which bother Grossberg — indeed, what really bothers him is the fact that the feature film, generically, specifies its politics through narrative in ways that are more difficult to refuse than the more affective pleasures of popular music.

The affective dimension of popular music — its capacity to call up identities and associations simply through sound — has recommended it to the advertising industry. The use of popular music within advertising and promotion is not new, of course; it has long been exposed to the kind of appropriations we have seen recently where large companies such as Microsoft take the meaning of lyrics espousing some kind of cultural myth (Bowie's 'Heroes') or sexual innuendo (The Stones' 'Start Me Up') and turn them into benign metaphors for consumer capitalism's dependence upon the ideologies of individualism. In Australia, the relation between popular music and the promotion of televised sport has been particularly strong. Channel 9's Wide World of Sport has an industry reputation as an innovator because of its pioneering use of rock music for segment headers and footers, intercut with exciting sporting footage which mimicks the formal tactics used in music video. Similarly, the 1990s Australian Rugby League campaign to broaden its supporter base benefited greatly from its identification with Tina Turner's 'Simply the Best'; the tradition continued in 1998 with the use of a Chumbarumba single over action footage from the game (although the 1999 campaign used a poem from Thomas Keneally to radically reposition the game). David Rowe has argued that we are witnessing a realignment of the relation between sport and rock music, generally. According to Rowe, and I would agree with much of this, sport was initially compromised for rock fans by its 'fraternization with straight society', its location in the school curriculum, and its place in national state ideology. Now, he suggests, the shift in the cultural and economic location of sport and the decline in the generational and ideological coherence of rock culture, has meant a cultural convergence between rock and sport (1995:10).

When we examine the proliferation of sites of consumption for popular music today, a key inclusion has to be the home computer. There, CDs are played, songs are sampled or downloaded, fan sites explored, and purchases made. At the moment, this is raising regulatory issues to do with copyright, taxation, and both producers' and consumers' protection as the statelessness of the Internet enables it to bypass most of our existing commercial regulation and copyright legislation. It is also a consequence of the relative novelty of merging one system of access and delivery with another, without the installation of the customary level of regulation.

Finally, in this review of the convergence of music with other forms of entertainment, it is worth acknowledging the role of the Walkman.[3] The Walkman is as much a lifestyle product as a new technology for consuming music; it can serve as an exercise accessory as well as a form of private entertainment usable in public spaces. The Walkman's insertion into our daily lives is not without consequences. It is a technology which paradoxically contributes to the everyday life of the individual who uses it, but atomises the experience of everyday life for the culture as a whole. The Walkman privatises consumption, replacing the shared experience of music with the personalised experience. While music may once have distinguished its context of consumption from that of, say, reading by noting how many aspects of music consumption are publicly or communally organised — how much it is a public or shared experience — listening to a Walkman is a solitary and private pursuit pretty much like reading.

All of the changes I have outlined above affect the role that popular music plays within our everyday lives. It is clear that at least some of the changes over the last decade or so have significantly affected the prominence or importance of music within our popular culture. I admit that nostalgia always creeps into this kind of argument. When once I described what I saw as a rearrangement of the power relations between the sound and the visuals in music video in the early 1980s (1983:64), I was called an apologist for the 1960s. That is a danger here too because it is precisely the kind of cultural investment in rock and popular music that is conventionally retrojected into the 1960s that I would argue seems to have diminished in the 1990s. What Grossberg calls the ideology of authenticity appears to be less comprehensively connected to popular music now than it was ten or fifteen years ago, and I would also argue that music is less comprehensively connected to a set of resistant styles and attitudes now than it used to be. Furthermore, there is now considerable evidence that consumption of music has become a less discrete activity, an activity that while it occurs across an ever widening range of media (CDs, tapes, vinyl, film, video, television, radio, home computers, the net), it is an activity that also occurs against an ever widening range of competitors for leisure time and cultural investment.[4]

Such an argument, however, is impossible to make without appearing to invoke the attitudes and prejudices of one cultural moment against those of another. Implicit in what I have had to say about popular music so far, in fact, may be a very dated conception of the core musical experience — that is, the live performance by musicians. Dance subcultures now constitute a significant part of the music audience with dance venues playing recorded music or using DJs who create their own music 'live' at the desk. Within this regime of consumption, the notions of authenticity that I would attach to the live performance by musicians, and what Grossberg means by the ideology of authenticity as well, are probably irrelevant. Certainly, the live production of a dance mix by the DJ is analogous to the live performance by musicians for that audience. In many clubs, the dancers face the DJ as they once would have faced a live band. But whether the DJ's performance incorporates all the other mythological and affective elements attached to a fan witnessing a concert performance by their favourite band is something that I simply don't know. It would be interesting to find out.

I want to move on now to consider a slightly less abstract set of indicators about the place of Australian music within our popular culutre. More pragmatic they might be, but they raise similar levels of concern because they demonstrate a substantial decline in the cultural influence of the popular music industry and in the support it receives from the government. It is possible to outline specific influences at work in contemporary Australia which raise concern about the place of Australian popular music within our own culture. Many of these influences are the product of policy decisions taken by government or commercial bodies. Taken in sum, they have the capacity to radically affect how popular music can contribute to our culture as well as, ultimately, the long-term survival of a local music industry. (Given that music plays a more prominent role in the everyday lives of teenagers and young adults, much of what I have to say in the following pages will be about this group's consumption of music, and the place music occupies within their lives at the moment).

One of the key changes in the industrial context within which Australian popular music must operate in the 1990s is the deregulation of radio, which occurred incrementally over the late 1980s. One of the key consequences of this deregulation was the removal of the local content regulation for radio and its replacement with a self-regulatory, and more restricted, code administered by the peak industry body, FARBS (Federation of Australian Radio Broadcasting Stations). This removed a key plank in government support for local music, a plank that had been in place since 1949. Unfortunately, it coincided with another shift within the radio industry which reduced the opportunities for new popular music across the board, finding its way onto radio playlists in Australia.[5] The narrowing of the range of radio formats available in metropolitan radio, the decline in formats favouring new and teen-oriented music, and the market domination by classic hits, easy listening, and talkback formats has been pronounced over the last decade:

> *Gradually, since the introduction of commercial FM radio, and increasingly rapidly since the upheaval in media ownership in 1986-7, teen radio has disappeared from metropolitan Australian radio. When the last Top 40 station in Melbourne converted to an 'easy listening' format in late 1988, we inhabited a moment when, for the first time in more than thirty years, there was not one top 40 station serving the teenage audience in any Australian capital city* (Turner 1993:143).

While there have been occasional attempts, such as that by Hitz FM in Melbourne, to address the gap this trend left in the market, the situation has remained largely unchanged through the 1990s. It should come as no surprise that in a recent survey of Australian leisure activities and taste cultures, 'easy listening' emerged as the most popular genre of music with almost half of the sample giving it either first, second or third preferences (Bennett et al., 1999). There is in fact, very little alternative. The grim financial climate within which radio operated in the late 1980s and early 1990s encouraged government assent to further de-regulation of corporate structures and of the competitive arrangements within metropolitan markets. As a result, there has been a dramatic reduction in real competition; in some markets, such as Brisbane, the two commercial stations competing for the rock FM audience are owned by the same company and share the same newsroom. It is hard to blame the companies concerned for this situation; it is clear that it was the result of the bitterly competitive environments produced by the policies of the National Radio Plan: the introduction of aggregation and government attempts to sell off new FM licences to AM broadcasters as a revenue raiser. Whatever the reasons however, the result is a narrow and inflexible set of radio formats, and a declining radio audience.

The 1996 ABA report on music programming and teen radio (Cupitt et al. op cit:5) recorded a significant decline in consumption of both radio and television by teenagers and young adults. Between 1990 and 1995, the researchers found there had been a decline in teenage weekly listening to radio of 20%; in the adult demographic it was less dramatic, but still in the order of 9%. It is hard not to conclude that the salient issue for teen listeners is the conservatism of FM formats, where the dominance of classic rock has seen the radio audience who loved listening to the Eagles in the mid-

1970s still listening to them in the late 1990s. Consequently, the demographic of FM's core audience has grown old comfortably with the formats while their sons and daughters are consigned to a music diet pretty much the same as their parents. This view is indirectly supported by the fact that while television viewing has declined significantly over this period too, the decline in teen audiences is not as marked as it is in radio. The critical period for television may well be earlier than this however, as the introduction of 'pay for play' in video programming dramatically reduced the amount of music video programming on television. The ABA's 1985 Report, *Young Australians and Music,* lists the programs which were screening in 1984. They included *Sounds* (Channel 7), *Solid Gold* (Channel 10, Sunday), *Nightmoves* (Channel 100), *Rock Arena* (Channel 2), *Continental Drift* (SBS), *Countdown* (Channel 2), *Wavelength* (Channel 9), and *Rock Around the World* (SBS). Some of these ran four nights a week. This is a wealth of riches compared to the current situation, where we have *Rage, Recovery, Video Hits,* and, for a very small minority, the cable channels *V* and *MTV.*

While the commercial broadcasting sector has adopted conservative tactics in order to survive, there has been an analogous withdrawal from and reorientation of government assistance programs for the popular music industry. It is a long way back to the levels of government involvement in the music industry which produced Ausmusic and Priority One. Marcus Breen (1996) has written the history of the federal Labor government's discovery of the popular music industry, detailing how it saw an ideal opportunity to serve both social and economic ends through supporting what was, at that time, a cultural industry which had received no support at all from the arts funding agencies at either state or federal level. Since the industry was already operating in a commercially successful manner, it did not require the levels of subsidy enjoyed by the film industry, the opera or the ballet. Rather, what Australian popular music received from its inclusion within governmental regimes of funding and organisation was acknowledged legitimacy as a national cultural form. Cultural nationalist objectives were initially paramount in the government's interest in popular music, but these soon mutated into (still defensible) social objectives organised around youth policy, and finally economic and political opportunism. As popular music emerged from this regime, legitimised but in some key ways disabled, it found itself transformed into an industry which no longer operated as well as it had originally against, in spite of, or in collaboration with, the international industry. As we stand now, Ausmusic has collapsed, and the residue of government funding occurs within arts programs administered by the Australia Council or its state equivalents. This resituates government support for popular music as falling into the category of arts grants, rather than industry assistance.

The internationalising process which has concentrated ownership, so that competition in the recording industry is shared between the so-called Big Six, has made life difficult for local or independent production and recording companies. Traditionally it has been the independents to whom the market looks for new directions, new sounds, and new talents. Little wonder, given the conservatism of the production industry and of radio formats, that industry figures for some time have shown a declining proportion of sales coming from new music, and an increase in compilations, re-releases and soundtrack albums. While this trend and its effects are not confined to Australia, it seems reasonable to assume that it cuts deeper into small national markets and small local industries like the Australian. In Australia, we starting to see a contraction of the infrastructure: the removal of the local music quota, the increasing effects of globalisation on artist rosters and promotion expenditure, and the evaporation of the market in the production of local advertising (again in response to a removal of local content requirements in the advertising industry) have meant that the number of viable recording studios is shrinking in response to the decline in the volume of work (Studio 301, for instance, one of the pioneers of local production for the majors and the independents, has now closed).

From all of these points of view, the strategic position of popular music in Australia — as a cultural form, as a cultural industry — is less favourable now than it was ten years ago. I am aware that there could be another reading of this situation: that we are approaching a fracturing of the industrial model of cultural production in the music industry — based upon the cheapness of recording equipment now, the ease with which CDs can be produced by individuals, the possibilities for marketing through, say, the internet and so on — and need to embrace a post-industrial, more community-based, model for local music cultures. My view is that we have approached such moments and such possibilities before, and found them to be chimeras. Further, we have to admit that it is in the interests of those currently in control of the industry to maintain the current shape and structure. So, while the music itself continues to claim its place within our everyday lives at the moment, the trends implicit in what I have described above threaten the longterm viability of the industry which produces it. The arguments I made about the local industry in Phil Hayward's book of six years ago now need substantial revision to accommodate worrying changes — not, most importantly, in the global market (as one might have thought) but in the way the market has been structured and regulated at home.

Now, I wouldn't be surprised if this seemed to be an overly negative reading of the current situation. Given my own cultural background, and my age I suppose, I have to admit that my default position in assessing the role of music within popular culture is to be alarmed and surprised when I find it is not dominant in people's lives. I find that I get alarmed and surprised more often than I used to; and when I look at the policy environment I have no difficulty in understanding why. More importantly, though, the unspoken assumption behind all I have said is a cultural nationalist one: that it is self-evidently desirable for us to have a local industry which is both commercially viable and eligible for government support as a culture industry, and which is able to preserve practices of access and equity which ensure a diversity of participants and outcomes. When I was working as a musician, it was commonplace to believe in the importance of providing local songs, local companies, a local industry. It may not be as commonplace now; perhaps it may not need to be. But it is pretty clear that these days local industries don't survive without a lot of effort and political will. There's plenty of effort at the moment but not a lot of will.

Notes

1 See also Simon Frith, 'Youth/Music/Television' in Simon Frith et al (eds.) *Sound and Vision: The Music Video Reader.* London: Routledge, 1993.

2 That is, incorporating modes of performance and consumption that predate the era of electronic recording and reproduction, with the attendant potential for mass distribution.

3 An excellent history of the Walkman, which also considers its cultural function for the user, is contained in Paul Du Gay, Stuart Hall, Linda Janes, Hugh Mackay and Keith Negus, *Doing Cultural Studies: The Story of the Sony Walkman*, London: Sage, 1997.

4 This point emerges very clearly from the ABA's 1996 report, *Music, New music and all that,* 1996, (Cupitt M. et al, op cit.).

5 A welcome change in the wind at the time of writing is the projected installation of a quota specifically for new local music for radio; we have yet to see how this will be defined, and what effects it might have.

References

Bennett, T., Emerson, M. & Frow, J. 1999, *Australian Everyday Cultures,* Melbourne: Cambridge University Press, forthcoming.

Breen, M. 1996, 'The Popular Music Industry in Australia: A study of policy reform and retreat', 1982-1996, unpublished PhD dissertation, VUT.

Burnett, R. 1996, *The Global Jukebox:The International Music Industry,* London: Routledge.

Cupitt, M., Ramsey, G. & Sheldon, L. 1996, *Music, New Music and All That: Teenage radio in the 90s,* Sydney: Australian Broadcasting Authority.

Du Gay, P., Hall, S., Janes, L., Mackay H. & Negus, K. 1997, *Doing Cultural Studies: The Story of the Sony Walkman,* London: Sage.

Frith, S. 1988, 'Introduction', in *Music for Pleasure: Essays in the Sociology of Pop,* London: Polity.

Gorham, R. & Nakach, A. 1993, 'Star Moves: Choreography, Choreographers and Australian Music Video', in *Perfect Beat,* 1:3:24.

Grossberg, L. 1993 'The Media Economy of Rock Culture: Cinema, post-modernity and authenticity' in Frith, S., Goodwin, A. & Grossberg, L. (eds), *Sound and Vision,* New York, Routledge.

Negus, K. 1992, *Producing Pop: Culture and Conflict in the Popular Music Industry,* London: Edward Arnold.

Rowe, D. 1995, *Popular Cultures: Rock music, sport and the politics of pleasure,* London: Sage.

Turner, G. 1983, 'Video Clips and Popular Music', *The Australian Journal of Cultural Studies,* 1:1; reprinted as 1984, 'Video Clips: The Altered State of Music', Metro:64.

Turner, G. 1992, 'Australian Popular Music and its Contexts' in Hayward, P. (ed) *From Pop to Punk to Postmodernism,* Sydney: Allen and Unwin.

Turner, G. 1993, 'Who Killed the Radio Star: The death of teen radio in Australia', in Bennett, T., Frith, S., Grossberg, L., Shepherd, J. & Turner, G. (eds.) *Rock and Popular Music: Politics, policies, institutions,* London: Routledge.

Valtwies, M. 1993, 'Success is in the Air: The Soundtrack, Music and Marketing of *Strictly Ballroom',* in *Perfect Beat,* 1:3:46.

MEETINGS ON THE CONCERT HALL STAGE

GORDON WILLIAMS

❖

Can an indigenous worldview be expressed through the symphony orchestra? Can the symphony orchestra, the repository of European musical thought, serve as a vehicle for the expression of indigenous aspirations?

Orchestra Dreaming, *which was presented at the Adelaide Festival in 1998, canvassed and celebrated the ways in which indigenous and orchestral music can meet, acknowledging the mutual innovation, adjustment and resolution which makes that meeting possible.*

In March 1998, Symphony Australia, jointly with the Adelaide Symphony Orchestra, presented *Orchestra Dreaming* as part of that years' Adelaide Festival. *Orchestra Dreaming* could be claimed as the first concert devoted to the theme of a meeting between Aboriginal and European orchestral music. It is appropriate that this concert be considered at Adelaide's *Musical Visions* conference which took place some months after the event (June 1998), and has the twin themes of popular music and Arnhem Land performance traditions.

Each of the works on the *Orchestra Dreaming* program — Peter Sculthorpe's *Kakadu*, Richard Mills' *Earth Poem/Sky Poem,* and particularly, the new work premiered in this concert, *Music is our Culture* (the product of a joint compositional effort by four Aboriginal musicians and one white composer)[1] — spoke to this issue of musical engagement in some way. *Earth Poem/Sky Poem* saw the combining of orchestra with traditional Yolngu music from the Top End. *Music is our Culture* acknowledged a modern Aboriginal musical culture in western popular forms. *Kakadu* however is a purely orchestral piece.

In effect, the program traced a history of engagement from relatively early techniques of quotation and utilisation by European composers *(Kakadu)*, to a slightly more venturesome juxtapositioning *(Earth Poem)*, to a near synthesis *(Culture)*.

Peter Sculthorpe's music, for example, maps a European-Australian nationalism which has gradually come to acknowledge Aboriginal precedence in this land. Early Australian art reflected a view of Australia as a vast emptiness, of the bush (in D.H. Lawrence's words), 'waiting… waiting… hoarily waiting'. But for what? The entrance of people? There were always people here, people who had named every hill, creek, soak or swamp, and Sculthorpe's music has gradually apprised itself of that reality. *Kakadu* also makes use of the first Aboriginal tune to be taken down by Europeans, members of Baudin's expedition in 1802. In expectation of a continuing rapprochement between black and white performing traditions, it was appropriate that *Orchestra Dreaming* began with a piece which quotes the first example of Aboriginal music to find its way into European cultural consciousness, from a composer who has done so much to turn the orchestral repertoire to face this country.

Just as Sculthorpe's music sees an advance on earlier engagements with Aboriginal culture, the two remaining works on the program displayed a more involved collaboration between Aboriginal Australian and European Australian musicians.

Richard Mills' *Earth Poem/Sky Poem* was devised in consultation with Djamina Gurruwiwi and the Galpu Wilderness Dancers And Elcho Island Dancers at Milingimbi and Galiwin'ku (Elcho Island) in the Northern Territory, back in 1993/94. The work juxtaposes orchestral music with songs taken from the repertoire of the Galpu clan of Elcho Island in Eastern Arnhem Land. The overall effect is one of collage; the music of both cultures expressed in their own way. In *Music is our Culture,* on the other hand, the first work for symphony orchestra by indigenous Australians, Aboriginal and European musical traditions intermix.

On paper, a fusion of the European symphony orchestra and Aboriginal music looks incredibly ambitious, if not impossible.

Consider that we associate classical orchestral music with polish, clean intonation, the ironing out of logical kinks. It's a style of music which aims for seamless development. Real life rarely seeps into orchestral performance, as it does into traditional Aboriginal ritual, where the proscenium could be considered to be the entire tribal domain — the time-scale eternity.

At a deeper ideological level, the orchestra, or more particularly its central repertoire, expresses a European goal-oriented view of the world — a sometimes avaricious compulsion to reach constructed climaxes. It is music which reflects the concerns of a society which has to a large extent engineered its environment.

Or at least it is when we are talking about orchestral music of the 18th and 19th centuries. There are aspects of 20th century orchestral culture, which augur well for future associations with Aboriginal music. Aspects related to the way the resources of orchestral music have been opened up this century so that orchestral music can abandon a formal analogy with argument, and express the experience of the moment, notions of stasis, looser structures. Couple this with the fact that popular Aboriginal music these days embraces western techniques — many of the basic tools of European composition (chords, harmonically-shaped melodies, simple forms) — and we have the basis for technical collaboration.

Yet, even considering the way orchestral music has been freed up in the 20th century such that it can incorporate outside influences, there would seem to be few natural meeting points between European and Aboriginal cultures. One assumes that we are talking about a fusion of the orchestra with *traditional* Aboriginal music. *Music is our Culture* saw the combining of orchestral music with a more modern, urban Aboriginal sound.

Music is our Culture developed out of a need felt by the then ABC orchestras to engage with Australia's indigenous music-makers: to produce a piece which is a genuine expression of the artistic aims of indigenous musicians in response to working with a western classical orchestra. A work which helps reshape western music-making with the benefit of indigenous insights.

When this idea first surfaced, Symphony Australia's Artistic Administrator, US-born Sam Dixon, struggled for months with the difficulties of finding a meeting point between the cultures. When the project was first broached with Jenny Newsome of Adelaide's Centre for Aboriginal Studies in Music, she suggested some guidelines which were more likely to guarantee an authentically indigenous orchestral work, a *real* improvement on the usual 'appropriation':

- the work to be created collaboratively by a team who were to initiate creative ideas all the way through;
- the team to comprise of musicians who are conversant with modern popular styles;
- the abandonment of a requirement for the orchestra to be treated as a monolith, and
- the acceptance of words and dance as essential musical elements.

She proposed a team comprising four musicians of different indigenous backgrounds:

1. Jardine Kiwat, from North Queensland, of Torres Strait Island descent, a fusion guitarist, singer, drummer and songwriter;

2. Grayson Rotumah, from northern NSW, also a guitarist, of Bandjalung and Melanesian descent;
3. Kerry McKenzie, a virtuoso didjeridu player from north central NSW, of Gamilraay descent, and
4. Jensen Warusam, a Torres Strait Islander, the only traditional person in the team, a former dancer with NAISDA, who also has knowledge of NE Arnhem Land styles.

How to assist this group compose for orchestra became the next question. Chester Schultz, an Adelaide composer with extensive experience in the language and musical revival of the Nunga people of Adelaide — and possessing arguably the most extensive knowledge of, and sensitivity to, traditional and 'Contact' Aboriginal music of any western-educated composer — assumed a unique role of facilitator, editor, orchestrator, translator, researcher, scribe and co-composer. A role requiring more self-effacement than the average composer is prepared to submit to. Richard Mills, composer of *Earth Poem/Sky Poem*, was engaged as Consultant Conductor for the workshop period and first performance.

Symphony Australia asked for a 30-minute work comprising song, dance and text, an ensemble of indigenous performers and an orchestra of no greater than the ASO's establishment strength (triple woodwind, a string strength of 12-10-7-6-5, brass, harp and percussion). A pre-recorded tape track could complement the live performance.

As important as the team was, *Music is our Culture* is as much a product of its method of composition which involved weekly or twice-weekly meetings of the composing team and workshop-rehearsals with orchestra roughly every two months.

In weekly sessions during 1997 the team grappled with issues of the participants' heritage, the mixing of musical styles, the solving of technical problems, how to express the conceptual themes musically, the peculiarities and possibilities of the western classical orchestra. Musical segments were sketched and at one stage the team experimented with the use of a 4-track cassette recorder in order to hear and evaluate more easily the approximate sound of multi-layered music which they could not, for practical reasons, play 'live' themselves. Significantly, musical ideas tended to come up as a 'storyline' evolved and the group grappled with linking the visual images.

How the team worked with orchestra is a question of much interest. The first couple of orchestral sessions consisted of testing various instrumentations of material composed in traditional and graphic notation and seeking out meeting points between Aboriginal and European instruments — essential for the team to get to know the palette that they were to deal with. At one stage in the first workshop in April 1997, Schultz asked Kiwat what other percussion instruments he might want to hear, and Kiwat replied: 'Whatever earthy sounds there are to go with lumut, warup, kulups and bilma, [the Torres Strait slit and hourglass drums and shakers and Arnhem Land clapsticks which the team brought along to the session]'. In June, Richard Mills set a deadline for presentation of the complete piece in sketch form, and the composing team played the work as a quintet in August. Thereafter, orchestral workshop sessions became more a matter of testing the orchestration and weighting of fully composed sections. It was a time for Schultz to change gears — from discreetly allowing the piece to evolve out of the discoveries of the indigenous creators, to pressing for firmer decisions about the orchestration, albeit negotiating agreement at every stage.

The path of such a collaboration is not exactly smooth. For example, it's fair to say that at the beginning of the project the Aboriginal musicians were unaware of such givens of orchestral culture as the firm dependence by orchestral musicians on notation — this was solved partly by finding musicians within the orchestra who were prepared to improvise and partly by Schultz assuming the role of educator/guide. Another ongoing conflict was the need to balance orchestral deadlines with the composing team's need for thinking space. Schultz conceded the creative potential in such tensions, but felt that the workshop structure was insufficiently different from the usual 'Young Composers' Workshop', where the composer is already fully trained, has an ear for orchestral sounds, and comes along with a nearly complete score which is then just tweaked into shape. Mills, on the other hand, believed that the project was 'wisely planned because there was time to explore and experiment without leaving the orchestral musicians sitting around in call-time twiddling their thumbs'.

There was always an issue of the degree to which traditional elements should be included. Symphony Australia was mindful of the fact that audience members would expect something sounding familiarly Aboriginal to emerge. In part, Kerry McKenzie's didjeridu guaranteed that. But, as the only traditional man in the group, Jensen Warusam most keenly felt the pressure to introduce traditional elements. 'This was an issue often discussed by the guys', said Schultz, who pointed out that three of the team are far removed from the traditional past. He agreed however, that without the hints of tradition visible in Warusam's choreography, and the use of certain instruments, there would have been a lack of poignancy; the message of dislocation might have been less dramatic.

In the end, the team fulfilled their brief, producing a half hour work for orchestra, indigenous musicians and dancers (Warusam and non-Aboriginal Juliette Bland). A narration (culled from the team-members' recorded accounts of their experiences) was read by actor, James Muir. Despite my partisan position, I regard *Music is our Culture* as one of the most successful fusion pieces in the repertoire. It not only conveyed the experience of Aboriginal people in the modern world, but blended a large array of styles, moving easily from one genre to another. Interestingly, the orchestra was not subjected to unusual formations or complements in the end.

I would ascribe the success of the work to the following ingredients:

(i) A judicious combination of talents

(ii) A productive structure for the creative process, providing:

  (a) Plenty of opportunity for the team to thrash out their ideas, but also opportunities for testing interim results, with editorial input by Mills and myself as the commissioner's representative

  (b) A series of deadlines at stages along the way

(iii) Getting the creative process the right way round; working out what needed to be said first and letting the piece evolve rather than rush too soon into a musical scheme.

It is gratifying to Symphony Australia that team members benefited from this project. When Jardine Kiwat first saw the full orchestra he thought: 'How the hell am I going to keep everybody busy?' Then he realised he didn't have to. '*Music is our Culture* stretched me in terms of working with a large group, not only thinking of something for everybody to do, but how to rest them. Now [when I'm working with my own group] I'm always thinking of a bigger picture'.

Music is our Culture premiered as part of *Orchestra Dreaming* at Thebarton Theatre, 13 March 1998 to an audience whose response *The Australian* critic, Stephen Whittington, described as 'rapturous'. In the closing minutes of *Music is our Culture* you can get some idea of the power of the piece. Though a team of five composers devised the work, it seems to tell one story, that of being stolen from traditions. There is a poignancy in the predicament of the 'stolen person' as the narrator tells us of life in the city at the end:

It's hard to go back...
Hard to go forward...
Hard to know why.
We've changed,...
I know I have,
looking for my traditions
in another man's place.[1]

At this point, musically, the high harp, warup, didjeridu and orchestra combine to produce a unique instrumental sound, an authentic contribution to the tonal palette of the orchestra from voices that are new to the medium. The last seven or so minutes are perhaps the most poetic moments in a piece which is full of poetry. Despite the 'realistic' concession that reconciliation has not yet been achieved, the music adroitly inserts hope beneath the understandable scepticism.

Part of the success of *Music is our Culture* derived from the blending of a modern urban Aboriginal music with orchestra, blending styles where blend is possible. But the *Orchestra Dreaming* concert raised a potentially more difficult problem. Richard Mills's *Earth Poem/Sky Poem* attempted a combination of western orchestral music with traditional Aboriginal music.

Mills' *Earth Poem/Sky Poem* came out of a 3-month residency at Milingimbi and Elcho Island in the Northern Territory. It was commissioned by the Darwin Symphony Orchestra and first performed by them in December 1993, subsequently opening the new NT Parliament House in Darwin in 1994. The recent performance by the Adelaide Symphony Orchestra was the first outside the Northern Territory.

Mills sees *Earth Poem* as a vision of the world of the Yolngu. Traditional songs about brolgas, crocodiles and magpie geese are embedded in an orchestral framework which basically describes the passing of a day, the orchestra providing an environment for songs from two series, one of which according to Steve Knopoff:

> *involves a cluster of spirit-beings centred around Banumbirr the Morning Star... The other series is an inland series related to the travels of the Wawilak Sisters and (for the Galpu, though not all clans who sing Wawilak songs) the great ancestral snake, [Wititj].*[2]

In traditional practice these songs would separately follow various prescribed sequences depending on the context in which they were being sung. In *Earth Poem/Sky Poem*, however, the orchestra basically acts as a frame for a roughly chronological presentation of the song-subjects. It is a spectacularly simple solution to the question of how to combine these two very different musical traditions.

I. Prelude
Yidakayi (Calling Songs)
II. Star music
Ba<u>n</u>umbirr (Morning Star Song)
Star Sonata (solo flute, clarinet)
III. Sunrise
IV. Land music
Wänga (Land) *Man'tjarr* (Leaves)
Ngatha (Food Gathering) *Gurtha* (Fire)
V. Cloud music
Cloud Sonata I. *Mangan* (Cloud Song) Cloud Sonata II
VI. Animal and bird music
Gurruma<u>t</u>tji (Magpie Geese) *Bäru* (Crocodile)
Bu<u>l</u>'mandji (Shark) *Weti* (Wallaby) *Gudurrku* (Brolga)
VII. Storm
Waltja<u>n</u> (Rain) *Gapu* (Water) *Wata* (West Wind)
VIII. Sunset
IX. Nocturne (solo violin)
X. Postlude

This is not to say, however, that *Earth Poem/Sky Poem* is a more ambitious or sophisticated piece than *Music is our Culture. Music is our Culture* grappled with issues of far greater social and emotional complexity. With five musicians exchanging their stories and talking and conferring over an 18 month period, it is no surprise that *Music is our Culture* also resulted in a more integrated union of elements. Yet, *Earth Poem/Sky Poem* attempts to combine musics which do not have obvious commonalities; to bring them together across what must be one of the greatest gulfs between cultures in the world.

It could be asked what degree of insight listeners gained into the complexity of Yolngu musical culture from this piece. For one thing, the appearance of 'painted-up' performers dancing in front of an orchestra was a constant reminder of the contrast between the two cultures — it was impressive in its clashing exoticness. Listeners also got to hear traditional music in a context which promoted the drama, colour and rhythm of the songs. The orchestral setting, with such devices as storms and nocturnes, also enhanced the impression that these songs are very much linked to the natural world of the Yolngu.

However, the audience probably would not have gained a deeper understanding of the musical processes at work in the Yolngu songs. Few listeners would have been aware, or become aware, of the ways in which Yolngu songmen juggle textual phrases or melodic alternatives.

That said, the work was still the result of a laudable amount of cross-cultural negotiation, sometimes at a deep, if not immediately apparent, level. Most obviously, there were long orchestral interludes in which the Galpu Dancers had to improvise choreography utilising traditional movements from their song repertoire.

Behind the scenes, negotiation with traditional performers provided an object lesson in cross-cultural interaction for concert administrators accustomed to dealing with classical music professionals.

One of the ways in which Mills adjusts to the Yolngu way of doing things in *Earth Poem* is to make use of two principal singers, one to represent each of the two moieties (or halves) into which the Yolngu divide their world. A world in which animals, humans, plants — *all things* — are either dhuwa or yirritja. Thus there are two main singers in *Earth Poem*. A dhuwa singer sings of subjects that are of the dhuwa moiety (eg. shark); a yirritja singer may sing only of what is yirritja (eg. crocodile). The work reflects this division throughout, and Symphony Australia therefore had to make sure that the Galpu Dancers brought down singers from each of the tribal moieties. *Earth Poem/Sky Poem* signalled the first time a Symphony Australia contract has specified that a touring group supply 'one (1) singer of the dhuwa moiety, one (1) singer of the yirritja moiety'.

As well, the difficulty of knowing exactly who would turn up was a new experience for classical music administrators. The program booklet (even the airline tickets) listed certain singers based on the *likelihood* that they would be able to appear. However, when the time came for the group to depart for Adelaide, certain members who had been earmarked to perform had to stay behind on Elcho to fulfil ceremonial obligations. Substitute performers had to be found, and discussions then had to take place to ensure that these 'understudies' could perform the traditional material according to custom and descent and other considerations.

Such efforts are worth it in order to give musicians the chance to perform together and let them and their audiences begin to appreciate each others' craft, but even in the surface details of *Earth Poem/Sky Poem* — as a musical product — there is something blatantly challenging and promising about the way both cultures are paired. In many ways *Earth Poem/Sky Poem* is a work of great beauty in that both cultures express themselves uninhibited by the other. There is a real sense of sharing the limelight — the Yolngu dancers are the feature when their songs are being performed; the orchestra has generous opportunities to shine. Both cultures can come together it seems to be saying, and it can be as simple as this.

But would Yolngu people regard *Earth Poem/Sky Poem* as 'ganma' — to make use of a Gumatj clan term which describes the confluence of salt water and fresh water in tidal estuaries, and, more importantly, symbolises for them their concept of the meeting and coalescence of difference? Well, I can't speak for Yolngu people, but I do see tempting clues to the possibility that musical meetings could be achieved at deeper structural levels, should they be desired. I'm not prescribing anything here. European and Aboriginal musicians could probably (and would need to want to) come up with better ideas than I can.

But there is the possibility of meeting at the level of creative invention, I would have thought. After all, the Yolngu possess a tradition of manipulating musical and symbolic material. Songmen select their textual phrases from a repertoire; there is sufficient variability in the accompaniments of clapsticks and didjeridu and the overlapping patterns of voice, sticks and didj to sustain long-term interest. And just as the symbolism of shared song subjects can be used to connect different strings of traditional songs, could not the manipulation of symbolism serve as an analogue to western music's key modulation? There is among the Yolngu of Yirrkala, as Steve Knopoff points out (1992), an understanding of human creation, and a tradition of creating new songs (Yuta manikay) out of traditional material. Aren't there grounds then for sitting down and talking about collaborations with our fellow citizens of the Top End?

And are we limited only to the Yolngu? Ethnomusicologists have always recognised a degree of creativity in Yolngu music-making; but have tended to dismiss this possibility in regard to the people of the Western Desert. Taking the lead from T.G.H. Strehlow, the common wisdom has been that desert music is a repertoire learnt from rote; that there is no modern-day creativity. As Strehlow once put it, as if sealing the question for ever in relation to the Arrernte people, the thoroughness of their forefathers in commemorating the landscape in song and verse had left them 'not a single unoccupied scene which they could fill with the creatures of their own imagination' (Strehlow 1947:6).

My own experience, however, suggests that the process of learning Central Australian songs is more a matter of re-creation than rote repetition; the young singer learns the techniques by which s/he may deduce the method of applying text to each songline's melody shape. Articles by Catherine Ellis and Ken Hale support this contention (1984).

As for a creative repertoire fixed for all time in the Dreamtime, one still hears of new verses being 'dreamt'. Sure the fact that the new material needs to well up from a realm remote from human activity, apparently impervious to human intercession, has ramifications for orchestral deadlines, but there is still a degree of creativity in traditional Central Australian music which could serve as a basis for collaboration. And Centralians are not fazed by working in our ways. Jenny Newsome tells the story of old *tjilpis* from the tribal lands up in northern South Australia correcting the part-singing of CASM students. How? Because they were recalling what they'd picked up about voice leading when they were in the Ernabella Choir.

Finally, why should our orchestras engage with these indigenous musics?

Well, Béla Bartók, who went out with a wax cylinder phonograph to record Eastern European folk music in the early years of this century, found that the richest music resulted from the so-called 'clash of cultures'. Australia hosts some of the most contrasting cultures on the face of the globe. Surely, when one considers the range of Aboriginal music that exists here (from the various traditional musics still being performed, to modern popular manifestations), there is much potential to explore.

But the best reason simply is this: we live in this land. The centre of our existence is here. Should we not have a repertoire that tells us how Sydney Dwarf Apples flower more prolifically after fire, or that the Red-tailed Black Cockatoo comes into Alice just before rain? The institutions and traditions, which were brought here from Europe, must adjust to the new environment. In the matter of our musical institutions, we must learn from the native musical traditions.

We live in Australia. We must sing about Australia. Or as they might say in Eastern Arnhem Land:

Ngialimurru Australia ga nhina. Ga ngilimurru balang Australia-dhi dar'taryun.[3]

Notes

1 *Music is our Culture:* narration — Jardine Kiwat, Grayson Rotumah, Kerry McKenzie, Chester Schultz and Jensen Warusam.

2 Steve Knopoff, personal communication, 15 April 1998.

3 Thanks to Dr Michael Christie, of the Northern Territory University, for correcting and improving my Dhuwala.

References

Hale, K. 1984, 'Remarks on Creativity in Aboriginal Verse' in Kassler, J.C. & Stubington, J. (eds.) *Problems and Solution,* Sydney: Hale and Ironmonger.

Knopoff, S. 1992, *'Yuta Manikay:* Juxtaposition of Ancestral and Contemporary Elements in the Performance of Yolngu Clan Songs', *Yearbook of Traditional Music:* 24, New York: The International Council for Traditional Music (ICTM).

Strehlow, T.G.H. 1947, *Aranda Traditions,* Melbourne: University of Melbourne.

Symphony Australia, formerly ABC Concerts, is a wholly-owned company of the Australian Broadcasting Corporation. It is the service organisation for the former ABC orchestras — the Adelaide, Melbourne, Queensland, Sydney, Tasmanian and West Australian Symphony Orchestras.

NOTES ON CONTRIBUTORS

Phil Bagust abandoned a secure career in surveying and drafting in 1991 for the uncharted waters of Communication Studies at the University of South Australia, which he now tutors in. He has recently completed a Masters thesis investigating the effects of the Internet on the environment movement — another interest. But it was probably public radio that started the rot. After subscribing as a teenager for the first time in 1982, he finally became a member in 1989 and an on-air presenter and management committee member in 1990. Now in charge of announcement production, the frequent frustration that goes with the medium have not yet made him entirely cynical about its charms.

Gerry Bloustien is an experienced film-maker and a lecturer in Communication Studies at The University of South Australia, where she teaches Screen Studies and Media Production. A hopeless musician, she is nevertheless a keen fan of a wide range of popular music and dance. Her doctural thesis, focusing on gender and representation, explored the significance of popular music and other related cultural texts in the everyday lives of a diverse group of teenage girls in South Australia. Her other current research interests and publications involve film music and, particularly, explorations of new forms of documentary. She served as Treasurer of the Australian-New Zealand chapter of IASPM from 1996 to 1997.

Andrew Bradley (aka Quro) has been a key player within Australia's, particularly Adelaide's, hip hop community for approximately a decade; as an MC and music artist, as a promoter and manager of events and as a freelance journalist (producer of Adelaide's longest running hip hop radio show, 93.7 Degreez in the Shade, writer for a weekly column in Adelaide street publication Rip It Up and various other hip hop related publications). His first recording was in 1993 with Finger Lickin' Good, a three piece group consisting of himself, Madcap and Groove Terminator. In the past two and a half years Andrew has been manager, promoter and frontman of the Fuglemen, who released their debut album 'Resuscitation' in late 1997. He also produced and released his solo album 'This Last Week I've...' in 1998 and has appeared on many locally and nationally produced albums. Now currently residing in Sydney, Andrew is working on the release of Fuglemen's second album, his second solo album and on material he is producing with Mostyn Space Unit as Reference Point.

Jenjo Brown currently teaches Media in the School for Humanities, Media and Cultural Studies at Southern Cross University in north-east NSW. She has a varied background emerging from interests in the arts and media, political activism, feminism and education. Her research interests centre on the cultural meanings of new technologies, especially in the sphere of contemporary music and with particular reference to difference and identity in the human-technology matrix. She is currently completing a doctoral thesis which explores an eclectic matrix of interests and intersections in voice, music, self, technology, productive processes and spaces, sound and silence.

Mark Evans is Co-Editor of *Perfect Beat: the International Journal of Research into Contemporary Music and Popular Culture.* He is an Associate Lecturer at the Centre for Contemporary Music Studies, Macquarie University, and is completing a PhD in 'Australian Church Music'.

Jon Fitzgerald lectures in popular music theory and history in the Bachelor of Contemporary Music program at Southern Cross University (Lismore, Australia). His doctoral thesis examined the development of popular songwriting in the early 1960s, and his research interests centre on the creative process. He is also an experienced performer and composer.

FRUIT are an Adelaide band, born June 1995, from a merger of two groups of three booked to play an acoustic evening. To add flavour to the night the six rehearsed a few songs together, the outcome being six new songs. What was to be an encore became a set and today FRUIT are a thriving 'indi' international touring band with music company, FRUIT Music. In the initial two years FRUIT's style leaned towards acoustic folk, ballads and jazz. Since a line up change in November 1997 the band has developed a more commercially powerful blend of funk, rock, pop and jazz whilst managing to maintain the writers' integrity and meet a range of markets both mainstream and niche.

Nancia Guivarra has found, since doing her paper, that along with her Meriam heritage, she is from the Bindal Juru people of Queensland. She is the producer of the Indigenous arts and culture program, 'Awaye!', on Radio National and is studying for her Masters in Journalism at the University of Technology in Sydney.

Philip Hayward is Head of the Centre for Contemporary Music Studies at Macquarie University. His recent publications include *Sound Alliances, Music at the Borders,* and most recently, *Widening the Horizons: Exoticism in Post-War Popular Music.*

Shane Homan is a Lecturer in the School of Communication & Media, University of Western Sydney, Nepean. A former professional drummer with various rock bands, his doctoral thesis *The Mayor's A Square: A Regulatory History of Sydney Rock Venues 1957-1997* was completed at Macquarie University in 1998. He has written many articles concerning Australian live performance and policy contexts, the most recent being 'Counter Sites: Mixed Audiences, Prejudices and Performance within the Australian Rock Pub' in Sally Macarthur & Cate Poynton (eds) *Musics and Feminisms,* AMC, 1999. He has also written on other popular music policy contexts, including 'Australian Music and the Parallel Importation Debate' in Helen Molnar and Helen Wilson (eds) 'Radio Futures' in *Media International Australia incorporating Culture and Policy,* May 1999. Dr Homan is Treasurer of the Australia-New Zealand chapter of IASPM.

Kipps Horn is a lecturer in music and education at the Royal Melbourne Institute of Technology. His research interests include the nature and practice of improvisation, arts education, and Greek music. His current doctoral study focuses on the performance of rebetika (a Greek urban popular music) in Melbourne.

Bruce Johnson is Associate Professor, School of English, University of New South Wales. His research areas have moved from Renaissance Studies to Twentieth Century Popular Culture, with emphasis on Australian music and oral cultures. Fellowships at numerous European universities reflect particularly strong connections with cultural and folkorist research in Finland. He is author/editor of several books (including *the Oxford Companion to Australian Jazz*), and has contributed to all major reference works on Australian music. He is currently Advisory Editor for the *Encyclopaedia of Popular Music of the World,* and contributing to the *Cambridge Companion to Jazz.* His book on music and modernity in Australia, *The Inaudible Music,* appears this year. He is a record producer, multi-award winning broadcaster, has served on government arts policy bodies, and established the Australian Jazz Archive in collaboration with The National Film and Sound Archive. He continues to be an active jazz musician.

Jardine Kiwat was a student at the Centre for Aboriginal Studies in Music (CASM) from 1982 – 1984. As well as being a member of Trochus, a four piece fusion band blending Torres Strait Islander songs and rhythms with jazz rock, ska and funk, he has worked as a lecturer and held positions on various boards and commitees. Jardine was co-founder of 'Tudtu (grandfather's place) Theatre', which educated school students about Torres Strait Islander culture through dance, stories and music. From 1996 – 1998, Jardine developed a new Indigenous music group, Malu Wildu, for the Music Viva in

Schools Program. Through a CD accompaniment to a booklet of music activites and through live performances, Malu Windu help educate primary school students in music performance.

Adé Kukoyi is the cofounder and managing director of Daki Budtcha Records. He was also the assistant producer of the international award winning opera film Black River, 1993 and has been a former producer and presenter on 4ZZZ Radio, Brisbane.

Richard Margetson worked as an actor in theatre, TV and radio until he shifted into radio in the 1990s initially as a hobby, training at Adelaide's community broadcaster 5MMM (now 3D Radio) and exploring his passion as a music collector. From there he became a producer at 5UV University Radio, creating *Radio Expresso,* which won 'Best Program' at the 1991 national Community Broadcasting Awards. He joined Triple J as coordinator of Triple J Newcastle, presenting music shifts and searching for local music for national airplay, before moving to Triple J Sydney, where he produced and presented a range of programs, principally *Weekend Breakfast.* In 1998 he returned to Adelaide as the Breakfast presenter for local ABC radio, 5AN. He collected the Ausmusic award for 'Outstanding Contribution to South Australian Music' that year. Currently he works as a package producer and field reporter for ABC radio and dreams of international rock stardom...

Tony Mitchell is a senior lecturer in Writing and Cultural Studies at University of Technology, Sydney and the Chairperson of IASPM. He is the author of *Popular Music and Local Identity: Rock, Pop and Rap in Europe and Oceania* (University of Leicester Press, 1996), *Dario Fo:People's Court Jester* (Methuen 1999) and (with Philip Hayward and Roy Shuker) *North Meets South: Popular Music in Aotearoa* (Perfect Beat, 1994). He is currently editing *Global Noise: Rap and Hip Hop outside the USA* for Wesleyan University Press, and his articles on popular music have appeared in *Popular Music, Ethnomusicology, Perfect Beat and Popular Music and Society.*

Jennifer Newsome is currently Coordinator of Academic Programs at the Centre for Aboriginal Studies in Music (CASM) at the University of Adelaide. She has lectured at the Centre since 1986, and played a central role in innovations in curriculum design at the Centre, which led to the accreditation of the first specialised tertiary awards for Aboriginal and Torres Strait Islander musicians in Australia. She has studied traditional indigenous music and dance through the Centre, and received her under-graduate and post-graduate training at the University of Adelaide, specialising in performance and undertaking research studies with Dr Cath Ellis. As a professional flautist she has been a founding member of several leading contemporary music ensembles in Adelaide.

David Page was born in Brisbane, descendant from the Munaldjali Clan of the Bundjalong Nation, South east Queensland. He began his career as a solo singer under the direction of the WEA Recording Company. In the 1980s, embarking on formal music studies, he enrolled as a student at CASM. Adelaide University's Centre for Aboriginal Studies in Music. As a composer David combined his talents with those of his brother, choreographer Stephen Page, to create music works for the Bangarra Dance Theatre. In 1996, David established his own music production company, Nikinali Company in Sydney.

Catherine Palmer currently works as a researcher/ writer/ ethnographer. Her interests include the role of music and sport in the construction of contemporary social identities, and has undertaken fieldwork with professional and amateur cyclists, rock climbers and skateboarders. She has taught Social Anthropology, Media Analysis and Cultural Studies at the University of Adelaide. She is currently working on a travel guide to cycling in France.

Motti Regev is Senior Lecturer in Sociology at the Open University of Israel. His published work, in English and Hebrew, covers various aspects of popular music in Israel and elsewhere. From 1997-1999 he served as General Secretary of the International Association for the Study of Popular Music (IASPM).

Robin Ryan, (Monash University) has published articles on Australian Aboriginal music and popular music in various journals and encyclopaedias. She recently wrote the foreword and introduction to Herb Patten's CD/booklet *How to Play the Gumleaf* (Currency Press), and is also involved as a specialist advisor/consultant to the editors of the *Companion to Music and Dance in Australia* (forthcoming, Currency Press). Robin plays in a band and her hobby is songwriting.

Paulene Thomas was originally a senior high school teacher trained in History and English as a Second Language. She worked in Himeji (Hyogo, Japan) from 1990 to 1993 as the Assistant Director of English Education for the Himeji City Board of Education. During this time she spent evenings taking classes in taiko at the Taiko Centre of Kyoto (one of the first two foreign students enrolled), then joined Shachi Taiko of Himeji for training in taiko and Japanese flute, going on to perform and attend taiko workshops in various parts of Japan. In 1995 with Harold Gent, (formerly of Katari Taiko of Vancouver, Canada) and Kaori Kamei (formerly of Kobe, Japan), she formed Ataru Taru Taiko, then the first taiko group in Australia. The group specializes in authentic traditional taiko and masked folk theatre and has performed widely in SA, Victoria and NSW. In 1997 they were the first Australian taiko group ever invited to perform in Japan.

Mandy Treagus has a day job in the English Department at the University of Adelaide, where she teaches Australian Cultural Studies. She has published on colonial women's fiction and popular music, and is currently researching the rise of female sport in the late Victorian era. She is also looking at issues of Australian identity in popular music. Mandy is a widely published songwriter, and has played in bands doing originals and covers, in styles ranging from jug (early seventies), new wave (late seventies), humorous satire (mid eighties) to rock (late eighties). Having got over an PhD-induced musical hiatus, she currently writes, sings and plays in the three-piece contemporary folk band Chicane. The artists on high rotation at her house include The Sundays, Ani Difranco, and the sadly defunct Cactus Child.

Ashley Turner is currently lecturing at the University of Adelaide's Centre for Aboriginal Studies in Music. He has also worked extensively in Indonesia consulting for the Ford Foundation, lecturing at the University of North Sumatra's Ethnomusicology Department, and conducting music research with the Malay people of Riau province. His publications include: 'Belian as a Symbol of Cosmic Reunification' 1991, in J. Kassler (ed.), *Metaphor — A Musical Dimension*, Sydney: Currency Press; 'Ekologi Kebudayaan Musik Masyarakat Melayu Petalangan di Riau' 1993, in *Jurnal Masyarakat Seni Pertunjukan Indonesia,* Jakarta: Gramedia; and 'Cultural Survival, Identity and the Performing Arts of Kampar's Suku Petalangan, in Bijdragen Tot de Taal, Land — en Volkenkunde, 153:4. He is also a violinist and has recorded across a wide range of musical styles.

Graeme Turner is Professor of Cultural Studies in the Department of English at the University of Queensland. He has published widely on Australian popular culture, television, film and music, and his books include *Making it National, The Media in Australia* (with Stuart Cunningham), and *British Cultural Studies.* In a former life, he was a professional musician, songwriter, and director of an independent record company.

Gordon Kalton Williams was Producer for the Adelaide Symphony Orchestra/Symphony Australia's *Orchestra Dreaming* concert and Project Manager for the *Music is our Culture* commission. He is currently Senior Writer for the Publications Unit of Symphony Australia, Sydney. Born in 1956, Williams is a music graduate from the University of Melbourne, and a graduate of NIDA's Playwrights Studio. He is the co-producer of two ABC Classic FM Specials on the influence of indigenous music on the concert hall, and is currently working on a screenplay on the life of T.G.H.Strehlow.